VERGIL

Aeneid Book 8

The Focus Vergil Aeneid Commentaries

For intermediate students
    Aeneid 1 • Randall Ganiban, editor: Available now
    Aeneid 2 • Randall Ganiban, editor: Available now
    Aeneid 3 • Christine Perkell, editor: Available now
    Aeneid 4 • James O'Hara, editor: Available now
    Aeneid 5 • Joseph Farrell, editor: Available now
    Aeneid 6 • Patricia A. Johnston, editor: Available now
    Aeneid 7 • Randall Ganiban, editor: In preparation
    Aeneid 8 • James O'Hara, editor: Available now
    Aeneid 9 • Joseph Farrell, editor: In preparation
    Aeneid 10 • Andreola Rossi, editor: In preparation
    Aeneid 11 • Charles McNelis, editor: In preparation
    Aeneid 12 • Christine Perkell, editor: In preparation

For advanced students
    Aeneid 1-6 • Ganiban, general editor; Perkell, O'Hara, Farrell, Johnston, editors: Available now
    Aeneid 7-12 • Ganiban and O'Hara, co-general editors; Farrell, Rossi, McNelis, Perkell, editors: In preparation

<small>VERGIL</small>

Aeneid Book 8

Adapted from the
commentaries of T.E. Page by

James J. O'Hara
University of North Carolina, Chapel Hill

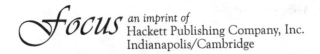 *an imprint of*
Hackett Publishing Company, Inc.
Indianapolis/Cambridge

A Focus book

Focus an imprint of
Hackett Publishing Company

Copyright © 2018 by Hackett Publishing Company, Inc.

24 23 22 21   2 3 4 5 6 7

For further information, please address
  Hackett Publishing Company, Inc.
  P.O. Box 44937
  Indianapolis, Indiana 46244-0937

  www.hackettpublishing.com

Cataloging-in-Publication Data is on file with the Library of Congress

ISBN-13: 978-1-58510-880-0

The paper used in this publication meets the minimum requirements of American
National Standard for Information Sciences—Permanence of Paper for Printed Library
Materials, ANSI Z39.48-1984.

∞

Table of Contents

Preface

In *Aeneid* 8 the hero Aeneas and his enemies prepare for the war between the Trojans and Italians that will play out in Books 9-12. The book features Aeneas' visit to Evander, a Greek immigrant now living at the future site of Rome, who becomes Aeneas' ally, tells a heroic story about Hercules' defeat of a fire-breathing monster, and gives Aeneas a tour of his city—which makes it a great book to read before, while, or after visiting Rome. The book ends with Venus bringing her son Aeneas new arms made by Vulcan, and with the poet's famous and fascinating description of the scenes from future Roman history on Aeneas' shield.

This volume is an introductory commentary on *Aeneid* 8 for use at the intermediate level of Latin or higher, though it may have something to offer to anyone working on the book. It provides a generous amount of basic information about grammar and syntax, as well as a complete vocabulary at the back of the book, so that students of varying experience will have what they need to understand Vergil's Latin. At the same time, it addresses issues of interpretation and style in the light of modern scholarly research, so that students of all levels may have a richer experience of the poem, and scholars may find insight on some questions or passages. There are appendices on meter and on stylistic features, and extensive bibliographical references that will help readers pursue areas of special interest. Two maps illustrate Evander's tour of the site of Rome, and the peoples and places mentioned on the shield of Aeneas.

Like the other volumes in this series, the commentary takes as its starting point the notes in the valuable school edition of T.E. Page's *Vergil: Aeneid 7-12* (1900). When still useful for today's student, Page's comments have been retained, but on nearly every line consideration has been given to the differing needs of today's student, and to the opinions of a century and more of scholarship that post-dates Page. Generally Page's notes have been revised, shortened, expanded, or completely replaced, not only on Vergil's Latin but also on literary, interpretive and even historical and archaeological questions. The General Introduction, Introduction to Book 8, maps, and the introductions to individual sections of the poem are all new, as are the appendices. The vocabulary to Book 8 is adapted with many changes from another source, as is indicated below. The general introduction is by Randall Ganiban, general editor of the commentaries on *Aeneid* 1-6 and co-editor with me of those on *Aeneid* 7-12. My appendices on meter and on stylistic terms are adapted from those in his 2008 *Aeneid* 2 commentary, and in fact this Preface draws upon his as a model and even repeats some of his language. The vocabulary for *Aeneid* 8 is adapted, with many changes, from that of John Tetlow's *The Eighth Book of Virgil's* Aeneid (1893); some of the changes follow the vocabularies of other commentaries in the series.

The Latin text of *Aeneid* 8 used here is based on that of F.A. Hirtzel (Oxford, 1900), except that at 75 I print *tenent* where Hirtzel has *tenet*; at 205 *furiis* where Hirtzel has *furis*; at 223 *oculis* where Hirtzel has *oculi*; at 519 *nomine* where Hirtzel has *munere*. I punctuate differently in several passages, most significantly at 532 and 563-6.

This edition places the Latin text and commentary on the same page. Often references are given to sections of Allen and Greenough's *New Latin Grammar* (1903; cf. Mahoney 2001), or to my appendix on stylistic terms and appendix on meter: the end of the Introduction to Book 8 will describe these references further.

For comments on talks on aspects of Book 8, I thank audiences or classes at UNC-Chapel Hill, the University of Wisconsin–Madison, Pennsylvania State University, Temple University, the University of Alabama-Huntsville, New York University, the University of Richmond, Wake Forest University, Middlebury College, Yale University, Baylor University, the 2012 American Philological Association Annual Meeting in Philadelphia, and the Vergilian Society's 2015 Symposium Cumanum. For reading through a draft of the commentary and making valuable learned comments, I thank Matthew Carter and John Miller; Shadi Bartsch also offered helpful comments and questions while working on her own translation of the *Aeneid*. For teaching with a draft of the commentary, and reporting back to me their own and their students' responses, I thank Erika Damer of the University of Richmond and Nandini Pandey of the University of Wisconsin–Madison. Reliable help and some good criticism came from my research assistants Erika Damer, Zack Rider, Alexandra Daly, and Tedd Wimperis. For making the maps, I am grateful to Gabriel Moss of the Ancient World Mapping Center at UNC, and for comments on the maps I thank my colleague Hérica Valladares. For working with drafts of the commentary, I thank more than one class of Latin 221: Vergil at UNC (a fifth-semester course). For crucial comments on my commentary, for cheerful collaboration, and for inviting me in the first place to join the team working on these Focus commentaries, I thank above all Randall Ganiban.

James J. O'Hara

Introduction to Vergil's *Aeneid*

Vergil's lifetime and poetry

Publius Vergilius Maro (i.e., Vergil)[1] was born on October 15, 70 BCE near the town of Mantua (modern Mantova) in what was then still Cisalpine Gaul.[2] Little else about his life can be stated with certainty, because our main source, the ancient biography by the grammarian Donatus (fourth century CE),[3] is of questionable value.[4] The historical and political background to Vergil's life (by contrast) is amply documented and provides a useful framework for understanding his career. Indeed, his poetic development displays an increasing engagement with the politics of contemporary Rome, an engagement that culminates in the *Aeneid*.

Vergil lived in a time of political strife and uncertainty. Two decades before his birth Rome fought a war with its allies (*socii*), the Social Wars of 91-88 BCE. A commander from that war, Sulla, then marched on Rome to secure an Eastern command and initiated a period of civil strife that ultimately led to his dictatorship in 81 BCE.[5] Later, in 49-45 BCE, when Vergil was in his early twenties, the Roman Republic was torn apart by new civil

---

1 The spelling "Virgil" (*Virgilius*) is also used by convention. It developed early and has been explained by its similarity to two words: virgo ("maiden") and virga ("wand"). For discussion of the origins and potential meanings of these connections, see Jackson Knight (1944) 36-7 and Putnam (1993) 127-8 with notes.

2 Cisalpine Gaul, the northern part of what we now think of as Italy, was incorporated into Roman Italy in 42 BCE. Mantua is located ca. 520 kilometers north of Rome.

3 This biography drew heavily from the *De poetis* of Suetonius (born ca. 70 CE).

4 Horsfall (1995: 1-25; 2006: xxii-xxiv) argues that nearly every detail is unreliable.

5 For "the importance of the Social (or Marsic) War (91-88 BC) as an analogue for the battles waged for Italy in the second half of Virgil's *Aeneid*," see Marincola (2010).

wars, as Julius Caesar fought and defeated Pompey and his supporters. Caesar was declared *dictator perpetuo* ("Dictator for Life") early in 44 BCE but was assassinated on the Ides of March by a group of senators led by Brutus[6] and Cassius. They sought to restore the Republic, which, they believed, was being destroyed by Caesar's domination and intimations of kingship.[7]

The assassination initiated a new round of turmoil that profoundly shaped the course of Roman history. In his will, Caesar adopted and named as his primary heir his great-nephew Octavian (63 BCE-14 CE), the man who would later be called "Augustus" (see below). Though only eighteen years old, Octavian boldly accepted and used this inheritance. Through a combination of shrewd calculation and luck, he managed to attain the consulship in 43 BCE, though he was merely nineteen years of age.[8] He then joined forces with two of Caesar's lieutenants, Marc Antony (initially Octavian's rival) and Lepidus. Together they demanded recognition as a Board of Three (*triumviri* or "triumvirs") to reconstitute the state as they saw fit, and were granted extraordinary powers to do so by the Roman senate and people. In 42 BCE they avenged Caesar's murder by defeating his assassins commanded by Brutus and Cassius at the battle of Philippi in Macedonia, but their alliance gradually began to deteriorate as a result of further civil strife and interpersonal rivalries.

Vergil composed the *Eclogues*, his first major work, during this tumultuous period.[9] Published ca. 39 BCE,[10] the *Eclogues* comprise a sophisticated

---

6   Kingship was hateful to the Romans ever since Brutus' own ancestor, Lucius Junius Brutus, led the expulsion of Rome's last king, Tarquin the Proud, in ca. 509 BCE, an act that ended the regal period of Rome and initiated the Republic (cf. *Aeneid* 6.817-18, 8.646-8 with notes below). In killing Caesar, Brutus claimed that he was following the example of his great ancestor—an important concept for the Romans.

7   For the reasons behind Caesar's assassination and the fall of the Republic, see the brief accounts in Scullard (1982: 126-53) and Shotter (2005: 4-19).

8   By the *lex villia annalis* of 180 BCE, a consul had to be at least forty-two years of age.

9   Other works have been attributed to Vergil: *Aetna, Catalepton, Ciris, Copa, Culex, Dirae, Elegiae in Maecenatem, Moretum,* and *Priapea*. They are collected in what is called the *Appendix Vergiliana* and are generally believed not to have been written by Vergil.

10   This traditional dating, however, has been called into question by some through re-evaluation of *Eclogue* 8, which may very well refer to events in 35 BCE. See Clausen (1994: 232-7).

collection of ten pastoral poems that treat the experiences of shepherds.[11] The poems were modeled on the *Idylls* of Theocritus, a Hellenistic Greek poet of the third century BCE (see below). But whereas Theocritus' poetry created a world that was largely timeless, Vergil sets his pastoral world against the backdrop of contemporary Rome and the disruption caused by the civil wars. *Eclogues* 1 and 9, for example, deal with the differing fortunes of shepherds during a time of land confiscations that resonate with historical events in 41-40 BCE.[12] *Eclogue* 4 describes the birth of a child during the consulship of Asinius Pollio (40 BCE) who will bring a new golden age to Rome.[13] By interjecting the Roman world into his poetic landscape,[14] Vergil allows readers to sense how political developments both threaten and give promise to the very possibility of pastoral existence.

The *Eclogues* established Vergil as a new and important poetic voice and led him to the cultural circle of the great literary patron Maecenas, an influential supporter and confidant of Octavian. Their association grew throughout the 30s.[15] The political situation, however, remained precarious. Lepidus was ousted from the triumvirate in 36 BCE because of his treacherous behavior. Tensions between Octavian and Antony that were simmering over Antony's collaboration and affair with the Egyptian queen Cleopatra

---

11 Coleman (1977) and Clausen (1994) are excellent commentaries on the *Eclogues*. For a discussion of the pastoral genre at Rome, see Heyworth (2005). For general interpretation of the *Eclogues*, see Hardie (1998: 5-27), with extensive bibliography in the notes, Volk (2008a), and Smith (2011).

12 Octavian rewarded veterans with land that was already occupied.

13 This is sometimes called the "Messianic Eclogue" because later ages read it as foreseeing the birth of Christ, which occurred nearly four decades later. The identity of the child is debated, but the poem may celebrate the marriage between Marc Antony and Octavian's sister Octavia that resulted from the treaty of Brundisium in 40 BCE; this union helped stave off the immediate outbreak of war between the two triumvirs. For more on this poem, see Van Sickle (1992) and Petrini (1997: 111-21), as well as the commentaries by Coleman (1977) and Clausen (1994).

14 In addition to the contemporary themes that Vergil treats, he also mentions or dedicates individual poems to a number of his contemporaries, including Asinius Pollio, Alfenus Varus, Cornelius Gallus, and probably Octavian, who is likely the *iuvenis* ("young man") mentioned at 1.42 and perhaps also the patron addressed at 8.6-13.

15 For the relationship between Augustus and the poets, see White (2005). White (1993) is a book-length study of this topic. For an overview of literature of the Augustan period from 40 BCE-14 CE, see Farrell (2005).

eventually exploded.[16] In 32 BCE, Octavian had Antony's powers revoked, and war was declared against Cleopatra (and thus in effect against Antony as well). During a naval confrontation off Actium on the coast of western Greece in September of 31 BCE, Octavian's fleet decisively routed the forces of Marc Antony and Cleopatra, who both fled to Egypt and committed suicide in the following year to avoid capture.[17] This momentous victory solidified Octavian's claim of being the protector of traditional Roman values against the detrimental influence of Antony, Cleopatra, and the East.[18]

Vergil began his next work, the *Georgics*, sometime in the 30s, completed it ca. 29 BCE in the aftermath of Actium, and dedicated it to Maecenas. Like the *Eclogues,* the *Georgics* was heavily influenced by Greek models, particularly the work of Hesiod (eighth century BCE) and of Hellenistic poets such as Callimachus, Aratus, and Nicander (third to second centuries BCE). On the surface, it purports to be a poetic farming guide.[19] Each of its four books examines a different aspect or sphere of agricultural life: crops and weather signs (Book 1), trees and vines (Book 2), livestock (Book 3), and bees (Book 4). Its actual scope, however, is much more ambitious. The poem explores the nature of humankind's struggle with the beauty and difficulties of the agricultural world, but it does so within the context of contemporary war-torn Italy. It bears witness to the strife following Caesar's assassination and sets the chaos and disorder inherent in nature against the upheaval caused by civil war (1.461-514). Moreover,

---

16   In addition to the political conflicts, there were also familial tensions: Antony conducted a decade-long affair with Cleopatra, even though he had married Octavia, Octavian's (Augustus') sister, as a result of the treaty of Brundisium in 40 BCE (see n. 13 above). Antony divorced Octavia in 32 BCE.

17   For the history of the triumviral period, see the brief accounts in Scullard (1982: 154-71) and Shotter (2005: 20-7); for more detailed treatments, see Syme (1939: 187-312), Pelling (1996), and Osgood (2006). For discussion of the contemporary artistic representations of Actium, see Gurval (1995).

18   This ideological interpretation is suggested in Vergil's depiction of the battle on Aeneas' shield (8.671-713). See in the commentary the notes to 8.626-728.

19   Recent commentaries on the *Georgics* include Thomas (1988) and Mynors (1990). For interpretation, see the introduction to the *Georgics* in Hardie (1998: 28-52) with extensive bibliography in the notes, and Volk (2008b). Individual studies include Wilkinson (1969), Putnam (1979), Johnston (1980), Ross (1987), Perkell (1989), Nappa (2005), and Thibodeau (2011). For allusion in the *Georgics*, see Thomas (1986), Farrell (1991), and Gale (2000).

Octavian's success and victories are commemorated both in the introduction (1.24-42) and conclusion (4.559-62) of the poem, as well as in the beginning of the third book (3.1-39). Thus once again, the political world is juxtaposed against Vergil's poetic landscape, but the relationship between the two is not fully addressed.[20]

Octavian's victory represented a turning point for Rome's development. Over the next decade, he centralized political and military control in his hands. He claimed to have returned the state (res publica) to the senate and Roman people in 27 BCE.[21] His powers were redefined, and he was granted the name Augustus ("Revered One") by the senate. It is true that he maintained many traditional Republican institutions, but in reality he was transforming the state into a monarchy. So effective was his stabilization and control of Rome after decades of civil war that he reigned as Princeps ("First Citizen") from 27 BCE to 14 CE, creating a political framework (the Principate) that served the Roman state for centuries.[22]

Vergil wrote his final poem, the Aeneid, largely in the 20s, during the first years of Augustus' reign, when the Roman people presumably hoped that the civil wars were behind them but feared that the Augustan peace would not last. The Aeneid tells the story of the Trojan hero Aeneas. He fought the Greeks at Troy and saw his city destroyed, but with the guidance of the gods and fate he led his surviving people across the Mediterranean to a new homeland in Italy.[23] As in the Eclogues and Georgics, Vergil interjects his

---

20 The overall meaning of the Georgics is contested. Interpretation of the Georgics, like that of the Aeneid (see below), has optimistic and pessimistic poles. Otis (1964) is an example of the former; Ross (1987) the latter. Other scholars, such as Perkell (1989), fall in between by discerning inherent ambivalence. For discussion of these interpretive trends, see Hardie (1998: 50-2).

21 Augustus, Res Gestae 34.

22 For general political and historical narratives of Augustus' reign, see the relatively brief account in Shotter (2005); longer, more detailed treatments can be found in A. H. M. Jones (1970), Crook (1996), and Southern (1998). A classic and influential book by Syme (1939) paints Augustus in extremely dark colors. For broader considerations of the Augustan age, see the short but interesting volume by Wallace-Hadrill (1993) and the more comprehensive treatments by Galinsky (1996, 2005) and Wallace-Hadrill (2008). For the interaction of art and ideology in the Augustan Age, see Zanker (1988).

23 For general interpretation of the Aeneid, see the overviews provided by Hardie (1998: 53-101), Perkell (1999), Anderson (2005), Johnson (2005), Fratantuono

contemporary world into his poetic world. In the *Aeneid*, however, the thematic connections between these two realms are developed still more explicitly, with Aeneas' actions shown to be necessary for and to lead ultimately to the reign of Augustus.

Vergil was still finishing the *Aeneid* when he was stricken by a fatal illness in 19 BCE. The ancient biographical tradition claims that he traveled to Greece, intending to spend three years editing his epic there and in Asia, but that early on he encountered Augustus, who was returning to Rome from the East, and decided to accompany him. Vergil, however, fell ill during the journey and died in Brundisium (in southern Italy) in September of 19 BCE. The *Aeneid* was largely complete but had not yet received its final revision. We are told that Vergil asked that it be burned, but that Augustus ultimately had it published. While such details regarding Vergil's death are doubted, the poem clearly needed final editing.[24] However, its present shape, including its sudden ending, is generally accepted to be as Vergil had planned.

Vergil and his predecessors

By writing an epic about the Trojan war, Vergil was rivaling Homer, the greatest of all the Greek poets. The *Aeneid* was therefore a bold undertaking, but its success makes it arguably the quintessential Roman work because it accomplishes what Latin poetry had always striven to do: to appropriate the Greek tradition and transform it into something that was both equally impressive and distinctly "Roman."

Homer's *Iliad* tells the story of the Trojan war by focusing on Achilles' strife with the Greek leader Agamemnon and consequent rage in the tenth and final year of the conflict, while the *Odyssey* treats the war's aftermath by relating Odysseus' struggle to return home. These were the earliest and most revered works of Greek literature, and they exerted a defining influence on both the overall framework of the *Aeneid* and the close details of its poetry. In general terms, *Aeneid* 1-6, like the *Odyssey*, describes a hero's return (to a new) home after the Trojan war, while *Aeneid* 7-12, like the *Iliad*, tells the

---

(2007), and Ross (2007). For the literary and cultural backgrounds, see Martindale (1997), Farrell (2005), Galinsky (2005), and Lowrie (2009).

24   We can be sure that the poem had not received its final revision for a number of reasons, including the presence of roughly fifty-eight incomplete or "half" lines. See commentary note on 8.41.

story of a war. But throughout the *Aeneid*, Vergil reworks ideas, language, characters, and scenes from both poems. Some ancient critics faulted Vergil for his use of Homer, calling his appropriations "thefts." Vergil, however, is said to have responded that it is "easier to steal his club from Hercules than a line from Homer."[25] Indeed, Vergil does much more than simply quote material from Homer. His creative use and transformation of Homeric language and theme are central not only to his artistry but also to the meaning of the *Aeneid*.

Though Homer is the primary model, Vergil was also influenced significantly by the Hellenistic Greek tradition of poetry that originated in Alexandria, Egypt, in the third century BCE. There scholar-poets such as Apollonius, Callimachus, and Theocritus reacted against the earlier literary tradition (particularly epic which by their time had become largely derivative). They developed a poetic aesthetic that valued small-scale poems, esoteric subjects, and highly polished style. Hellenistic poetry was introduced into the mainstream of Latin poetry a generation before Vergil by the so-called "neoterics" or "new poets," of whom Catullus (ca. 84–ca. 54 BCE) was the most influential for Vergil and for the later literary tradition.[26]

Vergil's earlier works, the *Eclogues* and *Georgics*, had been modeled to a significant extent on Hellenistic poems,[27] so it was perhaps a surprise that Vergil would then have turned to a large-scale epic concerning the Trojan war.[28] However, one of his great feats was the incorporation of the Hellenistic and neoteric sensibilities into the *Aeneid*. Two models were particularly important in this regard: the *Argonautica* by Apollonius of Rhodes, an epic

---

25 *...facilius esse Herculi clavam quam Homeri versum subripere* (Donatus/ Suetonius, *Life of Vergil* 46).

26 Clausen (1987, 2002), George (1974), Briggs (1981), Thomas (1988, 1999), and Hunter (2006) display these influences, while O'Hara (1996, expanded reprint 2017) provides a thorough examination of wordplay (important to the Alexandrian poets) in Vergil.

27 The *Eclogues* were modeled on Theocritus' *Idylls*; the *Georgics* had numerous models, though the Hellenistic poets Callimachus, Nicander, and Aratus were particularly important influences.

28 For example, at *Eclogue* 6.3-5, Vergil explains in highly programmatic language his decision to compose poetry in the refined Callimachean or Hellenistic manner rather than traditional epic. See Clausen (1994: 174-5).

retelling of the hero Jason's quest for the Golden Fleece,[29] and Catullus 64, a poem on the wedding of Peleus and Thetis. Both works brought the great and elevated heroes of the past down to the human level, thereby offering new insights into their strengths, passions, and flaws, and both greatly influenced Vergil's presentation of Aeneas.

Of Vergil's other predecessors in Latin literature, the most important was Ennius (239-169 BCE), often called the father of Roman poetry.[30] His *Annales,* which survives only in fragments, was an historical epic about Rome that traced the city's origins back to Aeneas and Troy. It remained the most influential Latin poem until the *Aeneid* was composed and provided a model not only for Vergil's poetic language and themes, but also for his integration of Homer and Roman history. In addition, the *De rerum natura* of Lucretius (ca. 94-55/51 BCE), a hexameter poem on Epicurean philosophy, profoundly influenced Vergil with its forceful language and philosophical ideas.[31]

Finally, Vergil drew much from Greek and Roman[32] tragedy. Many episodes in the *Aeneid* share tragedy's well-known dramatic patterns (such as reversal of fortune) and explore the suffering that befalls mortals often as a result of the immense and incomprehensible power of the gods and fate.[33] As

---

29   On the influence of Apollonius on Vergil, see the important book by Nelis (2001).

30   Ennius introduced the dactylic hexameter as the meter of Latin epic. Two earlier epic writers were Livius Andronicus, who composed a translation of Homer's *Odyssey* into Latin, and Naevius, who composed the *Bellum Punicum,* an epic on the First Punic War. Both Naevius and Livius wrote their epics in a meter called Saturnian that is not fully understood. For the influence of the early Latin poets on the *Aeneid,* see Wigodsky (1972); and on Ennius, Goldschmidt (2013).

31   See Hardie (1986: 157-240) and Adler (2003). The influence of the Epicurean Philodemus on Vergil (and the Augustans more generally) is explored in the collection edited by Armstrong et al. (2004). For Lucretius' influence on Vergil's *Georgics,* see especially Farrell (1991) and Gale (2000).

32   The earliest epic writers (Livius, Naevius, and Ennius; see above) also wrote tragedy, and so it is not surprising that epic and tragedy would influence one another. Latin tragic writing continued into the first century through the work of, e.g., Pacuvius (220-ca. 130 BCE) and Accius (170-ca. 86 BCE). Their tragedies, which included Homeric and Trojan war themes, were important for Vergil. However, since only meager fragments of them have survived, their precise influence is difficult to gauge.

33   Cf., e.g., Heinze (1915, trans. 1993: 251-8). Wlosok (1999) offers a reading of the Dido episode as tragedy, and Pavlock (1985) examines Euripidean

a critic has written, "The influence of tragedy on the *Aeneid* is pervasive, and arguably the single most important factor in Virgil's successful revitalization of the genre of epic."[34]

The *Aeneid* is thus indebted to these and many other sources, the study of which can enrich our appreciation of Vergil's artistry and our interpretation of his epic.[35] However, no source study can fully account for the creative, aesthetic, and moral achievement of the *Aeneid*, which is a work unto itself.

The *Aeneid*, Rome, and Augustus

While Aeneas' story takes place in the distant, mythological past of the Trojan war era, it had a special relevance for Vergil's contemporaries. Not only did the Romans draw their descent from the Trojans, but the emperor Augustus believed that Aeneas was his own ancestor.[36] Vergil makes these national and familial connections major thematic concerns of his epic.

---

influence in the Nisus and Euryalus episode. Hardie (1991, 1997), Panoussi (2002, 2009), and Galinsky (2003) examine the influence of tragedy, particularly in light of French theories of Greek tragedy (e.g., Vernant and Vidal-Naquet (1988)), and draw important parallels between the political and cultural milieus of fifth-century Athens and Augustan Rome. On tragedy and conflicting viewpoints, see Conte (1999, revised now in Conte 2007), and Galinsky (2003).

34 Hardie (1998: 62). See also Hardie (1997).

35 See Farrell (1997) for a full and insightful introduction to the interpretive possibilities that the study of intertextuality in Vergil can offer readers. For a general introduction to intertextuality, see Allen (2000). For the study of intertextuality in Latin literature, see Conte (1986), Farrell (1991: 1-25), Hardie (1993), Fowler (1997), Hinds (1998), and Edmunds (2001). For Vergil's use of Homer, see Knauer (1964b), Barchiesi (1984, in Italian), Gransden (1984), Cairns (1989: 177-248), and Dekel (2012). Knauer (1964a), written in German, is a standard work on this topic; those without German can still benefit from its detailed citations and lists of parallels. For Vergil's use of Homer and Apollonius, see Nelis (2001).

36 Augustus' clan, the Julian *gens*, claimed its descent from Iulus (another name for Aeneas' son Ascanius) and thus also from Aeneas and Venus. Julius Caesar in particular emphasized this ancestry; Augustus made these connections central to his political self-presentation as well. See, e.g., Zanker (1988: 193-210) and Galinsky (1996: 141-224).

As a result, the *Aeneid* is about more than the Trojan war and its aftermath. It is also about the foundation of Rome and its flourishing under Augustus. To incorporate these themes into his epic, Vergil connects mythological and historical time by associating three leaders and city foundations: the founding of Lavinium by Aeneas, the actual founding of Rome by Romulus, and the "re-founding" of Rome by Augustus. These events are prominent in the most important prophecies of the epic: Jupiter's speech to Venus (1.257-96), Anchises' revelation to his son Aeneas (6.756-853), and the scenes on the shield Vulcan makes for Aeneas, discussed in this commentary (8.626-728). Together these passages provide what may be called an Augustan reading of Roman history, one that is shaped by the deeds of these three men and that views Augustus as the culmination of the processes of fate and history.[37]

This is not to say that the associations among Aeneas, Romulus, and Augustus are always positive or unproblematic, particularly given the ways that Aeneas is portrayed and can be interpreted.[38] To some, Vergil's Aeneas represents an idealized Roman hero who thus reflects positively on Augustus by association.[39] In general this type of reading sees a positive imperial ideology in the epic and is referred to as "optimistic" or "Augustan." Others are more troubled by Vergil's Aeneas and advocate interpretations that challenge the moral and spiritual value of his actions, as well as of the role of the gods and fate. Such readings perceive a much darker poetic world[40] and have

---

37   See O'Hara (1990), however, for the deceptiveness of prophecies in the *Aeneid*, as well as the notes below to *Aen.* 8.40-1, 341, 533, 626-728, 629, 652, 720-8.

38   For general interpretation of the *Aeneid*, see n. 23 (above).

39   This type of reading is represented especially by Heinze (1915, trans. 1993), Pöschl (1950, trans. 1962), and Otis (1964). More recent and complex Augustan interpretations can be found in Hardie (1986) and Cairns (1989).

40   See, e.g., Putnam (1965), Johnson (1976), Lyne (1987), and Thomas (2001). Putnam's reading of the *Aeneid* has been particularly influential. Of the ending of the poem he writes: "By giving himself over with such suddenness to the private wrath which the sight of the belt of Pallas arouses, Aeneas becomes himself *impius Furor*, as rage wins the day over moderation, disintegration defeats order, and the achievements of history through heroism fall victim to the human frailty of one man" (1965: 193-4). For a different understanding of Aeneas' wrath, see Galinsky (1988). For *furor* and violence in Book 8, see notes to 184-279, 196, 219-20, 494.

been called "pessimistic" or "ambivalent."[41] Vergil's portrayal of Aeneas is thus a major element in debates over the epic's meaning.[42]

Randall Ganiban, *Series Co-Editor*

---

41   For a general treatment of the optimism/pessimism debate, see Kennedy (1992). For a critique of the "pessimistic" view, see Martindale (1993); for critique of the "optimistic" stance and its rejection of "pessimism," see Thomas (2001); and for brief historical perspective on both sides, see Schmidt (2001). For the continuing debate over the politics of the *Aeneid* and over the Augustan age more generally, see the collections of Powell (1992) and Stahl (1998).

42   Indeed some readers also question whether it is even possible to resolve this interpretive debate because of Vergil's inherent ambiguity. See Johnson (1976), Perkell (1994), O'Hara (2007: 77-103), and Conte (2007). Martindale (1993) offers a critique of ambiguous readings.

Introduction to Book 8:
Its Role in the *Aeneid*

Aeneid 8 is the poem's most Roman book, and the book most concerned with history and the historical process, and with the city of Rome. It features a visit to the site of Rome and stories about Italy's earlier history, and it ends with a depiction of Roman legend and history on Aeneas' shield. It presents what from Aeneas' perspective is the past, present, and future of Italy and especially Rome, though for Roman readers these are all stages in their legendary, historical, and recent past. Two major sections of Book 8, one telling a story about Hercules from early Italian history and one depicting the battle of Actium on the shield, present the struggle of "good" against "evil" in ways that different readers will see either as providing a reliable model for violent heroic action against an evil foe or as lending themselves to multiple perspectives that present differing views on right, wrong, and the ways in which human beings talk about their enemies. Both readings make Book 8 crucial for interpreting Aeneas' killing of Turnus at the end of Book 12.

The book should be seen in the context of its place in the second half of the poem and in the whole poem. *Aeneid* 8 follows Aeneas' landing at the mouth of the Tiber River in Book 7, the attempts to make an alliance with Latinus and the Latins, and the outbreak of war after Juno sends the fury Allecto from the underworld to sow hostilities between Trojans and Italians. After the events of Book 8, war will break out in full in Book 9 as Turnus attacks the Trojan camp in Aeneas' absence. Aeneas returns in Book 10, and then the death of Pallas, the son of Evander entrusted to Aeneas in 8.514-19, at Turnus' hands sends him into a rage like that of Achilles after the death of Patroclus in the *Iliad*. Book 11 sees a truce for funerals, an assembly of the Italians, and further battles, while Book 12 shows the events leading to the final confrontation between Aeneas and Turnus, in which the influence can be felt of the ideas and values of Evander, whom we meet in Book 8. Book 8 can thus be seen as the second book of the Iliadic half of the poem, after an Odyssean 1-6, and as such can be paired with Book 2 as two books about the death of Aeneas' past city Troy in Book 2, and the future city of his people, Rome, in Book 8. Some also see in the *Aeneid* a tripartite structure, in which Book 8 is the last of four books about Italy and Sicily,[1] featuring Sicily in Book 5, Cumae and the descent to the underworld in Book 6, the landing at the mouth of the Tiber in Book 7, and the events of Book 8.

Like other books in 7-12, the eighth book often reworks material from Homer's *Iliad* and *Odyssey*. Aeneas' visit to Evander's city draws on Telemachus' visit to Nestor in the *Odyssey* (the *Odyssey* was a model for many aspects of Books 1-6), and the poem adapts and rivals the *Iliad* both in the request for arms for her son by the hero's mother (Thetis in the *Iliad*, Venus here) and in the detailed description of the hero's shield (that of Achilles in the *Iliad*, Aeneas here). The book also has numerous debts to Apollonius of Rhodes' *Argonautica* (third century BCE), and it deals with material found in Ennius' Latin *Annales* (early second century BCE) and more recently in the early books of Livy's *Ab Urbe Condita* (written in prose in the decade or so before the *Aeneid*); the book often backdates to the age of Aeneas practices dated by those Roman authors to the period of the Roman kings (see 343 n.).[2]

It will be useful to summarize and comment on what happens in Book 8. The book starts with preparations being made for the war that broke out in Book 7, and with Turnus sending for allies (1-17). Then the river god Tiberinus appears to the worried Aeneas in a dream, welcomes him to Italy with deceptively encouraging words, and tells him to seek as allies Greeks living just up the river at the future site of Rome and to sacrifice to Juno (18-101). Aeneas finds Evander and the Arcadians sacrificing to Hercules, in a scene modeled on the visit by Odysseus' son Telemachus to Nestor in *Odyssey* 3 (102-305); the old man Nestor will be a model for Evander in several ways. Evander tells Aeneas that their sacrifice commemorates Hercules' killing of the monster Cacus who had stolen his cattle, resulting in the founding of the altar known to the Romans as the Ara Maxima. Evander's long story, which borrows from *The Homeric Hymn to Hermes* and a number of other texts, is thus an "aetion" or origin-story for the Ara Maxima and the worship of Hercules and also presents one model for violent heroic action against

---

1   "The central and important core of the poem"; Duckworth (1957: 3). Cf. Boyle (2003: 91).

2   On such "intertextuality" and the use of earlier texts, see the section "Vergil and his predecessors" in the above "Introduction to Vergil's *Aeneid*."

a foe. Book 8 presents a number of briefer aetiologies. The interest in aetiology matches that of third-century BCE Alexandrian poets like Callimachus (whose most famous poem was his *Aetia*) and Apollonius of Rhodes (whose *Argonautica* is full of aetia), but Book 8 also draws upon Roman material from Ennius, Varro, and other Latin authors. The whole *Aeneid*, of course, is an aetion for Rome, the Roman people, and the family of Augustus. Both Evander's Cacus story and the subsequent hymn to Hercules sung at the feast stress gore, violence, and justified angry punishment, as does Evander's later (481-504) harshly negative portrait of the exiled Etruscan king Mezentius, whom Aeneas will fight and kill at the end of Book 10. Evander's values present one perspective through which to view later events of the war, including Aeneas' killing of Turnus in revenge for the death of Pallas at the end of the poem; the end of the poem is profoundly influenced by Evander's way of looking at the world.

After the feast, Evander tells Aeneas a version of Latium's past (314-36), including the Golden Age ruled by Saturn and the decline that followed it—looking at things from a perspective different from that of the narrator at 7.45-9 and 177-91 or Latinus in 7.202-11. Evander then gives Aeneas (and us) a tour of the future site of Rome (337-61) as they walk from the Ara Maxima to Evander's home, which seems to be near the future site of Augustus' home on the Palatine, which archaeologists have excavated only in the last half century (see map 1). Some landmarks are described by Evander, others by the narrator from a contemporary perspective that contrasts Evander's poverty with Rome's opulence, not without some moralizing preference for Rome's simpler past. It is as though the Roman reader, like a visitor to Rome today, sees layers of different eras overlaid upon one another, as on the kind of reused manuscript called a palimpsest,[3] or on a multiply exposed photograph, or a modern website or slideshow offering a time-lapsed view of the city's growth (cf. Johanson (2009)).

The narrative cuts away to Olympus, where Venus flirts with her husband Vulcan and asks him for weapons for Aeneas (i.e., her son not with him but with the mortal Anchises). Thetis in the *Iliad* had asked for arms for her son Achilles (370-406); in this striking passage a character cites her own literary model as precedent. Vulcan and the Cyclopes begin forging the weapons, after Vulcan in a surprising and challenging simile is compared

---

3   For the image, cf. Edwards (1996: 27-8) on Freud's view of Rome.

to a chaste woman rising early to do weaving-work to support her family (407-53).

Evander also tells Aeneas that because of an oracle, an Etruscan army angry at its vicious exiled king Mezentius awaits a foreign leader like him (just as oracles in Book 7 told Latinus to expect a foreign leader). Evander gives Aeneas some Arcadian troops, including his son Pallas (454-519); Pallas' death at the hands of Turnus in Book 10 will lead to the poem's final scene in Book 12 in which Aeneas kills Turnus in revenge, as Pallas, Turnus, and Aeneas come to play the Iliadic roles of Achilles' friend Patroclus, his killer Hector, and Hector's killer Achilles. After Evander says he will send Pallas to war with Aeneas, omens in the sky frighten everyone but Aeneas, who says they refer to him and to his mother's promise to bring him weapons (520-40); the omens probably presage both Aeneas' victory and Pallas' death. Aeneas chooses men to accompany him to meet the Etruscans, Evander makes an emotional speech of farewell, and they depart (546-96). Near the Etruscan camp, Venus brings Aeneas the arms, and the hero gets a rare embrace from his divine mother (597-616).

As Aeneas looks at the arms made by Vulcan, the poet describes a selection of the scenes from future Roman history on the shield (626-728), in one of the most famous and memorable parts of the poem. The shield offers one of three great prophecies in the *Aeneid* that relate parts of the history from Aeneas' time to that of Vergil and Augustus: the others are Jupiter's prophecy to Venus in 1.257-96 and Anchises' review in the underworld of the souls of his descendants in 6.756-892. Vergil's description begins with Romulus (a descendant of Aeneas who will found Rome) and scenes from early Roman history, often featuring threats to the young city-state, like the sack by the Gauls, most of which featured in Ennius' early second-century BCE epic *Annales* (626-66). After brief references to the late-Republican figures Cato and Catiline in the underworld (666-70), Vergil spends the rest of his description on the Battle of Actium in 31 BCE, in which Augustus and Agrippa defeated Antony and his Egyptian wife Cleopatra ("shameful!"), and Augustus' triple-triumph—a glorious victory parade—in 29 BCE (671-728). Large structural patterns and some details allow a reader to associate Hercules' defeat of Cacus, Augustus' victory over Antony, and Aeneas' killing of Mezentius in Book 10 and especially Turnus in Book 12, but other details work against such associations to produce a more indeterminate picture in the poem as a whole (cf. 184-279 n., 626-731 n.). As the book closes Aeneas, though he does not understand what is depicted on the shield, marvels as he lifts onto his shoulder—as at the end of Book 2 he had lifted his father—the legends and glory of his descendants (730-1).

The book provides numerous challenges to interpretation. Tiberinus is helpful to Aeneas but deceives him (40-1 n.). Evander must think of his story of Hercules and Cacus as a model for a hero punishing a villain, but details of the presentation suggest a more blurred picture in which the violent hero and the monster he kills share many traits (184-279). In all his appearances Evander shows a remarkable fondness for gore, violence, and punishment (196 n.), a fondness that some readers may share but others find less attractive. The simplicity of Evander's home and city contrasts with the splendor of Augustan Rome (98-100 n., 366 n.), with some preference for the former. The method by which Venus seduces her husband into providing arms for her son—her son by an adulterous relationship with a mortal—shocked critics even in antiquity (370-453 n., 381-2 n., 406 n.) and provides a challenging context in which to view the shield. The shield lends itself to a variety of interpretive approaches. Its fantastic hyperbole and exaggeration might work as effective encomium of Augustus as world-conqueror, or might suggest to some readers that the shield is a piece of false propaganda more simplistic than the rest of the poem. The shield presents Actium as "the victory of order over disorder, of West over East, of male over female, of civilisation over barbarism."[4] But both the shield's treatment of Actium and the story of Hercules and Cacus can be seen as depictions that are *quoted* by the main narrator but are much simpler in their moral outlook than his own handling of the stories of Aeneas (cf., e.g., 299-300 n., 626-728 n., 720-8 n.). Different readers will either take the shield and the Hercules-Cacus story as a guide to how to read the rest of the poem, or the rest of the poem as a guide to how to read the shield and the Hercules-Cacus episode.

For bibliography on Book 8 in general, see Putnam (1965: 105-50), Fowler (1917), Wiesen (1973), George (1974), Clausen (1987: 61-82 and 2002: 153-84), Horsfall (1995: 162-9), Zetzel (1997), Boyle (1999), Tueller (2000), Bacon (2001), Nelis (2001: 327-64), Fratantuono (2007: 233-61), Binder (1971),[5] Novara (1989),[6] Feldherr (2014), and Quint (2015). Further references will be given below, especially on the Hercules-Cacus story (184-279), Evander's history of Italy (306-36) and tour of Rome (337-69), and the shield

---

4   Zetzel (1997: 198); see also 626-728 n., 675 n.
5   In German, reviewed in English by Gransden (1974).
6   In French, reviewed by Harrison (1989).

of Aeneas (626-731). Search engines will provide interesting images of works ancient and modern in various media on Hercules and Cacus, Aeneas and Pallanteum (see 107 n.), the shield of Aeneas, and the Battle of Actium.

Please note: the following commentaries on Book 8 will be cited by the author's last name without date: Page (1900), Conington (1963, orig. 1883-4), R.D. Williams (1972-3), Eden (1975), Gransden (1976), and Fordyce (1977). An ambitious commentary on Book 8 by Fratantuono and Smith is forthcoming from Brill. The way in which the volumes in this series have been adapted from Page (1900) has been described in the Preface, and some of his language remains in my notes. References to *Allen and Greenough's New Latin Grammar* ("AG"; see Mahoney (2001)) are provided by section number (e.g., "AG §333"), which will be the same in the 1903 edition, Mahoney's revision, or the version online at the Perseus Project (www.perseus.tufts.edu). *OLD* refers to the Oxford Latin Dictionary (2nd ed. 1996), and *VE* refers to Thomas and Ziolkowski, eds. (2014). Terms marked with an asterisk (e.g., "hypotactic*") are defined in Appendix B, on stylistic terms; for metrical features, see Appendix A on meter.

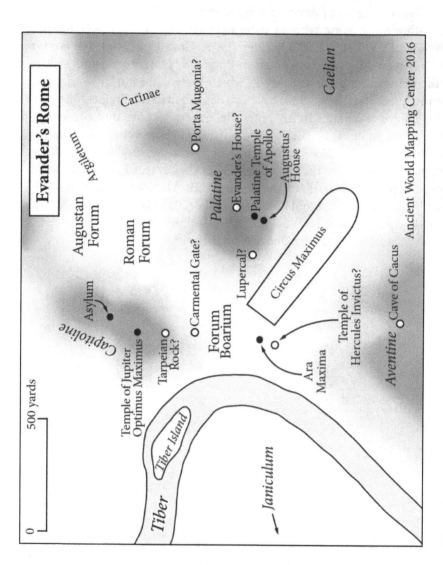

Map 1. Ancient World Mapping Center © 2017 (awmc.unc.edu). Used by permission.

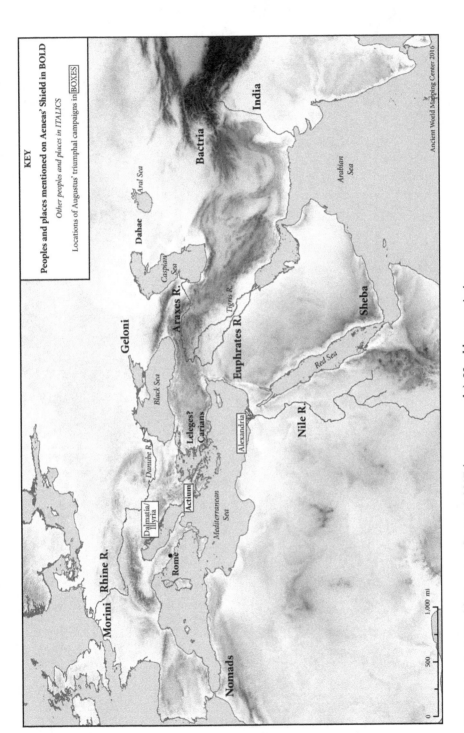

Map 2. Ancient World Mapping Center © 2017 (awmc.unc.edu). Used by permission.

LIBER OCTAVUS

Ut belli signum Laurenti Turnus ab arce
extulit et rauco strepuerunt cornua cantu,
utque acris concussit equos utque impulit arma,

1-101. Turnus and the Italians prepare for war, levying troops and sending embassies to the
Greek Diomedes to seek help against his old enemy Aeneas (1-17). Aeneas is torn by worry,
but after he finally falls asleep the rivergod Tiberinus tells him that he has found his home,
that the gods' anger against him has yielded, and that he should seek help from Arcadians
up the river—who live at the future site of Rome (18-65). Aeneas wakes, prays, and sacrifices
to Tiberinus and prepares to follow his advice (66-101). Both the embassy to Diomedes and
the dream of Tiberinus are charactized by deception: the embassy because it exaggerates the
Trojans' aims in Italy (see 12 n., 13 n.), Tiberinus because the reader knows that the anger of
Juno against Aeneas has not yielded at all (40-1 n.). But Tiberinus' advice will also help Aeneas
find the allies he needs for the coming war.

For commentaries cited by last name only, terms marked in the notes with an asterisk (*),
and the abbreviations VE and AG, see the end of the "Introduction to Book 8."

*1-17. Turnus gives the signal for war and raises troops, while Venulus is sent on an embassy to
Diomedes, to tell him about Aeneas' arrival and to ask for help.*

The book begins with three sentences, the first and third long and involving multiple
subordinate clauses (cf. 10 n.) in the hypotactic* style characteristic of much Roman prose,
especially historiography.

1-2. **belli signum...extulit:** "raised the signal for war." Probably a flag such as was raised during
the Republic as a signal for battle, along with the blowing of horns (Livy *Ab Urbe Condita*
10.19 *signa canere ac vexilla efferri*, Caes. *Bellum Gallicum* 2.20), but possibly the horns in 2
are the signal, and 1-2 here offer theme and variation*. **Laurenti:** adj. We never learn the name
of Latinus' city, where Turnus is in command because Latinus has locked himself away (7.600);
the name of his people the Laurentians is explained at 7.59-63. **rauco strepuerunt cornua cantu:**
alliteration* and onomatopoeia*, probably suggestive of the archaic* epic of Ennius; cf. 7.615
aereaque adsensu conspirant cornua rauco, Lucr. 2.619 *raucisonoque minantur cornua cantu*.

3. **utque...:** interestingly unusual Latin: Vergil could have said that Turnus drove forward
(*impulit*) his horses and smashed together or shook (*concussit*) his weapons, but he switches
the verbs and objects so that Turnus "roused" (lit. "struck"?) the horses and "drove (together)"
his arms. For similar switches, cf. Eden ad loc., Horsfall (2013) on *Aen.* 6.847-8, and Görler
(1999), who notes that such "shifting from a familiar to a less common syntactical object...,
like a fresh metaphor...makes us see things anew" (p. 282) and both produces "a stronger visual
aspect" and "makes us realize that horse-riding is all shaking and tossing" (p. 281); see also
Conte on enallage* in 525-6 n. For *concussit*, cf. how Hercules strikes Cacus' cave-top in 237
(with *impulit* in 239), and 354 *aegida concuteret*. For *impulit arma*, cf. 528-9 *arma...| pulsa
tonare*; 12.332 *Mavors clipeo increpat*; 12.700 *horrendumque intonat armis*; as well as Callim.
Hymn to Delos 136, where Ares strikes his shield with his sword.

extemplo turbati animi, simul omne tumultu
coniurat trepido Latium saevitque iuventus   5
effera. ductores primi Messapus et Ufens
contemptorque deum Mezentius undique cogunt
auxilia et latos vastant cultoribus agros.
mittitur et magni Venulus Diomedis ad urbem
qui petat auxilium, et Latio consistere Teucros,   10
advectum Aenean classi victosque penatis

4-6. **extemplo turbati animi**: supply *sunt*. The phrase occurs also at 11.451; *turbatus* is often used near *trepidus* (Lucr. 3.834 *belli trepido concussa tumultu*; Hor. *Carm.* 3.27.17 *quanto trepidet tumultu*). **tumultu**: used elsewhere of an "uprising" in Italy or Gaul (Cic. *Phil.* 8.3), but the sense of "tumult" or "confusion" is equally present here; cf. 371 *mota tumultu*, of Venus. **trepido**: conveys excitement, not fear: cf. 11.300, *Geo.* 4.69 *trepidantia bello* "eager for war." **simul…**: note the asyndeton* or lack of conjunction connecting this and the previous clause. **omne…coniurat…Latium…iuventus**: *coniurat* and *iuventus* are both technical terms for a military oath sworn by males of fighting age; cf. Caes. *B.G.* 7.1 *de senatusque consulto certior factus, ut omnes iuniores Italiae coniurarent*, a decree that "all those of military age should take the oath together"; cf. too Augustus *Res Gestae* 25 *iuravit in mea verba tota Italia sponte sua*. Twenty years before Vergil's birth, a number of Italian cities united to fight a war against Rome, the Social War (war with the *socii*) of 91-88 BCE, and that war provides a historical backdrop for the war between Italians and Trojans and their allies in *Aen.* 7-12. Cf. 678 *hinc Augustus agens Italos in proelia Caesar*, Toll (1997), Johnson (2001), Ando (2002). **saevitque iuventus | effera**: the verb and adj. may reflect the natural ferocity of the Latins or, as the fourth-century commentator Servius says, the madness inspired by Allecto (7.323-571). For savagery in the *Aeneid*, cf. Knox (1997).

6-7. Three warriors from the Catalogue at the end of Book 7: Messapus (7.691), Ufens (7.745), and Mezentius (7.648), also there called *contemptor divum*, and about whom Evander will soon tell tales of extraordinary cruelty (8.482-8; see notes).

8. **cultoribus**: abl. of separation; they empty the fields of their farmers by taking them away as soldiers. Cf. *Geo.* 1.507 *squalent abductis arva colonis*, of the effect of war.

9. **Diomedis**: gen. Greek hero who nearly killed Aeneas in *Il.* 5.239-453 and emigrated to Italy after the Trojan War; cf. Horsfall (2003: 163-4), Fletcher (2006). Aeneas' first speech in the poem mentions him (1.96-7); Diomedes' story and his rejection of this embassy's request for aid are reported at 11.225-95.

10. **qui petat…**: "to seek aid and inform him (*edoceat* 13) that…," subjunctives in a relative clause of purpose. The infinitives in the indirect statements of 10-17 are dependent on *edoceat*, in a long sentence suggestive of the style of historical prose.

11. **advectum**: supply *esse*. **classi**: this form of the ablative only here, *classe* seven times. **Aenean**: Gk. acc. sing.: nom. *Aeneas*, gen. and dat. *Aeneae*, acc. *Aenean* (*Aeneam* occurs in other authors), abl. *Aenea* (AG §44). **victosque penatis**: the phrase is used by Aeneas' foe Juno at 1.68.

inferre et fatis regem se dicere posci
edoceat, multasque viro se adiungere gentis
Dardanio et late Latio increbrescere nomen:
quid struat his coeptis, quem, si fortuna sequatur,   15
eventum pugnae cupiat, manifestius ipsi
quam Turno regi aut regi apparere Latino.
    Talia per Latium. quae Laomedontius heros

---

12. **inferre:** cf. 1.6 *inferretque deos Latio*. **fatis regem se dicere posci:** for Aeneas, an exaggeration or lie (cf. next note); more accurate for what Latinus has been saying (cf. 7.254-8, 272 *hunc illum poscere fata*). For more echoes of 1.1-22 in these lines, cf. 1.2 *fato*, 1.21 *populum...regem*.

13. **multas...gentes:** another exaggeration or lie, as often in embassies and other speeches in the *Aeneid*, as no allies had as yet joined him; cf. the exaggerations of Ilioneus (7.236-8 *multi nos populi, multae...gentes*), and Aeneas (8.146-9), noted by Heinze (1993: 423 n. 72).

14. **Dardanio:** possibly suggesting that his connection with the Italian Dardanus (cf. 7.207) would induce the Italians to join him.

15-16. **struat...cupiat:** subjunctives in indir. question dependent on *manifestius...apparere*; cf. 2.60, 4.235. The first verb has a bad sense as in the common phrases *struere crimina, insidias, odium*. **si fortuna sequatur:** literally "if fortune should follow (him)" (subjunctive in a future less vivid protasis), but here as at 4.109 with the sense of "favorable fortune" as in the phrase *fortuna secunda*. **manifestius ipsi...:** "more obviously clear to him (the person addressed) than to Turnus...." Diomedes who knows the Trojans could judge better than Turnus or Latinus what they intended.

17. **Turno regi...regi...Latino:** giving both kings their official title. The use of Turnus' name in the first and last lines of 1-17 is an example of ring composition.

18-35. Aeneas is worried, and his thoughts shift in all directions, like the light reflected from water, but after he falls asleep the rivergod Tiberinus appears to him to lessen his cares.

    The description of Aeneas' doubt and sleeplessness and the simile* illustrating them both link Aeneas, through intratextual or intertextual echoes, to distressed or lovelorn heroines such as Dido in Book 4, Ariadne in Catullus 64, and Apollonius' Medea (including perhaps Medea in the translation of Apollonius in Vergil's youth by Varro of Atax; see 26 n.). Readers should think about how Aeneas is like and unlike them; see esp. Reed (2007: 186-9), Lyne (1987: 125-32), and further references in notes below. This will be Aeneas' last moment of profound doubt in the poem, though cf. the hesitation at 12.486-7, quoted on 19 below, and at 12.940 before killing Turnus.

18. **talia per Latium:** supply a verb like *gerebantur* (suggested by Servius). **Laomedontius:** Trojan, of the race of Laomedon who cheated Apollo, Poseidon, and Hercules, and so the word always has the potential to suggest treachery. Cf. 157-9 n., 291 n., 7.105, *Geo.* 1.502 with Thomas (1988) who notes that the adj. "seems to be Callimachean (*Aet.* 1, fr. 21.4 Pf.)," Wiesen (1973: 744-6), Petrini (1997: 54-5).

cuncta videns magno curarum fluctuat aestu,
atque animum nunc huc celerem nunc dividit illuc   20
in partisque rapit varias perque omnia versat,
sicut aquae tremulum labris ubi lumen aënis
sole repercussum aut radiantis imagine lunae
omnia pervolitat late loca, iamque sub auras
erigitur summique ferit laquearia tecti.   25

---

19. **aestu:** suggests a boiling, troubled sea. **fluctuat:** may describe either a storm of passion or, as here, the "wavering" of doubt. Reed (2007: 187): "the text elaborates an image that melds [Aeneas] with Dido in her distressed-heroine persona." **curarum:** in 35 Tiberinus will take away Aeneas' *curae*. Cf. 4.532 *magnoque irarum fluctuat aestu*, of Dido's passion; its models in Catullus 64.62: *et magnis curarum fluctuat undis* (Ariadne) and Lucr. 6.73-4 *magnos irarum volvere fluctus*; *Aen.* 12.486-7 *heu quid agat? vario nequiquam fluctuat aestu* | *diversaeque vocant animum in contraria curae* (Aeneas' doubt in battle); 12.527 *fluctuat ira intus*. See Lyne (1987: 125-32), Petrini (1997: 55), Dyson (1997).

20-1. Repeated from 4.285-6, where Aeneas is unsure how to approach Dido; cf. also 10.680 *haec memorans animo nunc huc nunc fluctuat illuc* (the suicidal Turnus). **partis:** can refer to geographical "directions" (*OLD* 13) or figuratively to "aspects of a problem" (*OLD* 14).

22-5. **sicut aquae…:** "as when in bronze basins of water the quivering light flung back by the sun or the moon's radiant form…." Like other epic poets such as Homer, Apollonius, and Lucretius, Vergil often uses extended similes* to comment upon his narrative; in this book see also 243-6, 391-2, 407-13 (implied simile), 589-91, 622-3. Here the sun's or moon's rays strike the water causing a light to be "dashed back" (*repercussum*) and, as the water is somehow (see Apollonius quoted below) agitated, this light plays about on the walls and ceiling. Today the effect can be produced with the face of a watch or cellphone. **imagine lunae:** is strictly parallel to *sole* and so cannot be "the reflection of the moon" in the water, but rather the moon whatever its form, crescent or full. The simile* is from Apollonius, *Arg.* 3.755-60, where it describes the trembling of Medea's heart: "as when a ray of sunlight bounds through a house, leaping from water freshly poured into a cauldron or maybe a bucket, and glances here and there, when shaken [note the absence of a cause of motion in Vergil] with a swift whirl" (Race (2008)), but borrows language from Lucretius' lines on stars reflected in standing water at *DRN* 4.211-15 (Clausen (2002: 154)). The simile also interacts with the one at *Aen.* 7.462-6 linking Turnus' anger with water boiling over. For discussion of the simile, cf. Johnson (1976: 84-7), Lyne (1987: 125-32), Clausen (1987: 61-4; 2002: 153-6), Reed (2007: 187-9), and, on links with the shield of Aeneas, Feldherr (2014: 290-2).

25. **laquearia:** cf. 1.726 *laquearibus aureis*, another reminder here of Dido and her gilded palace (the word occurs only in these two passages), and Lucr. 2.28 *laqueata aurataque templa*, in a description of aspects of wealth the philosopher does not need. In this book Evander's poverty will be presented as admirable (98-100 n.).

nox erat et terras animalia fessa per omnis
alituum pecudumque genus sopor altus habebat,
cum pater in ripa gelidique sub aetheris axe
Aeneas, tristi turbatus pectora bello,
procubuit seramque dedit per membra quietem.　　　30
huic deus ipse loci fluvio Tiberinus amoeno
populeas inter senior se attollere frondes
visus (eum tenuis glauco velabat amictu
carbasus, et crinis umbrosa tegebat harundo),
tum sic adfari et curas his demere dictis:　　　35

---

26. **nox erat...**: complicated intertextuality and intratextual self-echoes here. Within the poem, cf. 3.147 *nox erat et terris animalia somnus habebat*, before Aeneas' dream of the Penates, and 4.522-7, which describes how all of nature is asleep, but for Dido (who in 532 *magnoque irarum fluctuat aestu*). Reed (2007: 189) says this is the "sleeplessness motif that is commonly given to lovelorn heroines" such as Dido in *Aen.* 4 and Medea in Apoll. Rhod. *Arg.* 3.751-60 — lines containing the light simile Vergil has just adapted (22-5 n.). Vergil also adapts the Latin translation of Apollonius here by his older contemporary Varro of Atax (frag. 8 Morel, 10 Courtney), preserved for us at Sen. *Controv.* 7.1.27, who notes both Vergil's imitation and Ovid's view of the Varro passage. Readers may also think of Agamemnon at the start of *Il.* 10, after Achilles has turned down the embassy and things look grim for the Greeks; cf. Clausen (2002: 156), and below 36-65 n. for Agamemnon's Deceptive Dream in *Il.* 2. In 2.267-8, all the Trojans sleep peacefully before the Greeks attack.

27. **alituum**: alternate gen. plur. of *ales*, used fives times in Lucretius and once each in Manilius and Statius; *alitum* is more common.

30. **seramque...**: "rest at last" (lit. "late rest").

31. **ipse**: "in visible presence," not merely revealing himself by voice; cf. 352-3 *ipsum...Iovem*. **fluvio...amoeno**: abl. of quality or of description (AG §415), cf. 7.30. On the river's name, see 72 n.

32. **senior**: sea and river gods are generally depicted as old; cf. 5.823 *senior Glauci chorus*.

33-4. **tenuis glauco...carbasus**: his clothing is "grey" (at 12.885 the fountain-nymph Juturna covers herself with a *glauco...amictu*) and "thin," or almost transparent, like water, being composed of fine flax or linen.

35. **adfari...demere**: probably historic infinitives, though they could be seen as dependent on *visus* in 33; the line is also used at 2.775, of the prophetic words of the shade of Creusa to Aeneas, and 3.153 of his dream-vision of the Penates. All three speakers seek to console Aeneas; see O'Hara (1990) 88-9.

"O sate gente deum, Troianam ex hostibus urbem
qui revehis nobis aeternaque Pergama servas,
exspectate solo Laurenti arvisque Latinis,
hic tibi certa domus, certi (ne absiste) penates;
neu belli terrere minis; tumor omnis et irae   40
concessere deum.

36-65. *Tiberinus tells Aeneas that he has reached his home, and that all the gods' anger has yielded. As a sign of this, he will find a white sow with thirty white young, indicating that after thirty years Ascanius will found Alba. He tells him to seek the alliance of Arcadians living in nearby Pallanteum, who are at war with the Latins, and promises to conduct him safely up the Tiber, then reveals that he is the god of that river.*

    The prophetic dream-appearance of the rivergod to Aeneas resembles his dreams of Hector (2.268-97), the Penates (3.147-81), and Anchises (5.719-45), and shares material with the prophecies of Jupiter (1.257-96) and Helenus (3.374-462). It also resembles the Deceptive Dream of Agamemnon in *Iliad* 2.1-40, and Iris' appearance to Turnus in 9.1-24, for besides providing useful encouragement and crucial advice about where to get allies, Tiberinus' claim that the gods' anger against him has yielded is false (40-1 n.). Tueller (2000: 361) also suggests that we may see echoes of Callimachus' influential dream of the Muses in *Aetia* 1, fr. 2 Pf.; this book will feature many stories about the origins (*aetia*) of Rome and its customs. On rivers throughout Book 8, especially on the shield of Aeneas, cf. Feldherr (2014).

36. sate gente deum: Aeneas is the son of Venus, and on his father Anchises' side is descended from Jupiter through Jupiter's son Dardanus.

37. revehis: because Dardanus had come from Italy (7.219, 240). **aeternaque Pergama:** *Pergama* is plural for Troy, and is metrically convenient for the hexameter; *aeterna* is predicative, as Aeneas' actions in a sense will make Troy eternal. But the words are also slightly deceptive, for as Book 12 shows (12.791-840), and the reader knows, Rome will not be Troy.

38. solo Laurenti arvisque Latinis: abl. of place, or possibly of agent (Eden ad loc.) with *expectate*; if agent, then with the pathetic fallacy*, as Servius says.

39. hic: not true of the particular spot where Aeneas is, but true with reference to *arvis Latinis*, and so "in this country," in Latium. **ne absiste:** *ne* + pres. imperative in second person prohibitions is archaic* and in Vergil's day poetic (AG §450a). Vergil elides *ne* only here and at 10.11, another parenthetical imperative.

40-1. terrere: passive imperative. **tumor omnis et irae | concessere deum:** Cf. 6.407 *tumida ex ira tum corda residunt* (Charon); Cic. *Tusc.* 3.26 *cum tumor animi resedisset.* The words *tumor* and *irae* can be seen as a hendiadys*. After we have seen the actions and attitudes of Juno and Allecto in Book 7, however, Tiberinus' claim must seem simply false. If the half-line (see next paragraph) were completed in a way like that suggested by Servius on *Aen.* 3.340, *profugis nova moenia Teucris*, his honesty could be saved. But gods who seek to encourage Aeneas regularly deceive him, and both Aeneas' ignorance about the extent of Juno's hostility and the anger of the gods in general are important themes in the poem, starting with the poet's question at 1.11: *tantaene animis caelestibus irae?* See Eden, who says on 41 that when encouragement is

iamque tibi, ne vana putes haec fingere somnum,
litoreis ingens inventa sub ilicibus sus
triginta capitum fetus enixa iacebit,
alba solo recubans, albi circum ubera nati.   45
[hic locus urbis erit, requies ea certa laborum,]

---

needed "mis-representation is permitted and expected," Johnson (1976: 99-105, 166 n. 67), O'Hara (1990: 24-39, 116-22), Feeney (1991: 129-55), Tueller (2000: 367).

Line 41 is the first example in Book 8 of a "half-line," a line left unfinished at the time of Vergil's death. In his *Life of Vergil*, Donatus claims that on his deathbed Vergil wanted the *Aeneid* burned but ultimately left it in the hands of Varius and Tucca to edit, with the proviso that they not add anything or remove the incomplete lines: *ea conditione, ne quid adderent quod a se editum non esset, et versus etiam imperfectos, si qui erant, relinquerent*. There are roughly fifty-eight incomplete verses in the entire *Aeneid* (the number is disputed because some half-lines may have been completed by later readers and thus now seem complete). There are two other half-lines in Book 8 (469, 536). Some half-lines have seemed to modern readers to work so well that some think Vergil meant to leave them incomplete (cf. 3.340, 4.361), but this seems extremely unlikely. On half-lines see Sparrow (1931), Goold (1990: 109-12), who says "The conclusion is inescapable: Virgil had no intention of leaving half-lines in the *Aeneid*," and O'Hara (2010).

42. **iamque...:** "and now, so that you do not think..., you shall find lying..."; *tibi* is ethical dative (AG §380).

43-6. **litoreis...laborum:** repeated (except that *hic locus* in 46 is substituted for *is locus*) from 3.390-3, where Helenus prophesies (slightly inaccurately) that Aeneas will found a city in the place where this portent occurs. These notes are adapted from the notes there of Perkell (2010).

43. **ilicibus sus:** the monosyllabic verse ending, with clash of ictus and accent, is archaic* (see Appendix A on meter, and Dainotti (2015: 206-16)), and thus appropriate to this traditional oracle. The sow prodigy is a traditional feature of the Aeneas legend; other versions are found in Lycophron (1255-60) and Dionysius of Halicarnassus (1.56); see Horsfall (2006: xxxiii-xxxiv). Helenus in 3.393 says the sow will mark the site of the future city; Tiberinus says that it signifies the foundation of Alba Longa from Lavinium in thirty years—as many years as the sow has offspring. **litoreis:** occurs only rarely of a riverbank.

44. **triginta...:** "shall lie having given birth (*enixa*) to a litter of thirty young," the huge number of offspring being prodigious in itself (Horsfall (2006) on 3.391). **capitum:** descriptive gen. after *fetus*; *caput* is used in counting men or animals, cf. *per capita*.

45. **solo:** abl. of place where, without preposition. **albi...nati:** sc. *iacebunt*. The anaphora* of *alba/albi* suggests an etymological link with Alba Longa (48 n.).

46. Editors condemn this line as an interpolation from Book 3 for one good reason (i.e., that it is present in only one of the three major manuscripts, R, and Servius does not comment on it) and for one reason involving a weak argument, namely that Aeneas' city will not in fact be on the spot where the sow lies, whereas in Book 3 Helenus spoke more generally about "that place." But misstatements or deception in prophecies are common in the poem, and Tiberinus has just lied about the anger of the gods (40-1 n.), though it is true that without this line the passage reads smoothly and keeps the focus on Ascanius' city (cf. 1.267-71).

ex quo ter denis urbem redeuntibus annis
Ascanius clari condet cognominis Albam.
haud incerta cano. nunc qua ratione quod instat
expedias victor, paucis (adverte) docebo.   50
Arcades his oris, genus a Pallante profectum,
qui regem Evandrum comites, qui signa secuti,
delegere locum et posuere in montibus urbem

---

47. **ex quo:** without 46, "and in accordance with this," as if *ex quo prodigio*; though it might mean "thereafter," as if *ex quo tempore*. **ter denis:** cf. Jupiter's prophecy at 1.267-71, which says that Aeneas will live for three more years, Ascanius will reign for thirty (*triginta*) and found Alba Longa, and then after Trojans rule for three hundred years, Romulus will be born and found Rome. The prediction that Aeneas himself has only three more years as a mortal is omitted.

48. **cognominis:** a *cognomen* is a name which "corresponds" or "answers" to something, and in poetry the word often calls attention to etymology. The name of the city *Alba* reflects the omen of the white sow, and the ambiguous term *clarum nomen* (*clarus* = famous, bright, white) underscores the derivation; cf. O'Hara (2017: 201). So at 7.671 *Tibur* has the *cognomen* of *Tiburtus*, 8.331 *Thybris* that of King Thybris, 11.246 *Argyripa* that of Argos, and cf. 12.845 *pestes cognomine Dirae* "plagues (i.e., creatures from Hell) rightly named Dreadful."

49. **haud incerta cano:** *cano*, "I foretell" (cf. 7.79), here in litotes* with a double negative, as in *Ecl.* 6.9 *non iniussa cano*. In structure both passages resemble the famous statement about treating only myths that have been treated before at Callim. fr. 612 Pf.; cf. his Gr. *amarturon ouden aeido*; Tueller (2000: 364). **quod instat:** the clause is direct object of *expedias*.

50. **paucis:** sc. *verbis*.

51. **Arcades:** nom. pl. masc., with Greek short *-es*. **profectum:** < *proficisci*, here "descended from" (*OLD* 4c). *Pallantium* was a city of Arcadia in Greece founded by a Pallas, whom Servius calls Evander's grandfather, and Vergil makes Evander migrate from there and found the city of *Pallanteum* on the Palatine Mount (*montibus* 53, see map 1), so that both city and hill derive their name from that of Pallas. The connection is "a figment of early Hellenizing antiquarianism" (Fordyce) based on the resemblance of names; cf. Livy 1.5 with the good note of Ogilvie (1970), Dion. Hal. *Rom. Ant.* 1.31, Varro *LL* 5.53 with other derivations, O'Hara (2017: 202). For early stories about Greeks in Rome or even founding Rome, cf. Gruen (1992: 6-21), Hall (2005). Tiberinus helps fulfill the Sibyl's prophecy to Aeneas at 6.96-7 of unexpected help "from a Greek city."

52. **secuti:** supply *sunt*. Instead of this repeated *qui* and hendiadys* (*Evandrum, signa*), prose would say "followed the standards of Evander."

Pallantis proavi de nomine Pallanteum.
hi bellum adsidue ducunt cum gente Latina; 55
hos castris adhibe socios et foedera iunge.
ipse ego te ripis et recto flumine ducam,
adversum remis superes subvectus ut amnem.
surge age, nate dea, primisque cadentibus astris
Iunoni fer rite preces, iramque minasque 60
supplicibus supera votis. mihi victor honorem
persolves. ego sum pleno quem flumine cernis

---

54. **Pallanteum:** the name produces a spondaic line. Later ages will develop the word "palace" from the location of Augustus' house on the Palatine (362 n., see map 1). For the four-syllable spondaic line ending, cf. 341 *Pallanteum*, 345 *Argileti*, 11.659 *Thermodontis*, 12.83 *Orithyia*, and with words not proper names 8.167 *intertextam, Ecl.* 4.49 *incrementum, Geo.* 1.221 *abscondantur.* On spondaic lines, see Appendix A on meter, Cic. *ad Att.* 7.2.1, Ross (1969: 130-1), Lyne (1978: 15-16), Dainotti (2015: 196-8).

55. **bellum adsidue:** Conington: "mention of constant war between the Latins and the Arcadians is inconsistent with the long peace of 7.46." For apparently deliberate and significant inconsistency in the portrayal of the situation in Italy, cf. O'Hara (2007: 96-8). Later, Evander will tell Aeneas about the Arcadians' harassment by Turnus' Rutulians (474) and by the exiled Etruscan king Mezentius (569-71).

57. **ripis et recto flumine:** a sort of hendiadys*, with the single idea of following the river's curves expressed by two words connected by *et.* The ablative is that of direction or route (AG §429a "way by which"), like *ibam forte Via Sacra* (Hor. *Serm.* 1.9.1). *Recto* in such phrases as *recto itinere, recta via,* and in this poem *recto...limite* (6.900; some print *litore* there) implies not necessarily that the road or thing traversed is "straight," but that the traveler "goes straight along it." Servius reports a different view, that *recto* means "pacified" (*edomito, frenato et in tranquillitatem redacto*), which would make 57-8 ("I will lead you with a controlled current, so that you may overcome the adverse current with your rowing") correspond nicely with 86-9 ("The Tiber controls its current, so that their rowing would be easy"). But it is a less natural meaning for the common word *recto.*

58. **superes...ut:** purpose clause.

59. **surge age:** in other divine appearances to Aeneas at 3.169 Penates, 10.241 Cymodocea. **primis...:** "when first the stars set," i.e., at dawn.

60-1. **Iunoni...:** at 3.435-40 Helenus also tells Aeneas to overcome the anger of Juno by prayer and become a *victor* (as in 8.61), although Aeneas will never overcome or even fully understand the anger of Juno; cf. 40-1 n. **mihi...:** "to me you will pay your offerings when victorious," i.e., Juno demands *instant* service, but *my* honors will come later.

62. **ego sum...quem:** Tiber reveals his identity: "I am the one whom you see...." The shade of Creusa had told Aeneas in 2.781-2 that his destiny lay in Hesperia, *ubi Lydius arva | inter opima virum leni fluit agmine Thybris.*

stringentem ripas et pinguia culta secantem,
caeruleus Thybris, caelo gratissimus amnis.
hic mihi magna domus, celsis caput urbibus exit.".   65
    Dixit, deinde lacu fluvius se condidit alto
ima petens; nox Aenean somnusque reliquit.
surgit et aetherii spectans orientia solis
lumina rite cavis undam de flumine palmis
sustinet ac talis effundit ad aethera voces: 70

---

64. caeruleus Thybris: so often called "the yellow Tiber" (e.g., 7.31; Hor. *Carm.* 1.2.13) that *caeruleus* is surprising, but the adjective is commonly applied to sea and river deities. *Thybris* is Vergil's "normal form of the name" of the river (Horsfall (2013) on 6.87 and (2000) on 7.303), for which Evander provides an etymology at 330-1, while *Tiberinus* (31) has "archaic*, sacral, and literary associations" as in the line of Ennius quoted in 72 n.; Cairns (2006: 71). On Vergil's names for Tiber, cf. also Reed (2007: 5-6) and index s.v.

65. hic...: "here is my mighty dwelling; my source (*caput*) rises (from) among lofty cities." *Hic* may be strictly "here," i.e., at the mouth of the stream, thus drawing a distinction between the position of his "dwelling" and his "source," but it is better taken generally as "in this land," as in 39. The god informs Aeneas that Latium is his home and that the upper part of his course lies amid towering cities (i.e., of Etruria). In the reply of Aeneas in 74-5, in exact answer to the double statement of Tiberinus, Aeneas tells the rivergod that (1) wherever he dwells and (2) wherever he rises he shall be equally honored.

66-80. *Aeneas wakes up, prays to Tiberinus for protection from danger, promises that he will always worship him, and prepares to sail up the stream.*

    Aeneas' actions match Tiberinus' words: cf. *surgit* (68) and *surge* (59), the reference to dawn in 68 and 59, and *rite* in 69 and 60; the injunction to pray to Juno will be fulfilled in 84-5.

66. deinde: disyllabic by synizesis, the normal prosody of this word; see Appendix A on meter. **lacu:** cf. 74 *lacus*. Vergil vaguely regards the rivergod as dwelling in some deep pool beneath the river. Such a *lacus* would typically exist at the river's head so as to form "the source" from which it flows (cf. 75 *fonte*, and *Geo.* 4.319, 364), but, as rivers were supposed to be fed from subterranean sources, there is no reason why the god should not find a *lacus* ready to receive him at any point of the river's course and even near its mouth.

68. aetherii...solis: common in Lucr.; cf. *DRN* 3.1044 *aerius sol*, 5.215. **spectans...:** looking to the east in prayer is common (cf. 12.172), as is taking water in the hands before prayer (cf. Turnus at 9.23).

"Nymphae, Laurentes Nymphae, genus amnibus unde est,
tuque, o Thybri tuo genitor cum flumine sancto,
accipite Aenean et tandem arcete periclis.
quo te cumque lacus miserantem incommoda nostra
fonte tenent, quocumque solo pulcherrimus exis,   75
semper honore meo, semper celebrabere donis
corniger Hesperidum fluvius regnator aquarum.
adsis o tantum et propius tua numina firmes."
sic memorat, geminasque legit de classe biremis
remigioque aptat, socios simul instruit armis.   80

---

71. **Nymphae, Laurentes Nymphae:** as Aeneas learns he has reached his goal Vergil evokes *Od.* 13.356-60, where Odysseus on his return to his homeland of Ithaca prays to "Naiad nymphs, daughters of Zeus." Clausen (2002: 158) notes that Vergil "offers an Italian place-name incorporated in an elegant Hellenistic phrase." Cf. *Ecl.* 6.55-6 *Nymphae,* | *Dictaeae Nymphae* and the Greek models in the note of Clausen (1994), and for the repetition Wills (1996: 51). **genus...:** as nymphs are the goddesses of fountains, the rivers which spring from them trace their "origin" or "birth" to them.

72. **tuque...:** adapted from the alliterative* Enn. *Ann.* 1.26 Sk. = 51 W (discussed at Macrob. *Sat.* 6.1) *teque, pater Tiberine tuo cum flumine sancto,* and cf. 9.816, *Geo.* 2.147 *tuo perfusi flumine sacro,* Lucr. 1.38 *hunc tu, diva* (= Venus), *tuo recubantem corpore sancto.* The use of the possessive adjective and *sancto* together belongs to earlier Latin poetry, and its archaic* character suits the language of prayer, in which old forms of speech are often retained. **genitor:** rivergods are often called "father"; cf. *pater* at 7.685. **Thybri:** Greek vocative with short *i.*

73. **arcete:** "keep (me) at a distance from..."; Servius calls this hypallage (= enallage*).

74-5. **quo...cumque...fonte...quocumque solo:** for these river-terms cf. 65 n. For the ritual *quicumque es* used in addressing an unknown god, cf. 4.577, and 9.22 with the note of Hardie (1994). Aeneas knows the identity of Tiberinus but not his origin.

76. **honore:** "service," "worship"; practically "sacrifices."

77. **corniger:** rivers are often represented as bulls (cf. Hom. *Il.* 21.237, of the Xanthus; Hor. *Carm.* 4.14.25 *tauriformis Aufidus*). **fluvius:** probably nom. "you shall be worshipped as the stream that is lord...," but it may be an archaic* vocative; cf. Livy 1.24.7 *audi tu, populus Albanus.* **regnator:** cf. *Geo.* 1.482 *fluviorum rex Eridanus.* There the Eridanus is described as "king of rivers" because of its size, while the reference here is to the Tiber's historic fame.

78. **adsis...:** "only be with me and with more present power (= the adverb *propius*)..."; for *adsis* or similar forms used in prayers, cf. O'Hara (2011) on 4.578, Harrison (1991) on 10.254-5. As yet the god has only appeared in a vision, and Aeneas prays for a more certain proof (cf. *firma* in the similar request at 2.691) of the divine assistance which he had promised. This is given in 81-3.

79-80. **biremis:** acc. **remigio:** abstract noun for *remigibus,* cf. 3.471. **armis:** equally applicable to "oars" or "weapons."

Ecce autem subitum atque oculis mirabile monstrum,
candida per silvam cum <u>fetu</u> concolor <u>albo</u>
procubuit <u>viridi</u>que in litore conspicitur sus:
quam pius Aeneas tibi enim, tibi, maxima Iuno,
mactat sacra ferens et cum grege sistit ad aram.   85
Thybris ea fluvium, quam longa est, nocte tumentem

81-101. Aeneas sacrifices the sow and her young to Juno. The Tiber holds back its current so that Aeneas' men can row easily upstream as the landscape "marvels" at them. At noon the next day they approach the city of Evander.

81-3. **ecce autem:** also at 7.286; adds vividness. The rest of the line resembles 2.680, *cum subitum dictuque oritur mirabile monstrum*, of the omen of Iulus' burning hair that persuades Anchises to leave Troy. Cf. also *Geo.* 4.554 *subitum ac dictu mirabile monstrum*, of the birth of the bees. **mirabile monstrum:** occurs in a fragment of Cicero's poetry (fr. 22.20 M) and may be from Ennius. The order of the words in the three-line sentence is carefully arranged so as to lead up to the final monosyllable *sus* which produces a rhythmically unusual line-end with clash of ictus and accent (cf. Hor. *AP* 139 *parturient montes, nascetur ridiculus mus*). In 43 the effect of the ending is to give an archaic* oracular character to the line, while here it suggests astonishment. See Appendix A on meter, Dainotti (2015: 206-16), and for the framing hyperbaton* of *candida...sus*, Dainotti (2015: 258-9).

84. **tibi enim, tibi, maxima Juno:** here the narrator's words suggest those of Aeneas' prayer, with *enim* and the repeated pronoun emphasizing that the sacrifice is to Juno (cf. 60), the bitter enemy of the Trojans. For *tibi*, cf. 3.119 *taurum tibi, pulcher Apollo*, as well as 6.18 and 251, and for the archaic*-sounding emphatic *enim* cf. 10.874 *Aeneas agnovit enim laetusque precatur*; *Geo.* 2.509 *geminatus enim* "repeated, yes, repeated" with Thomas (1988) ad loc.; Ovid *Met.* 15.581-2 *"rex," ait, "o salve; tibi enim, tibi, Cipe, tuisque | hic locus et Latiae parebunt cornibus arces,"* and its common use in *enimvero*.

85. **mactat...et sistit:** could be described as hysteron proteron*, or *mactat* can be seen as "offer as a sacrifice," followed by "set it on the altar."

86. **ea..., quam longa est, nocte:** "all night long"; cf. 4.193 *hiemem inter se luxu, quam longa, fovere*, "all winter long." The present tense, followed by perf. *leniit*, is a little unusual, but is similar to the usage in *dum* clauses (AG §556). The chronology of Aeneas' journey to the site of Rome, in which he takes a long time to travel, with divine help, about twelve miles, does not make perfect sense (cf. Fordyce here).

abl.

leniit, et tacita refluens ita substitit unda, *ablative of separation*
mitis ut in morem stagni placidaeque paludis *imp. subj.*
sterneret aequor aquis, remo ut luctamen abesset. *result clause*
ergo iter inceptum celerant rumore secundo: 90
labitur uncta vadis abies; mirantur et undae,
miratur nemus insuetum fulgentia longe *pres. act. ppl*
scuta virum fluvio pictasque innare carinas.
olli remigio noctemque diemque fatigant
et longos superant flexus, variisque teguntur 95

87-9. refluens ita substitit...ut: *ut* (88) introduces a result clause, but *ut* (89) a clause of purpose, "in order that." Literally *refluens* must mean that the Tiber checked its stream and stood all but still, but the word also suggests the literary motif of rivers flowing backwards, which often appears as an *adynaton* (impossibility) or sign that the world is turned upside down (cf. Eden here, Eurip. *Medea* 410 with the note of Mastronarde (2002)). See also the ambiguous reference in 240 below to the Tiber (*refluit*).

89. sterneret aequor aquis: also at 5.821, with *sternitur*; "spread out a smooth surface on (with?) his waters." *Aquis* can be local ablative, or instrumental ablative. **luctamen:** apparently a Vergilian coinage.

90. rumore secundo: describes the cheering of the crew. The phrase occurs in Enn. *Ann.* 244 Sk. = 243 W, and in Sueius fr. 7 M. (an older contemporary of Catullus who Macrob. *Sat.* 6.1.37 says is Vergil's source here), as well as Hor. *Epist.* 1.10.9 *quae vos ad caelum fertis rumore secundo*. Cf. too 10.266 *clamore secundo*; 5.338 *plausuque volat fremituque secundo*.

91-2. uncta: pitch was used on ships to make them waterproof; cf. 4.398 *natat uncta carina*, Enn. *Ann.* 376 Sk. = 374 W *labitur uncta carina*. **abies:** metonymy* for ship, first here. **mirantur et...miratur:** see 7.516. The marveling of the waves and woods, stressed by the anaphora*, is an example of the pathetic fallacy* in which human emotions are attributed to nature; one may also speak of personification*. Their wonder also suggests the voyage of Jason and the Argonauts, thought by Romans to be the first sea-voyage: cf. Catullus 64.1-15, where the sea-nymphs marvel at the Argonauts (*admirantes*, 15) and its model in Apollonius, *Arg.*1.544-52. Petrini (1997: 49) argues that this evocation of the world's first ship suggests that Aeneas brings an end of innocence to Pallanteum and Italy; for the innocence of Italy cf. Parry (1966), but see O'Hara (2007: 96-101) for different passages that depict Italy as both peaceful and warlike.

93. scuta: hung on the sides of the ships for show (cf. 1.183 *celsis in puppibus arma*), and so said to "float along the stream" as the vessels themselves do. **virum:** gen. pl. **innare:** with abl. of place *fluvio*; more common with acc. as at 651; again with abl. at 691.

94. noctemque diemque: "give night and day no rest." On the epic double *-que*, see Austin (1955) on 4.83: "this use of double *-que* is a mannerism of high epic style, very common in Virgil, Lucan and Statius; it is never found in classical prose. It goes back to Ennius, who took it over from Homer's use of *te...te*."

arboribus, viridisque secant placido aequore silvas.
sol medium caeli conscenderat igneus orbem
cum muros arcemque procul ac rara domorum
tecta vident, quae nunc Romana potentia caelo
aequavit, tum res inopes Evandrus habebat.   100
ocius advertunt proras urbique propinquant.

---

96. **viridisque secant:** though on the river, they seem to be cutting through the trees that over-
hang it. Servius suggests they are cutting through the reflection of the trees. **placido aequore:**
elision between the fourth and fifth foot is rare: cf. Gransden here, Austin (1955) on 4.420,
Soubiran (1966: 536-7).

97. **sol medium...:** cf. *Il.* 8.68 "But when the sun had reached the middle of heaven" (sim. at
16.777) and *Geo.* 4.426-7 *medium sol igneus orbem | hauserat.*

98-100. **procul:** the second syllable is lengthened in arsis (see Appendix A on meter). **Romana
potentia:** likely allusion to an etymology* of *Roma* < ῥώμη, "strength," found in several texts;
see Maltby (1991) s.v. *Roma*, and Watson (2003) on Hor. *Epod.* 16.2. **Evandrus:** the form that
Vergil always uses except at 10.515 (Evander). These lines offer the first of several contrasts
between the humble huts of Evander's time (*tum*, 100) and the lofty and (in later passages)
wealthy metropolis of Vergil's (*nunc*, 99, from the poet's own perspective); cf. 25 n., 104-5 n.,
348 n., 360-1 n., 366 n., 407-53 n. There is a similar contrast at Prop. 4.1, Tib. 2.5.23-6, Ovid
Fast. 5.91-4. Martindale (1993: 51) claims that Vergil offers an "erasure" of the problematic
contrast between lofty present and humble past at Rome, but it is Vergil who in several passages
draws the contrast, which some readers will see as criticism of Augustan Rome. For anxieties
about wealth and spending in the late Republic and early empire, see Edwards (1993: 137-
206), Wallace-Hadrill (2008: 315-55).

102-305. At the site of Rome Aeneas meets Evander, who tells him of Hercules' fight against
Cacus; at a feast priests sing a hymn about Hercules' exploits.

When Aeneas arrives at Pallanteum, Evander and the Arcadians are celebrating annual rites
in honor of Hercules at the Ara Maxima (102-25). The opening lines draw heavily from Telemachus' arrival at Pylos, *Od.* 3.1-50, where he finds Nestor sacrificing and is greeted by his son
Peisistratus as Aeneas is greeted by Evander's son Pallas. The Homeric model provides both structure and a number of details, but hospitality scenes in Callimachus' *Aetia* 3 (where Hercules
is entertained by Molorchus) and *Hecale* also contribute; cf. Tueller (2000), improving on
earlier work by George (1974) in part because of new papyrus finds of Callimachus. The whole
episode serves as a long "aetion" or origin story for the Ara Maxima, built to honor Hercules
after his defeat of the monster Cacus (Tueller 2000). The Ara Maxima (cf. also 102-25 n.) does
not survive, but we know its location in the Forum Boarium from inscriptions; see Coarelli
(2007: 318-19). Aeneas explains who he is, through a novel genealogy stressing a connection
to the Arcadians through Mercury (126-51), which can be read in the light of a Homeric

Forte die sollemnem illo rex Arcas honorem
Amphitryoniadae magno divisque ferebat

genealogy that Aeneas explains to Achilles in the *Iliad*. Evander responds by saying that when
young he had met and felt great love for Aeneas' father Anchises; there may be erotic overtones
to Evander's love for Anchises (152-83). Evander tells the story of Hercules and Cacus at great
length (184-279), with a stress on Cacus' monstrosity and Hercules' violence (cf. 184-279 n.,
194 n., 196 n., 219-20 n., 230-2 n., 260-1 n.) that makes this version distinct from that of
Livy 1.7, written in the decade or so before the *Aeneid*. On the background and possible function
of the story, see 184-279 n. The scene ends with feasting and with a song sung in honor of
Hercules' labors (280-305).

*102-25. The Trojans' ships startle Evander and the Arcadians as they are sacrificing to Hercules.
Evander's son Pallas hurries to stop them from interrupting the rites, but when Aeneas says they
are Trojans fighting against the common Latin enemy, the stunned Pallas welcomes him as a guest
and tells him to come speak to his father.*

The worship of Hercules was popular at Rome; Livy 1.7 describes it as instituted by Romulus
according to the rules laid down by Evander, whose history he records almost in the same
way as Vergil does. A temple of Hercules Victor stood between the Palatine and the river near
the well-known Ara Maxima (186, 271) or *Ara Maxima Herculis Invicti*, and this is clearly the
spot which Virgil describes here, *ante urbem* (104) (see map 1). Hercules is important in the
Aeneid both when mentioned and when the poem merely alludes to him. He is a half-divine
hero who like Aeneas attains divinity through *labores*, and a civilizing hero with affinities with
both Aeneas and Augustus (cf. 6.801-5), but he is also an ambivalent figure of brutal violence,
who in *Aen.* 10.464-5 will be helpless to save Pallas from Turnus. See Hor. *Carm.* 3.3.9-16,
3.14, Prop. 4.9, and in general on Hercules Galinsky (1990), Feeney (1991: 156-62; 1998: 55-
6), Hardie (1993: 65-7), Newman (2002), Stafford (2012), Loar (2017); for further references,
see 184-279 n.

102. **Forte die...illo:** Aeneas arrives at the site of Rome on the day of the festival honoring
Hercules at the Ara Maxima, Aug. 12. By having Aeneas arrive on this day, Vergil arranges
it so that the next day, Aug. 13, when Aeneas receives the shield from his mother (608-16),
is the date of the start of Augustus' triple-triumph in 29 BCE, which will be depicted on
Aeneas' shield (714-28); cf. Gransden and Eden here, Horsfall (1995: 162-3), Feeney (2007:
160-2). The reference to *Romana potentia* in 99 helps prepare the reader to pick up details
like this.

103. **Amphitryoniadae:** the name *Hērcŭlēs* does not fit the hexameter in most cases; here as
often a patronymic is used. Hercules' real father is Jupiter; this seven-syllable patronymic uses
his mortal step-father's name and is borrowed from Cat. 68.112 *falsiparens Amphitryoniades*.
It first appears in Hesiod *Theog.* 317. Below we see *Alcides* (203: from Amphitryon's father),
Tirynthius (228), and the adjective *Herculeus* (270, 288). The long Greek name also produces
a rare and strikingly Hellenistic four-word line, here and in 214. See 157-9 n., 263 n., 341 n.,
and 521 n., and on the slow solemnity of four-word lines, see Dainotti (2015: 79).

ante urbem in luco. Pallas huic filius una,
una omnes iuvenum primi pauperque senatus   105
tura dabant, tepidusque cruor fumabat ad aras.
ut celsas videre rates atque inter opacum ⟵ *indirect statement*
adlabi nemus et tacitos incumbere remis,
terrentur visu subito cunctique relictis
consurgunt mensis, audax quos rumpere Pallas   110
sacra vetat raptoque volat telo obvius ipse,
et procul e tumulo: "iuvenes, quae causa subegit
ignotas temptare vias? quo tenditis?" inquit. *to where*
qui genus? unde domo? pacemne huc fertis an arma?"

nom, pl, masc.

104-5. **ante urbem:** in front of Evander's small settlement on the Palatine. Demosthenes *de Falsa Legatione* 86 refers to it as a violation of custom to hold a sacrifice to Hercules *within* the walls of Athens. **in luco:** the sacred grove containing the altar and temple of the god. Feeney (2007: 283 n. 152) notes that *ante urbem in luco* repeats a phrase used in the same metrical position in 3.302 describing "the futile and backward-looking sacrifices of Andromache," in contrast to here where the rites look to the Roman future. **Pallas:** first mention in the poem of Evander's son, whose death at the hands of Turnus in Book 10 will cast Aeneas in the role of Achilles seeking revenge for the death of Patroclus. Distinguish *Pallās* from *Pallăs* Athena (435). **huic:** Evander (supply *est*). **pauperque senatus:** for the theme of Evander's lack of wealth, cf. 98-100 n.

107. **ut…:** they saw the ships (*rates*), and what they were doing (*adlabi*), and that silent men were bending over the oars (*tacitos incumbere remis*). For the reading *tacitis*, which requires that we supply an unstated subject for *incumbere*, see Page and Fordyce. Lorrain's famous seventeenth-century painting "The Arrival of Aeneas at Pallanteum, the Site of Rome" can be found on the internet and at Liversidge (1997: pl. 11) (along with paintings from *Aeneid* 8 of Aeneas asleep and Hercules-Cacus).

110-11. **audax quos rumpere…sacra:** "to break off (*rumpere = interrumpere*) the solemn feast." Fordyce on *audax*: "here Pallas is fearless in confronting possible danger, but the word presages his later story. Servius is right when he says that the implication of *audax* in Virgil's use is *virtus sine fortuna*, 'ill-starred gallantry' (or, as he puts it on ix. 3, *fortis sine felicitate*): it is so applied to Turnus four times (vii. 409, ix. 3, 126, x. 276)."

112-14. Pallas questions strangers as one would in Homer, e.g., *Od.* 1.170 "Who are you and where are you from? Where is your city, your parents?" **genus:** acc. of specification, as in 5.285 *Cressa genus*, more common in Greek (cf. *Od.* 15.267, ἐξ Ἰθάκης γένος εἰμί, AG §397b, Smyth (1920) 1600-1). **unde domo:** idiomatic expression, also in a series of questions at Hor. *Epist.* 1.7.53, combining the interrogative adverb *unde* with an abl. of place from which (AG §427); cf. 10.141, *Maeonia generose domo*, 183, *qui Caerete domo*.

abl of means

tum pater Aeneas puppi sic fatur ab alta 115
paciferaeque manu ramum praetendit olivae:
"Troiugenas ac tela vides inimica Latinis,
[quos illi bello profugos egere superbo.] *relative clause*
Evandrum petimus. ferte haec et [dicite lectos *indirect statement*
Dardaniae venisse duces socia arma rogantis."] 120
obstipuit tanto percussus nomine Pallas:
"egredere o quicumque es," ait "coramque parentem
adloquere ac nostris succede penatibus hospes."
excepitque manu dextramque amplexus inhaesit.
progressi subeunt luco fluviumque relinquunt. 125
        Tum regem Aeneas dictis adfatur amicis:

---

116. **paciferaeque:** cf. 7.154 *ramis velatos Palladis omnis.*

117. **Troiugenas:** four syllables, with consonantal *i*; the compound appears in Lucr. 1.465 and Cat. 64.355, and is put in the *carmen* of the legendary *vates* Marcius by Livy (25.12.5). The similar *Graiugenae* (127) is used by Pacuvius fr. 364 R^2 = 14 W and Lucretius 1.477.

118. **profugos:** "poor exiles" (cf. 1.2 *fato profugus*, of Aeneas): Fordyce: "*profugos egere* is a striking piece of diplomatic exaggeration and *superbo bello* is hardly justified by the fact that Latinus had allowed his pledge to be broken." Thomas (2004: 136) says that this claim and that of 146 (see note below) precisely contradict Aeneas' claim in 143 not to have approached Evander "through craft," right before he exaggerates again in 146-50.

119. **ferte haec:** "report these words/this message." The plural imperative is a little odd but may imply that others came along with Pallas.

121. **nomine:** the great name of "Troy" amazes him.

124. **excepitque...:** in the Homeric model for the scene (102-305 n.), Nestor's son Peisistratus in greeting Telemachus and the disguised Athena "took their hands" (*Od.* 3.35). **dextramque amplexus inhaesit:** "...and clung to the right hand he embraced," as Evander does at 558; for similar Homeric formulae, see Kirk (1990) on *Il.* 6.253.

126-51. *Aeneas tells Evander that he has no fear of him as a Greek and offers a complex genealogical explanation that they are both descended from Atlas. He says that he has come to ask for help against their common enemies, who he says want to control all of Hesperia.*

In *Il.* 20.200-41 Homer's Aeneas explains his lineage to Achilles, pointing out that Dardanus' father was Zeus (Jupiter) himself, a point triply stressed to Latinus by Ilioneus at *Aen.* 7.219-20 (*ab Iove principium generis, Iove Dardana pubes | gaudet avo, rex ipse Iovis de gente suprema*). But Jupiter is omitted here (cf. 129 n.), as Aeneas puts weight instead on a novel connection through Atlas and Mercury. Like Turnus' embassy to Diomedes (cf. 12 n., 13 n.), Aeneas exaggerates the threat of the Latins to all of Italy and the wrong done to him by Latinus (147-9 n.).

126. **dictis adfatur amicis:** cf. *dictisque ita fatur amicis* at 2.147, when Priam addresses the treacherous Sinon.

"optime Graiugenum, cui me Fortuna precari
et vitta comptos voluit praetendere ramos,
non equidem extimui Danaum quod ductor et Arcas
quodque a stirpe fores geminis coniunctus Atridis;　　　130
sed mea me virtus et sancta oracula divum
cognatique patres, tua terris didita fama,
coniunxere tibi et fatis egere volentem.
Dardanus, Iliacae primus pater urbis et auctor,
Electra, ut Grai perhibent, Atlantide cretus,　　　135

---

127. **Graiugenum:** the archaic* gen. plur. in -*um* for -*arum* and -*orum* is common in Vergil with
(1) proper names or (2) names which describe a class of persons (cf. 129 *Danaum* and 7.50-1).
cui...precari: the verb usually takes the accusative, not the dative as here, of the person
addressed.

129-30. **equidem:** Vergil always uses this word with the first person and as Servius says seems
to think of it as = *ego quidem*; cf. 471. **quod...fores:** the subjunctive marks a possible reason for
him to have been afraid, which the speaker does not endorse (AG §592); *fores = esses*, but we
would have expected *fuisses* after *extimui* as Servius notes. **a stirpe:** "by lineage," i.e., as being
of Greek stock. Thomas (2004: 133-6) argues that Aeneas goes out of his way to suppress his
descent from Jupiter, the god who in the *Georgics* (esp. 1.125-46) ends the Golden Age and
below will be contrasted with the Saturn of the Golden Age (306-69 n.). **geminis...Atridis:**
Agamemon and Menelaus, not necessarily literally twins; *geminus* is often used loosely of a pair.

131. **sed mea me virtus:** self-praise in which a stranger declares his name and fame to his host is
Homeric; cf. *Od.* 9.19, "I am Odysseus son of Laertes, a concern to all men for my tricks, and
my fame reaches heaven," and Vergil's *sum pius Aeneas...fama super aethera notus* in 1.378-9.

132. **tua terris didita fama:** harsh asyndeton*.

133. **coniunxere:** combines with *cognatique patres* at the start of 132 to answer *coniunctus Atridis*
in 130. **fatis egere volentem:** Aeneas says that destiny drives him, but his own will consents;
cf. Seneca's poetic paraphrase at *Epist.* 107.11 of the Stoic Cleanthes frag. 527 von Arnim:
ducunt volentem fata, nolentem trahunt. Evander in 335 uses *egere* of the divine forces that
drove him to Italy.

134. **Dardanus:** Aeneas begins his genealogy with Dardanus (cf. 7.207), just as the Homeric
Aeneas does when speaking to Achilles in *Il.* 20.215 and as Ilioneus does as 7.219-20 (quoted
126-51 n.). On the genealogy here, see Thomas (2004-5: 134-5), who stresses that Aeneas
omits his connection to Jupiter, stressed elsewhere, Clausen (1987: 119-20), Cairns (1989:
121), Nakata (2012) (see 139 n. below), and Wimperis (2017).

135. **ut Grai perhibent:** not expressing doubt but referring to Greek tradition as an authority
which his Greek hearer could not question. Aeneas' words also resemble the "Alexandrian
footnote" often used by learned poets speaking in their own persona to allude to a source text
(as Vergil here evokes *Il.* 20), or to suggest disbelief by attributing a claim to a source other
than the poet. See Ross (1975: 78), Thomas (1988) on *Geo.* 1.247 (*ut perhibent*, which also
occurs at *Aen.* 4.179), Horsfall (1990; 2016: 111-34), and Hinds (1998: 1-5).

advehitur Teucros; Electram maximus Atlas
edidit, aetherios umero qui sustinet orbis.
vobis Mercurius pater est, quem candida Maia
Cyllenae gelido conceptum vertice fudit;
at Maiam, auditis si quicquam credimus, Atlas,   140
idem Atlas generat caeli qui sidera tollit.
sic genus amborum scindit se sanguine ab uno.
his fretus non legatos neque prima per artem
temptamenta tui pepigi; me, me ipse meumque
obieci caput et supplex ad limina veni.   145

---

136. **advehitur:** pres. tense for a vivid past event (AG §469). But does Dardanus found Troy (so that *Teucros* is proleptic, as Servius says), or come to a city already founded by the Cretan Teucer? The ambiguity reproduces a problem in *Aen.* 3, where the Trojans wrongly intepret an oracle about their "ancient mother" as a command to go to Crete, whence Teucer came to Troy (cf. 3.108); the correct interpretation is to seek Italy, the land of Dardanus (3.167-8). Cf. Nakata (2012) and Wimperis (2017).

139. **conceptum...fudit:** as often, participle and main verb where English would use two verbs. For Mercury's parentage and his grandfather Atlas who holds the heavens, cf. 4.246-58; for Atlas and Aeneas cf. 731 n. Mercury, a key to the genealogy here, will be a model for some aspects of the Hercules-Cacus story; cf. 210-12 n., 224 n., Casali (2010: 39). Nakata (2012: 352) suggests that "Aeneas fabricates a genealogy featuring an unexpected connection as a basis for an alliance" by conflating three different mythological Atlases—one North African, one Italian, and one Arcadian—listed by Servius on 8.134, who calls Aeneas' conflation a mistake: *ex nominum similitudine facit errorem et dicit Electram et Maiam filias fuisse Atlantis maximi.* Servius' reaction is not the only one imaginable for this passage, for there is much mythological innovation throughout the *Aeneid.* But it is not unreasonable to think that many readers would think that Aeneas, after saying that the Daunians have cruelly attacked him (118 n.), and before referring to their plan to take over all of Italy (147-9 n.), has also fabricated this genealogical connection. Eden on 130 suggests the influence of second-century BCE Roman drama: "Accius' tragedy *Atreus* seems to have expounded this Atlas-connection of its hero and may have influenced Virgil here."

140-1. **auditis:** dat. with *credimus,* "give credence to." **quicquam:** adverbial accusative. **Atlas | idem Atlas:** *idem* strongly identifies *Atlas* with *Atlas* in line 136, stressing the innovative idea that he is the common ancestor of Aeneas and Evander. Vergil uses such epanalepsis* with Atlas also in 4.247-8.

143-4. **non legatos...pepigi:** "I did not settle on an embassy (lit. 'ambasadors') or on first approaching you by craft." *Legatos* is governed loosely by the general sense of *pepigi < pango,* which usually refers to hammering out an agreement or treaty. On *per artem,* cf. Thomas cited above 118 n. **me, me ipse meumque:** on the emphatic first-person repetition, see the examples collected in Wills (1996: 80, 266).

gens eadem, quae te, crudeli Daunia bello
insequitur; nos si pellant nihil afore credunt
quin omnem Hesperiam penitus sua sub iuga mittant,
et mare quod supra teneant quodque adluit infra.
accipe daque fidem. sunt nobis fortia bello   150
pectora, sunt animi et rebus spectata iuventus."|
    Dixerat Aeneas. ille os oculosque loquentis
iamdudum et totum lustrabat lumine corpus.
tum sic pauca refert: "ut te, fortissime Teucrum,
accipio agnoscoque libens! ut verba parentis   155
et vocem Anchisae magni vultumque recordor!

---

146. Daunia: i.e., the Rutulians, since Turnus is the son of Daunus (12.22).

147-9. nihil afore...quin...: "that nothing will be lacking to keep them from...," i.e., that they
will have everything they need for completely subjugating Italy (for the subjunctives after *quin*,
see AG §558). Both Aeneas here and his enemies above in 12-15 make the exaggerated claim
(similar to the "Domino Theory" popular in U.S. foreign relations during the 1950s to 1980s)
that only they stand in the way of their foe's plans for dominating Italy. Fordyce on 146 calls
this "total misrepresentation: for the Italians have done no more than repel the Trojan in-
comers and there has been no suggestion that they even have designs on anything that is
not their own"; on deception, cf. 118 n., Fratantuono (2007: 238). **supra...infra:** the *mare
superum* or Adriatic, and the *mare inferum, Tuscum*, or *Tyrrhenum*. Line 149 is largely repeated
from *Geo.* 2.158 in Vergil's "Praise of Italy."

150. accipe daque fidem: the phrase is borrowed from Ennius' version of the Aeneas story (*Ann.*
32 Sk. = 78 W); cf. Goldschmidt (2013: 92), who says it "metapoetically" calls attention to
Vergil's "revision of Ennius." **fortia bello:** *bello* is ablative of specification (AG §418), though in
151 *rebus spectata* means that their qualities have been "seen" and so "tested" in or by "action."

*152-83. Evander replies by saying that he is happy to recognize Aeneas, since when young he had
felt great love for Anchises when Anchises visited Arcadia, and that his son Pallas still treasures
the gifts Evander received from Anchises. Then he promises his alliance and invites Aeneas to
join the feast.*

Evander's recollections of Aeneas' father's visit to his hometown recalls visits in Homer and
in Apollonius (cf. 157-9 n., 160 n.), and may have erotic connotations (160 n.).

152-3. ille...: he "scans" his face and body because they remind him of those of Anchises, even
though Aeneas has not identified himself except as a Trojan. For the gradual recognition of
a son by resemblance to his father, cf. Helen and Menelaus' words about Telemachus at Hom.
Od. 4.140-54, and those of the disguised Athena to Telemachus at *Od.* 1.207-12.

154-6. fortissime Teucrum: answers Aeneas' opening *optime Graiugenum* (127). **ut...
libens...ut...recordor:** "how..., how..." **accipio agnoscoque:** also in the much darker context
of the deceptive omen at 12.260. **verba...vocem...vultumque:** three alliterative* disyllabic
accusatives.

nam memini Hesionae visentem regna sororis
Laomedontiaden Priamum Salamina petentem
protinus Arcadiae gelidos invisere finis. *"gelidos finis" : acc. pl.*
tum mihi prima genas vestibat flore iuventas,   160
mirabarque duces Teucros, mirabar et ipsum
Laomedontiaden; sed cunctis altior ibat

157-9. **nam memini...**: cf. Dido's memory of a visit to Sidon from Teucer: *atque equidem Teucrum memini Sidona venire* (1.619), the words of Antenor to Helen at *Il.* 3.204-8 about a visit of Odysseus and Menelaus to Troy, and Lycus' memory of a visit from Heracles in Apollonius, *Arg.* 2.774-810; cf. Nelis (2001: 360-1) and 160 n. below. **Hesionae:** sister of Priam, wife of Telamon the king of Salamis, and mother of Ajax and Teucer. Part of her father Laomedon's punishment for cheating Poseidon and Apollo was to expose Hesione to a sea-monster: Hercules saved her, and when refused his promised reward sacked Troy; cf. 18 n., 291 n., and Gantz (1993: 400-1). **visentem...petentem...invisere:** going to see (for the verb, cf. Cat. 11.10 *Caesaris visens monimenta*) his sister [and so] seeking (the pileup of participles is striking) Salamis (*Salamina* = Gk. acc.) he [went further West and] visited Arcadia. Line 158 is a striking four-word hexameter; cf. 103 n. and for other such lines beginning with Laomedon's name, see *Geo.* 1.502, *Aen.* 3.248, 4.542.

160. **tum mihi prima genas vestibat flore iuuentas:** *vestibat* is an older form of *vestiebat*, which will not scan; cf. 436 *polibant*, and *VE* pp. 846-7. **flore:** "bloom." The whole line suggests the beauty of a young man who is vigorous and attractive, including being attractive to other men: cf. *ora puer prima signans intonsa iuventa* (Euryalus beloved of Nisus, 9.181), *flaventem prima lanugine malas* (Clytius beloved of Cydon, 10.324), as well as the non-erotic *pueri et primaevo flore iuventus* 7.162; cf. Lucr. 5.888-9 *puerili aevo florente iuventas | occipit et molli vestit lanugine malas*; Pac. 362 R. = *inc. fab.* 34 W *nunc primum opacat flora lanugo genas*; and in a model for this scene at Apollonius, *Arg.* 2.779, where Lycus says Heracles visited him "when I was just growing down on my cheeks" (cf. above 157-9 n.). This line and other features of Evander's story (cf. 163-4 n., 165 n., 166-7 n.) have led some scholars to see an erotic attraction or even encounter in Evander's description of his meeting with Anchises. Cf. Putnam (1995: 32-3), Lloyd (1999), Reed (2007: 185), Quint (2015); cf. the Nisus and Euryalus story in 9.176-83, with Fantuzzi (2012: 187-266), and more generally on Roman attitudes to same-sex relationships, see Williams (2010).

162. **sed cunctis...**: "but towering above all...," with the name emphatically last. Aeneas would have known his father only as the man crippled by Jupiter's lightning after boasting of sleeping with Venus (cf. 2.648-9). Cf. the lead character on meeting the baseball-playing ghost of his father in the 1998 film *Field of Dreams*: "I only saw him years later when he was worn down by life."

Anchises. mihi mens iuvenali ardebat amore
compellare virum et dextrae coniungere dextram;
accessi et cupidus Phenei sub moenia duxi.   165
ille mihi insignem pharetram Lyciasque sagittas
discedens chlamydemque auro dedit intertextam,
frenaque bina meus quae nunc habet aurea Pallas.
ergo et quam petitis iuncta est mihi foedere dextra,
et lux cum primum terris se crastina reddet,   170

163-4. **ardebat...:** "burned with a young man's longing to address"; the inf. may follow either
ardebat (cf. *ardor* in 7.393) or *amore* (cf. 12.282 *amor...decernere*). More possible erotic
undertones of the story (160 n.), but cf. too the non-erotic 3.298-9 *miroque incensum pectus
amore | compellare virum* (Aeneas and the prophet Helenus).

165. **cupidus:** adverbial; both the word and his taking him on a tour may add more erotic undertones (160 n.). **Phenei:** a town in Arcadia, mentioned in the Catalogue of Ships (*Il.* 2.605)
and at Cat. 68.109 *Pheneum prope Cylleneum* (associated there with tunnels built by
Hercules). Servius on 3.167 says that Pheneus was the birthplace, according to one tradition,
of Dardanus.

166-7. **ille mihi...discedens:** to Lloyd (160 n.) these gifts from Anchises to Evander look like
the gifts of a lover. In epic, hosts give gifts to guests on departure, expecting that the guest
will reciprocate when it is his turn to be host. Aeneas brings or sends gifts to Dido and to
Latinus when he arrives in Books 1 and 7, but there are no clear examples in Homer, Apollonius,
or Vergil of a guest giving gifts on departure, as Anchises does here. One possible exception
is Bellerophon at *Il.* 6.216-21, as Ready (2010: 135 n. 7) notes, but Heubeck, West, and
Hainsworth (1988) on *Od.* 1.311-13 and 318 think that may refer to two different occasions.
Od. 21.13-41 tells of how Odysseus when young exchanged gifts with another young man
when both were visiting a friend; cf. Donlan (1982: 150). **pharetram...chlamydemque:** Eden:
"Greek loan-words fall with natural ease from the Greek Evander." **auro...intertextam:** for
the four-syllable spondaic line ending, cf. 54 and note.

168. **frenaque bina meus quae nunc habet aurea Pallas:** in the bold double hyperbaton* here
meus is put outside the relative clause and *aurea* within it. **bina:** the distributive form is often
used, esp. in poetry, not to mean "two each" but "a pair of."

169. **iuncta est:** the perfect tense means the alliance has now been sealed with the joining of
hands (though possibly the perfect tense could refer to the past friendship with Anchises).
After the death of Pallas, Aeneas will look back grimly to this clasping of hands: *dextraeque
datae* (10.517). **mihi:** "by me," dat. of agent, or perhaps "for me," ethical dat. (AG §380).

auxilio laetos dimittam opibusque iuvabo.
interea sacra haec, quando huc venistis amici,
annua, quae differre nefas, celebrate faventes
nobiscum, et iam nunc sociorum adsuescite mensis."
Haec ubi dicta, dapes iubet et sublata reponi   175
pocula gramineoque viros locat ipse sedili,
praecipuumque toro et villosi pelle leonis
accipit Aenean solioque invitat acerno.
tum lecti iuvenes certatim araeque sacerdos
viscera tosta ferunt taurorum, onerantque canistris   180
dona laboratae Cereris, Bacchumque ministrant.
vescitur Aeneas simul et Troiana iuventus
perpetui tergo bovis et lustralibus extis.

[handwritten note: ἀπὸ κοινοῦ → from common]

171-4. Line 171 repeats 1.571 (Dido to Ilioneus) with the change of *tutos* to *laetos*, then in 173
celebrate faventes is repeated from her words at 1.735; for more associations of Aeneas' two
hosts Evander and Dido, see 584 n. Lines 172-4 also resemble Peisistratus' words to Mentor
(the disguised Athena) in *Od*. 3.43-50.

176. **sedili:** dat., with *locat*. Macrob. *Sat*. 3.6 and Servius here say that at feasts to Hercules, the
worshippers did not recline but sat.

177. **toro et villosi pelle leonis:** hendiadys* for a "cushion" consisting of a lion skin; *toro, pelle,*
and *solio* (178) are instrumental abl. with *invitat* which almost means *accipit* (Fordyce cites
Cic. *Verr*. 2.4.25 *ecquis est qui senatorem...tecto ac domo non invitet?*). The lion-skin suggests
Hercules, soon to be featured in Evander's story (185-275), and associates Aeneas with him
in advance of that story; cf. Gransden here, Tueller (2000).

180-1. **viscera:** the flesh, all that is left when the skin is removed; cf. 1.211 and Servius there.
onerantque canistris | dona: enallage* for "load baskets with..." **dona laboratae Cereris:**
"the gifts of Ceres [which they had] prepared," metonymy* for "bread," as Ceres is the goddess
of grain; the simple word *pan* never occurs in Vergil (Clausen (2002: 6)).

183. **perpetui tergo bovis:** another enallage* for the whole or unbroken back portion of an
ox, or "long chine of beef," a Homeric term used for the special cut given as a sign of honor at
Il. 7.321, *Od*. 14.437, and without an adjective at *Od*. 4.65. **lustralibus extis:** "sacrificial" or
"expiatory entrails"; like *tergo*, abl. after *vescitur*. The inner organs were usually burned on the
altar or, in the case of sea-gods, flung into the waves (5.237-8), but according to Livy (1.7) in
sacrificing to Hercules they were eaten at the commencement of the feast.

Postquam exempta fames et amor compressus edendi,

184-279. Evander tells Aeneas why his people honor Hercules. Pointing to shattered rocks nearby, he explains that they once formed the cave of the fire-breathing monster Cacus, who terrorized the area until he stole cattle that Hercules had taken from Geryon. The mooing of the cattle betrayed their hiding place, and Hercules tore the top off of the Aventine Hill to get at Cacus. Although Cacus filled the cave with smoke and flame, Hercules killed him, and these annual rites and the Ara Maxima were instituted in memory of the exploit.

The story of Hercules (see also 102-25 n.) and Cacus that Vergil puts in the mouth of Evander draws upon numerous earlier Greek and Roman texts, and resonates thematically with several parts of the *Aeneid*. Certain or possible intertexts include the *Homeric Hymn to Hermes* (210-12 n., 224 n., 263 n.; see Secci (2013: 204-9), Clauss (2017)), Homer's story of Odysseus and the Cyclops (226-7 n., 240 n.), lost satyr plays of Sophocles and Euripides (210-12 n.), Callimachus' stories of Heracles and the Nemean lion (260-1 n.), and mythical descents to the underworld (243-6 n.). The suggestions of the Cyclops and the portrayal of Cacus as a monster tie in with the use elsewhere in the poem of gigantomachy as a symbol for the fight of order against disorder, including on Aeneas' shield later in Book 8 (636-731 n.); cf. Hardie (1986: 85-156), O'Hara (2007: 96-103). There are also elements shared with the Herculean tales in the hymn at 285-305, as well as intratextual connections to Vergil's depictions of the Cyclops (198-9 n., 230-2 n.), Chimaera (198-9 n.), Mezentius (230-2 n.), Turnus (223 n., 229 n.), and Augustus on the shield of Aeneas (196 n., 202 n.).

The story of Cacus' theft of Hercules' cattle and death at his hands is securely dated to no source earlier than Livy 1.7, written a decade or so before the *Aeneid*. In Livy Cacus is a fierce and strong human herdsman, not a monster (*pastor accola eius loci, nomine Cacus, ferox viribus*), and it is Vergil (and/or Evander) who makes him a half-human fire-breathing son of Vulcan. Much later and perhaps unreliable sources (*Origo Gentis Romanae* 6-7, Solinus 1.7) cite second-century BCE sources (G. Gellius, Cassius Hemina) for the story, and some scholars have thought it appeared slightly earlier in Fabius Pictor or Ennius. Diodorus Siculus (fl. 60-30 BCE?) has Hercules entertained at Rome by men named Pinarios (cf. 269 n.) and Kakios, and says the Scalae Caci leading from the Forum up the hill of the Palatine recall this man, although Vergil puts his monstrous Cacus on the Aventine (see map 1). An Etruscan seer is named Cacu on a fourth-century BCE mirror from Bolsena (Small (1982: 4, 113 and passim), *Lexicon Iconographicum Mythologiae Classicae* vol. 3/1, 175-7), and may be the same character, before his name's resemblance to Greek *kakos* and a Roman (Augustan?) author's goals made him the bad guy. After Vergil, Dion. of Hal. *Ant. Rom.* 1.39-42 gives two versions of the story, one he calls more "mythic" and one "truer" and attributed to historians, in which Hercules and Cacus are ordinary mortals; cf. too Prop. 4.9 and Ovid *F.* 1.543-86, 5.643-52. See Winter (1910), Alföldi (1965: 228-30), Ogilvie (1970) on Livy 1.7.3-15, Fontenrose (1959: 339-42), Small (1982) but with the caution about the unreliability of sources by Horsfall (1984).

Within the *Aeneid* the story functions as an aetion for the Ara Maxima and the worship of Hercules, and offers a model for a hero punishing a villain, but one that can be looked at from different perspectives. Evander sees it as a simple tale of good and evil (Evander, "Goodman," Gk. *eu + andr-*), tells of the punishment of Cacus ("Badman," Gr. *kakos*, although with

rex Evandrus ait: "non haec sollemnia nobis,   185
has ex more dapes, hanc tanti numinis aram

---

different accent and vowel quantity), and he exults in the tale's simple morality and bloody gore (see 196 n.). This tells us much about the worldview of Evander, who will play a crucial role in the rest of the *Aeneid*, calling in Book 11 for Aeneas to avenge the death of Pallas in Book 10, which he does at the end of Book 12. Details of the presentation could also suggest to Vergil's readers a more blurred picture in which hero and villain share many traits, for "it is notoriously hard to distinguish between the emotions and tactics of the 'evil' Cacus and the champion of 'good man' Evander"; Hardie (1993: 66). Hercules can be seen as a hero justly punishing a monster, or as a violent brute killing a thief who in stealing his cattle has done no more than Hercules has just done in stealing the cattle of Geryon, who in some sources is a sympathetic figure (202 n.). The story of Hercules and Cacus is paired in Book 8 with the pictures on the shield Vulcan makes for Aeneas, which present numerous threats to Rome (626-731 n.) and center on the Battle of Actium in 31 BCE (675-713). Readers may see that Hercules defeats Cacus as soon Aeneas will defeat Turnus (for links between Turnus and Cacus, see 196 n., 198-9 n., 223 n., but also 229 n. for Turnus linked to Hercules), and as one day Augustus will defeat Antony and Cleopatra at Actium. In Evander's mind, the parallel will be with Mezentius whom he describes as a monster deserving punishment (481-504). Different readers will see Hercules as a positive model to be emulated or a troubling "hero" of whose *furor* (cf. 219-20 n.) the rest of Vergil's *Eclogues, Georgics,* and *Aeneid* would seem to disapprove; cf. Perkell (1999: 38), Panoussi in *VE*, pp. 515-16, with further references. Petrini (1997: 64) contrasts Evander's hero with the Hercules who at 10.465-6 is helpless to help Pallas (see quotation at 299-300 n.).

On the function of the story, cf. Hardie (1986: 110-18; 1993: 65-7), Clausen (1987: 69-72; 2002: 161-6), Ferenczi (1998-9), Galinsky (1990), Feeney (1991: 156-62; 1998: 55-6), Newman (2002), Gildenhard (2004), Morgan (1998) (positive view of the violence), Secci (2013), who questions Evander's credibility, and Wimperis (2017). Contrast Fordyce (1977: 223-7), arguing against a political reading that would equate Hercules and Cacus with Augustus and his enemies, with Walsh's Introduction to the posthumous Fordyce, arguing for just such a reading (pp. xxiv-xxvi).

184. **postquam...:** a Homeric formula, "when they had put aside the desire for drink and food," fourteen times in *Od.* (incl. 3.67, from the Telemachus-Nestor scene), seven times in *Il.*; cf. a different version at *Aen.* 1.216 *postquam exempta fames epulis mensaeque remotae,* 723 *postquam prima quies epulis mensaeque remotae.* **amor edendi:** from Lucr. 4.869.

185-6. **non haec..., has..., hanc:** tricolon* with polyptoton* for the three direct objects, each time with the stressed demonstrative introducing a half-line. Conington: "Livy 1.7 says that this worship of Hercules at the Ara Maxima was the only foreign worship adopted by Romulus; and this apology of Evander points to the same feeling, the jealous dislike of strange gods." Evander likes tricola*; cf. 541-84 n.

vana superstitio veterumque ignara deorum
imposuit: saevis, hospes Troiane, periclis
servati facimus meritosque novamus honores.
iam primum saxis suspensam hanc aspice rupem,   190
disiectae procul ut moles desertaque montis
stat domus et scopuli ingentem traxere ruinam. |
hic spelunca fuit vasto summota recessu,
semihominis Caci facies quam dira tenebat

---

187. **superstitio:** used in a good sense 12.817, but here, as ordinarily, in a bad one; cf. Servius here
who calls it *timor superfluus et delirus*, Cic. *ND* 1.117 where it is defined as *timor inanis*, as
opposed to *pius deorum cultus = religio*. It is the "empty dread" which induces men to "neglect
the old gods" and seek new and inferior objects of worship, but cf. also 349-50 n. for Hardie's
words about the "uncomprehending dread" described there.

188-9. **saevis...periclis | servati:** the participle explains the cause of their performing the
rites. Savagery, danger, and salvation will be important both in the Hercules-Cacus story
and on scenes from Roman history on the shield of Aeneas (626-731 n.). **facimus...:** can
be taken "absolutely" in its sacrificial sense (cf. *Ecl.* 3.77 *cum faciam vitula* "when I sacrifice
with a calf"), or as one of two verbs for which *honores* is direct object. **novamus:** probably
means "renew" from year to year (cf. 173 *annua*, 185 *sollemnia*), rather than "institute,"
"newly introduce."

190-2. **aspice rupem,...ut...:** the remains of Cacus' cave on the Aventine (see map 1) are described
in challenging Latin. The verb takes as dir. objects first the noun *rupem*, then the *ut*-clause +
indicative where *ut* = "how" and introduces something like an exclamation or matter-of-fact
indirect question not requiring a subjunctive (Fordyce ad loc. lists parallels; see also Clausen
(1994) on *Ecl.* 4.50-2, Horsfall (2013) on 6.855-66 *aspice ut | ...ingreditur*). *Rupem* can also
be seen as a colloquial proleptic accusative; Palmer (1988: 79); cf. AG §576, as in Matthew
6:28, "Consider the lilies of the field, how they grow...." *Saxis suspensam* = "vaulted with
rocks" with abl. of means or material. Within the *ut*-clause there are three statements:
disiectae procul...moles (supply *sunt*); *desertaque montis stat domus* ("a mountain dwelling...")
and *scopuli...traxere ruinam* ("...have crashed down," "have suffered a collapse" as in 2.465-6 *ea
(turris)...ruinam...trahit* and 2.631—for more resemblances to the Fall of Troy in Book 2,
cf. 241-2 n.).

194. **semihominis:** four syllables; the *i* of *semi-* is treated as a consonant. This is our first sign that
Cacus will not be an ordinary man as in Livy but a monster (cf. 184-279 n.; Cacus is *semiferus*
at 267). **Caci facies:** "shape" or "form of Cacus." Such a noun + gen. is used in Homer, Greek
tragedy, Ennius, and Lucretius; here the periphrasis emphasizes his hideousness, just as 7.650
corpore Turni stresses the beauty of Turnus; cf. also 205 *Caci mens* and 2.601 *Tyndaridis facies*.
quam: the relative pronoun is postponed to fourth position in its clause, an extreme example
of a poetic mannerism that emphasizes the words before it.

solis inaccessam radiis; semperque recenti   195
caede tepebat humus, foribusque adfixa superbis
ora virum tristi pendebant pallida tabo.
huic monstro Volcanus erat pater: illius atros
ore vomens ignis magna se mole ferebat.
attulit et nobis aliquando optantibus aetas   200
auxilium adventumque dei. nam maximus ultor

---

196. **caede tepebat humus:** Evander will talk about gore and slaughter more than any character
in the poem: cf. 184-279 n., *tristi...pallida tabo* (197), *elisos oculos et siccum sanguine guttur*
(261), *ossa super recubans antro semesa cruento* (297 and note), along with the stress on slaughter
and killing in the hymn to Hercules (294-5, 296-7, and notes on centaurs, Cretan bull, and
Cerberus), and, in his story of Mezentius, *sanie taboque fluentis* (487; cf. 485 n.). This fondness
for killing (cf. also 345-6 n., 563-6 n.) and for justified punishment (cf. 291 n., 494 n., 500-
1 n.) is related to his crucial role in the poem calling for Aeneas to avenge the death of Pallas
by killing Turnus; cf. 11.178-9 *dextera causa tua est, Turnum gnatoque patrique | quam debere
vides.* Cf. O'Hara (2018). **superbis:** "proud," because of Cacus' trophies of victory, and also
suggesting insolence and outrage; used of Priam's palace at 2.504 *barbarico postes auro spoliisque
superbi.* Note the challenging reference to *superbia* for both Hercules at 8.202 *spoliis superbus,*
and Augustus on the shield at 721-2 *dona recognoscit populorum aptatque superbis | postibus.*
See Fowler (2000: 49-54), Reed (2007: 124) and 721-2 n. below, and cf. 8.118 *bello...superbo.*
Turnus will hang heads of his victims on his chariot at 12.511-12. Romans may also have
thought of how Antony in 43 BCE had Cicero's head and hands displayed on the Rostra in
the Forum; cf. Plut. *Cic.* 49: "a sight that made the Romans shudder, for they thought they saw
there...an image of the soul of Antony."

198-9. **illius:** i.e. *Vulcani*: Cacus is a fire-breathing monster like the Chimaera on Turnus' helmet
(7.785-6); cf. Hardie (1986: 116-19, 266), who notes that these lines liken him to a volcano
like Etna. Vulcan will play a major role later in this book in creating the shield of Aeneas (370-
453, 608-731). **atros:** probably as at 7.456-7 *atro | lumine fumantis,* of the mingled smoke and
flame (cf. 252), but also with the associated idea of "deadly." **magna...:** cf. 3.656 *vasta se mole
moventem,* of the giant Cyclops (cf. 184-279 n. on gigantomachy); 5.372-3 *immani corpore qui
se | ...ferebat,* of the huge boxer Butes; 9.597; 12.441 *portis sese extulit ingens. Se ferre* always
gives a sense of size, stateliness, or pride.

201. **auxilium adventumque dei:** hysteron proteron*; *adventus* is used of the arrival or epiphany
of a god (though Hercules will only become a god later, like Aeneas). Cf. Lucr. 1.6-7 *te, dea,
te fugiunt venti, te nubila caeli | adventumque tuum;* Ovid, *F.* 1.240 *adventum...dei,* and, for
the etymology of the Aventine hill, cf. below 235 n. **maximus ultor:** the first word anticipates
the establishment of the Ara Maxima (cf. 102-305 n., 271-2 and note), the second shows the
centrality of vengeance in Evander's ideology, which will play an important role in *Aen.* 11-12
(cf. 184-279 n., 291 n., 494 n.).

tergemini nece Geryonae spoliisque superbus
Alcides aderat taurosque hac victor agebat
ingentis, vallemque boves amnemque tenebant.
at furiis Caci mens effera, ne quid inausum   205
aut intractatum scelerisve dolive fuisset,

---

202. **Geryonae:** gen., like *Anchisae*. One of Hercules' labors (292 n.) was to acquire the cattle
of three-bodied Geryon in Spain, as Vergil notes at 7.661-2 *victor* | *Geryone exstincto* in
describing Hercules' Italian son Aventinus. Geryon's death at his hands was described in
a famous lost poem of Stesichorus, apparently sympathetically (see Gantz (1993: 402-8),
Horsfall (2000: 433-4), Nisbet and Hubbard (1978) on Hor. *Carm.* 2.14.8); sympathy is
also suggested by Vergil's borrowings in describing Euryalus' death at 9.435-7. Pindar, in
frag. 81 SM, describes Geryon as praiseworthy compared to Hercules, and Pindar, frag. 169
SM, is quoted by a character in Plato *Gorgias* 484b1-c3 who says that Hercules took Geryon's
cattle "without purchasing or being given them" due to the natural right of the stronger to take
possessions from the weaker. (Cf. too Homer *Od.* 21.25-30, for a strongly negative portrait
of Hercules as killing a host and stealing his horses.) The Hercules-Cacus story thus presents
Cacus as stealing cattle from Hercules that the latter had stolen from Geryon. Geryon is one
of the monsters whose forms appear to Aeneas at the entrance to the underworld (6.289); cf.
also Evander's story of fighting a three-souled monster (563-7). **spoliisque superbus:** cf. 196 n.
Evander thinks of his story as one of good versus evil, but many details like this blur the
difference between Hercules and Cacus.

203. **hac:** abl. of place or route, referring to the *Forum Boarium* in the low ground by the Tiber,
which is named (this story suggests) for Hercules' cattle (see map 1). The origins of Roman
place-names will often be alluded to in this and subsequent scenes; cf. O'Hara (2017: xxix,
204-12). Evander may actually be pointing, as often in this book. **victor:** Servius on 8.363
sees an allusion both here and there to the worship of Hercules Victor at Rome; see Loar
(2017).

205-6. **at furiis Caci mens effera:** some manuscripts have, and Hirtzel (1900), Mynors (1969)
and Conte (2009) print, the gen. *furis*, a word for "thief" that does not occur elsewhere in
epic but appears in the imitation of this scene at Prop. 4.9.13-14; Casali (2010: 38) sees *furis*
as an allusion to the alternate story of Cacus as not a monster but a simple thief. *Furiis*, printed
by Geymonat, is well attested and thematically appropriate; cf. 4.376 *furiis incensa* and esp.
219 *furiis* and 228 *furens*, of Hercules, and for more discussion Eden here, and Casali (2010:
38). **ne quid... | ...fuisset:** "that nothing...might have been left..."; the plup. subjunctive is
rare in purpose clauses, and may suggest completed action, and even Cacus' thinking of a
future perspective from which to look back on his deeds (so Page; cf. AG §441-2 on the plup.
subjunctive for wishing that something had not happened). Cf. 4.415 *ne quid inexpertum frustra*
moritura relinquat, Ovid on Orpheus at *Met.* 10.12 *ne non temptaret et umbras*.

quattuor a stabulis praestanti corpore tauros
avertit, totidem forma superante iuvencas.
atque hos, ne qua forent pedibus vestigia rectis,
cauda in speluncam tractos versisque viarum 210
indiciis raptor saxo occultabat opaco;
quaerenti nulla ad speluncam signa ferebant.
interea, cum iam stabulis saturata moveret
Amphitryoniades armenta abitumque pararet,
discessu mugire boves atque omne querelis 215
impleri nemus et colles clamore relinqui.
reddidit una b*o*um vocem vastoque sub antro
mugiit et Caci spem custodita fefellit.

207-8. quattuor...praestanti corpore tauros | ...totidem...iuvencas: repeated from the
description of the rebirth of bees from a slaughtered bull at *Geo.* 4.538, 540, and 550-1;
praestanti corpore (abl. of description) is also used of the nymphs used to bribe Aeolus at *Aen.*
1.70 and of Turnus at 7.783. Where was Hercules when Cacus was taking his cattle? Livy
1.7.5 describes Hercules as asleep while heavy with food and drink (*cibo vinoque gravatum*)
when Cacus steals the cattle; Parkes (2007) points to 7.659-63 and suggests he was off with
the priestess Rhea fathering Aventinus.

209-12. hos...cauda in speluncam tractos...occultabat: he dragged them by the tail into the
cave and hid them, but where English would use two verbs, Latin expresses the first action
with a passive participle. **qua:** = *aliqua*, with *vestigia*. Dragging the cattle backwards so that
no tracks would lead towards his cave is a trick borrowed from the *Homeric Hymn to Hermes'*
description (75-8) of the young god's theft of Apollo's cattle. Cf. Clauss (2017) on the *Homeric
Hymn* as well as Callimachus and Apollonius, and Secci (2013); Sutton (1977) suggests that
Vergil's models included lost Greek satyr plays involving theft of horses, Heracles tearing apart
a bad man's house and killing him, and even animals dragged backwards (in both Sophocles'
Ichneutae and Euripides' (*Second*) *Autolycus*). The "mystery" of the missing cattle led Dorothy
Sayers to include the Hercules-Cacus story in early anthologies of mystery/detective stories
(Sayers (1928) and (1929)). **quaerenti:** dative of reference (AG §378) "for anyone searching
no tracks led...."

213. stabulis: not English "stables" but "stopping-place(s)" outdoors.

214. Amphitryoniades: for the four-word line with the long Greek patronymic, cf. 103 n.; note
here the grand alliteration* and assonance* with *a*.

215. mugire: this and the next two verbs are historic infinitives.

218. custodita: "though closely guarded" the cow frustrates Cacus' hopes.

hic vero Alcidae furiis exarserat atro
felle dolor: rapit arma manu nodisque gravatum   220
robur, et aërii cursu petit ardua montis.
tum primum nostri Cacum videre timentem
turbatumque oculis; fugit ilicet ocior Euro
speluncamque petit, pedibus timor addidit alas.
ut sese inclusit ruptisque immane catenis   225
deiecit saxum, ferro quod et arte paterna
pendebat, fultosque emuniit obice postis,
ecce furens animis aderat Tirynthius omnemque

219-20. hic vero...exarserat...rapit: a pluperfect followed by the present marks great rapidity; the first action is already past, so quickly is it succeeded by the second (cf. Aeneas' eagerness to arm at 12.430-1). **Alcidae:** dative of reference or ethical dative (AG §379-80). **furiis:** the same word is used of Cacus in 205 if that reading is correct, and would blur the difference between Hercules and Cacus; for Hercules, cf. also *furens* 228. The two uses of *furor*-words, as well as *fervidus ira* in 230, connect Hercules with Aeneas as he kills Turnus (see 184-279 n., 230-2 n.).

221. robur: his famous club, which he uses to kill Cacus in Livy 1.7.7 (and later Propertius 4.9.15 and Ovid *Fasti* 1.575-6). But the club will not be used on Cacus here, as the killing will be by hand and gorier (260-1 n.). **ardua montis:** neuter pl. adj. used as a substantive with partitive genitive.

222. nostri: substantive: "our (people)." But see next note for the text.

223. oculis: could be taken with *videre*, "catch sight of," or as abl. of specification with *turbatum*, "with troubled eyes." Servius mentions a reading *oculi*, i.e., *nostri...oculi*, which Gransden prefers, which would bring the narrator Evander more vividly into the story. **fugit...ocior Euro:** at 12.733, of Turnus fleeing Aeneas after his sword breaks.

224. pedibus timor addidit alas: a metaphor not used before this passage (Fordyce). Casali (2010: 39) notes that Hermes has winged sandals (cf. 4.223), and so Vergil's novel metaphor alludes to his model for the cattle-theft; Hermes/Mercury also featured prominently in the earlier genealogies (139 n.).

226-7. saxum: in lines in a more hypotactic* style, the rock is like that with which the technologically backward Homeric Cyclops seals his cave in *Od.* 9 (cf. Hardie (1986: 115), Secci (2013: 203) and my 230-2 n.) but here is a sort of portcullis that Cacus had hung using iron chains and his father Vulcan's technological skill (*ferro quod et arte paterna*); now he breaks the chains and lowers it, then "fortified with its barrier the well-built-up entrance." **obice:** scans as a dactyl, as if *obiice*. **postis:** may be the "door-posts" or the entrance generally.

228. animis: "with rage"; cf. 256. **omnemque:** the final vowel is elided before the vowel starting 229, so the line is hypermetric, as befits the chaotic action; cf. Appendix A on meter, Harrison (1991: 281), and Goold (2002).

accessum lustrans huc ora ferebat et illuc,
dentibus infrendens. ter totum fervidus ira   230
lustrat Aventini montem, ter saxea temptat
limina nequiquam, ter fessus valle resedit.
stabat acuta silex praecisis undique saxis
speluncae dorso insurgens, altissima visu,
dirarum nidis domus opportuna volucrum. | 235
hanc, ut prona iugo laevum incumbebat ad amnem,
dexter in adversum nitens concussit et imis
avulsam solvit radicibus, inde repente
impulit; impulsu quo maximus intonat aether,

refers to the crag

---

229. **accessum lustrans huc ora ferebat et illuc:** often Hercules will prefigure Aeneas, but here cf. Turnus seeking an entrance to the Trojan camp: _huc turbidus atque huc | lustrat equo muros aditumque per avia quaerit_ (9.58-9, cf. frustrated _irae_ and _dolor_ 9.66). The word _lustrans_ can mean both "scanning" visually, as here, and "traversing" as in 231.

230-2. **dentibus infrendens:** here not Cacus but Hercules is likened to monsters and animals, for the phrase is used at 3.664 of the Cyclops (otherwise linked to Cacus, 226-7 n.) and at 10.718 of the wild boar to which Aeneas' enemy Mezentius is likened. **ter...ter...ter:** emphatic repetition; for three attempts as an epic motif cf. e.g. _Il._ 16.702-3 of Patroclus, with Janko's note. **fervidus ira:** as he kills Turnus at the end of the poem Aeneas is _furiis accensus et ira | terribilis_ 946-7 and finally _fervidus_ 951 (cf. 219-20 n.).

233-4. **stabat:** "there stood" or "there was." Vergil's readers would know that there was no longer such a formation on the top of the Aventine, which was flat. Tueller (2000) suggests Vergil provides an aetion for its present shape; such aetia figure in much of Book 8. **praecisis:** "broken off," "precipitous," so that the _silex_ stood up perpendicular from the top (_dorso_) of the cave. **visu:** supine, abl. of specification.

235. **dirarum...volucrum:** scavengers attracted by Cacus' bloody victims (195-7). That the Aventine is full of birds (usually _aves_) may offer an etymology for the hill; at 201 _adventus_ may offer another, from the arrival of Hercules, while at 7.655-63 Aventinus is named from the hill. Varro, _LL_ 5.43 mentions all three derivations; cf. O'Hara (2017), Parkes (2007).

236-9. **prona...incumbebat:** difficult Latin: the rock leaned sloping away from the ridge and towards the river, which was on the left (presumably Hercules', as he approaches the rock from downstream, though the point of reference is challenging throughout this passage). **dexter:** Hercules leans against the rock from the right (_dexter_ modifies him), strikes it with a mighty blow (_concussit_), loosens it by tearing it from its roots (_avulsam solvit..._, with long syllables for heavy effort, and a participle and verb where English would have two verbs), then drives it forcefully forward (_impulit_). The Trojan tower pushed over at 2.460-7 is similarly wrenched loose (_convellimus_) and then driven forward (_impulimus_); cf. 241-2 n. **impulit; impulsu:** for the verb followed by a related noun, see Wills (1996: 325-8), who shows (311-28) that Ovid is particularly fond of such "category shifts," following a word in one part of speech by a related word in another. Cf. _Aen._ 4.565 _non fugis hinc praeceps, dum praecipitare potestas?_

dissultant ripae refluitque exterritus amnis.   240
at specus et Caci detecta apparuit ingens
regia, et umbrosae penitus patuere cavernae,
[non secus ac si]qua penitus vi terra dehiscens
infernas reseret sedes et regna recludat
pallida, dis invisa, superque immane barathrum   245
cernatur, trepident immisso lumine Manes.
ergo insperata deprensum luce repente
inclusumque cavo saxo atque insueta rudentem

[handwritten left margin: conditional of comparison clause]

[handwritten below text:]
— likens Cacus' cave with the underworld
— contrasts light and dark

---

240. **dissultant ripae:** possibly describing the physical effect as the rock falling between them
seems to drive the banks apart (Vergil is not explicit) and/or suggesting their leaping back in
(personified) amazement at the sound. The next clause suggests water physically pushed back,
while saying it flows backwards in terror (with personification*, and pathetic fallacy*; cf. 87
and note, 9.124-5). Tueller (2000) suggests that, besides explaining why the top of the Aventine is flat (233-4 n.), Vergil also offers an aetion for the Tiber island, which sits a kilometer or
two from the top of the Aventine (see map 1). Sansone (1991) compares the Cyclops' throwing
a mountain-top at Odysseus' ship, especially the description at *Od.* 9.484-5 of the sea-water's
reaction to being hit by the boulder; again Hercules as well as Cacus is linked to the Cyclops
(cf. 230-2 n.), which Sansone says contributes to the "fundamental ambivalence" of the
episode. Cf. also Hardie (1986: 115-16).

241-2. **specus et...regia:** hendiadys*, with Cacus' cave oddly being called a palace, in anticipation
of it being compared to Pluto's palace in the simile at 243-6; Lyne (1989: 128-9). **penitus
patuere:** "lay open utterly" (literally "far within"). Cf. Enn. *Ann.* fr. 429 Sk. = 427 W *late
specus intus patebat.* Putnam (1965: 34-6) compares 2.479-88 where Pyrrhus tears a hole in the
door of Priam's palace; for echoes of Book 2, see also 190-2 n., 236-9 n., 249 n.

243-6. **non secus ac si...:** the conditional clause of comparison takes the subjunctive, like the
protasis to a future less vivid condition (AG §524). The simile* is developed not from a Homeric
simile but, as Macrob. *Sat.* 5.16.12-14 notes, from the narrative at *Il.* 20.61-5 where Hades
fears that Poseidon's earthquake will break open the underworld; see also Hardie (1986: 112)
for resemblance to Hes. *Theog.* 850. **barathrum:** used at *Od.* 12.94 and *Aen.* 3.421 of
Charybdis, several times in Plautus, in Catullus 68.108 linked to the pits dug by Hercules
at Pheneum (cf. 165 n.), and often of the underworld (cf. Lucr. 3.966). Fowler (1917: 62-4)
suggests allusion to the *mundus,* a circular hole that three days a year gave Rome access to the
underworld; cf. Varro as quoted by Macrob. *Sat.* 1.16.18, with the note of Kaster (2011) on
Macrob., and Forsythe (2005: 132).

248. **insueta rudentem:** a verb usually used of animals; *insueta* is adverbial accusative. The name
of Hercules' previous monstrous foe, Geryon (202), suggests Gr. γηρύω, "say," "sing," "cry out."

desuper Alcides telis premit, omniaque arma
advocat et ramis vastisque molaribus instat.   250
ille autem, neque enim fuga iam super ulla pericli,
faucibus ingentem fumum (mirabile dictu)
evomit involvitque domum caligine caeca
prospectum eripiens oculis, glomeratque sub antro
fumiferam noctem commixtis igne tenebris.   255
non tulit Alcides animis, seque ipse per ignem
praecipiti iecit saltu, qua plurimus undam
fumus agit nebulaque ingens specus aestuat atra.
hic Cacum in tenebris incendia vana vomentem
corripit in nodum complexus, et angit inhaerens   260
elisos oculos et siccum sanguine guttur.
panditur extemplo foribus domus atra revulsis

249-50. **omniaque...:** Hercules uses anything he can get his hands on to throw at Cacus,
including tree branches and (as in *Il.* 7.270 and 12.161) rocks as large as millstones (*molaribus*).
Another resemblance (cf. 241-2 n.) to the Trojans defending Troy: *nec saxa nec ullum | telorum
interea cessat genus* (2.467-8). Hardie (1990) notes that *molaris* occurs only once in the *Aen.*
and only once in Ovid, *Met.*, in a passage in which Cadmus is likened by allusion to Vergil's
Hercules (3.59).

251. **super:** = *superest.*

253. **caeca:** usually "blind," here "blinding."

254. **glomerat:** cf. English "conglomerate."

256-7. **tulit...:** "put up with," "endure"; cf. *non/haud tulit* at 9.622, 10.578, 12.371. **animis:** "in
his fierce courage/wrath." **seque ipse:** after the objects he had thrown before. **qua...:** when
blinded by a smoke-breathing monster, one must attack where the smoke is thickest.

260-1. Evander dwells on the gruesome aspects of Hercules' violence (cf. 196 n.); contrast Livy,
Propertius, and Ovid, who say that he killed Cacus with his club (221 n.). **nodum:** literally
"knot," a wrestling hold, such as he used when killing the Nemean lion and Antaeus. **angit:**
applies better to *guttur* than to *oculos*; he grips his throat until first his eyes are almost forced
from their sockets, and then he dies of suffocation (*elisos* and *siccum* are both proleptic). *Angit*
usually describes mental distress before the Augustan period; cf. Brown (1987) on Lucr. 4.1134,
but then *Geo.* 3.497 of plague. Tueller (2000) suggests imitation of a Greek verb in a lost
passage from Callimachus' *Aetia* on killing the Nemean Lion. With *elisos*, cf. baby Hercules
killing the snakes below at 289 *geminosque premens eliserit anguis.*

abstractaeque boves abiurataeque rapinae
caelo ostenduntur, pedibusque informe cadaver
protrahitur. nequeunt expleri corda tuendo   265
terribilis oculos, vultum villosaque saetis
pectora semiferi atque exstinctos faucibus ignis.
ex illo celebratus honos laetique minores
servavere diem, primusque Potitius auctor
et domus Herculei custos Pinaria sacri   270
hanc aram luco statuit, quae maxima semper
dicetur nobis et erit quae maxima semper.

---

263. **abiuratae:** "denied on oath," but there is no room in Vergil's story for Cacus to be accused and then deny having stolen the cattle as in Dion. Hal. *Ant. Rom.* 1.39.3, and as Mercury does in *Hymn to Hermes* 274-7. Vergil may be alluding as he often does to an alternate story (cf. O'Hara (2007: 85-91)); Servius and others try to stretch the word to mean "unlawfully taken." For the detail as undermining Evander's credibility, cf. Secci (2013), O'Hara (n.d.). With this grand four-word line, cf. *Geo.* 1.470 *obscenaeque canes importunaeque volucres* and esp. *Aen.* 11.870 *disiectique duces desolatique manipli*; see also 103 n.

265. **nequeunt expleri:...:** "they cannot satisfy their hearts with gazing on...," cf. 1.713 *expleri mentem nequit ardescitque tuendo* and *Il.* 22.370-5 where the Greeks gaze at the corpse of Hector. But the construction is different from the English: *expleri* is a passive form used like a Greek middle, with *corda* used as its object (AG §397c) or as an accusative of respect (AG §397b); *corda* can also be called a "retained accusative," with the case "retained" from an imagined active construction.

268. **minores:** Evander oddly speaks of how "later generations" celebrate an event from his own lifetime, using language that would sound more natural coming from the narrator. Some have thought 268-72 not fully polished (see also 271-2 n.), but G. Williams (1983: 131) argues that the ambiguous language deliberately both presents Evander's viewpoint and also suggests that of the Augustan age.

269. **auctor:** "founder." Livy 1.7 says that when Evander instituted this feast, the *Potitii* and *Pinarii* were invited to perform the ceremonies, but the *Pinarii* arrived only after the *exta* had been consumed, and were consequently not allowed afterwards to share that portion of the feast, the legend probably indicating that their position was inferior to that of the *Potitii*. In 312 BCE the *Potitii* taught "public slaves" (contrast Vergil's *lecti iuvenes* 179) how to perform these rites, and as a divine punishment supposedly became extinct within a year (Livy 9.29); but cf. also 281 n. on the consul Valerius Potitus. In Vergil's time, therefore, the *Pinarii* would be the "guardians" (cf. *custos* 270) of the rite. On the myth, cf. Mueller (2002).

271-2. **quae Maxima semper...:** the repetition of the line-end in consecutive lines, criticized by many editors, emphasizes the correspondence between the name of the altar and its real distinction, and between the altar of Evander's day and Vergil's; cf. Feeney (2007: 162), and the imitation at Propertius 4.9.67-8. The story has been told as an aetion of the Ara Maxima (cf. 102-305 n.), which does not survive but whose location in the Forum Boarium we know

quare agite, o iuvenes, tantarum in munere laudum
cingite fronde comas et pocula porgite dextris,
communemque vocate deum et date vina volentes."　　275
dixerat, Herculea bicolor cum populus umbra
velavitque comas foliisque innexa pependit,
et sacer implevit dextram scyphus. ocius omnes
in mensam laeti libant divosque precantur. ▌

---

from inscriptions; see Coarelli (2007: 318-19). **statuit:** the subject must be *Potitius et domus...
Pinaria*, although the singular verb and *auctor* stress the role of Potitius.

273. **munere:** "celebration"; a *munus* is the performance of some solemn act or rite in someone's
honor. **laudum:** heroic deeds worthy of praise, as in 287.

274-5. **porgite:** = *porrigite*, and is an archaism* said by Servius to be Ennian, cf. *operis inc. frag.*
19 Sk. and the notes of Skutsch (1985), Warmington (1935-40: vol. 1, 562), and also found in
comedy and Cicero's poetry. **communem:** Evander cheerfully (and with ringing alliteration*
of *c, p, v,* and *d*) calls for Trojans and Arcadians to celebrate what he calls a god they both worship,
but the Trojans have had little reason to reverence Hercules before (see 291 n. on his sack of
Troy). Some suggest he means "summon the god to share in the feast" (see Eden); Morgan
(2005) argues that this word reflects Hercules' Italian character as a god who bridges divides
between groups.

276. **dixerat...:** i.e., as soon as he had finished speaking, but the inverted *cum*-clause (AG §546
n. 4a) is a little odd here. **populus:** sacred to Hercules, who wore it on his journey to the underworld; Theoc. 2.121, *Ecl.* 7.61 *populus Alcidae gratissima, Geo.* 2.66, *Aen.* 5.134. Distinguish
pōpulus from *pŏpulus, -i* (325). **bicolor:** white/silver on the under, green on the upper, side of
its leaves.

278. **scyphus:** a cup especially associated with Hercules; cf. Servius here, Macrob. *Sat.* 5.21.16-
19, Plut. *Alex.* 75 "drinking a *skyphos* of Herakles," Sen. *Ep. Mor.* 83.23 *ille Herculaneus ac
fatalis scyphus.* Wills (1987) notes that the word occurs once only (i.e., it is a "hapax legomenon")
in Homer (*Od.* 14.112) and once in Theoc. (*Idyll* 1.143), suggesting that Vergil used it only
once for that reason.

abl absolute

Devexo interea propior fit Vesper Olympo.   280
iamque sacerdotes primusque Potitius ibant   *appositional ger*
pellibus in morem cincti, flammasque ferebant.
instaurant epulas et <u>mensae</u> grata secundae   *abl of means*
dona ferunt cumulantque oneratis <u>lancibus</u> aras.
tum Salii ad cantus incensa altaria circum   285
populeis adsunt evincti tempora ramis,

280-305. As night approaches, the sacrifice and feast are renewed, and the Salii sing the praises of Hercules in a hymn recounting many of his heroic deeds.

The hymn to Hercules resembles the hymn Orpheus sings to Apollo at Apoll. Rhod. *Arg.* 2.704-13 (cf. 293 n.), as well as notions in the time of Cicero and Vergil of the songs of praise sung by early Romans; see 285 n., Lucr. 5.1444-5 *carminibus cum res gestas coepere poetae | tradere*, Habinek (2005: 8-33), Lowrie (2009: 48-60). Consistent with Evander's Hercules-Cacus story and with his later characterization (cf. 196 n.), his people's hymn stresses deadly and unstoppable violence and dwells on killing and gore, often presenting versions of myths that are more deadly than other versions, or that praise curious incidents (294-5 n.), and it mentions Hercules' sack of Troy before a Trojan audience (291 n.). Cf. (in German) Buchheit (1963: 122-4), Hardie (1986: 111-12), Heiden (1987), Galinsky (1990: 288-9), Habinek (2005: 32), Lowrie (2009: 57-8), Secci (2013), Miller (2014), and Clauss (2017).

280. **Devexo...Olympo:** the heavens "are carried" or "move" downwards, i.e., towards night. *Vesper Olympo* occurs at *Ecl.* 6.86, *Aen.* 1.374.

281. **primusque Potitius:** repeated from 269. Dio 51.21.1-2 notes that the suffect consul who officiated at the thanksgiving in 29 BCE after Actium was the similarly named Valerius Potitus; cf. Miller (2014: 457 n. 61).

283. **mensae...secundae:** in Roman times, a second course served on new small tables, often of wine and dessert (*Geo.* 2.101); in heroic times it may simply indicate more feasting, as in the scene at 7.134, though Vergil may also be playing on the ambiguity, as Miller (2014) argues.

284. **oneratis lancibus:** "with plates that have been filled (with offerings)."

285. **Salii:** "leaping" priests of Mars. Horace *Epist.* 2.1.86 mentions the *Saliare...carmen* of Numa, Rome's second king, who is said to have instituted several priesthoods, including that of the Salii. Vergil's reference to them on Aeneas' shield (663-5) fits that story, but here he backdates them to Evander's reign; cf. Goldschmidt (2013: 53-54, 90-100) (and below 343 n. on the Lupercal). Romans of Vergil's day could not understand the words of the extant hymn, but there is no sign that it had anything to do with Hercules, although there is late evidence that the Salii worshipped Hercules at Tibur. Cf. Varro *LL* 7.2, Quint. *IO* 1.6.40, the discussion of this passage at Macrob. *Sat.* 3.12.1-9, Eden ad loc., Rudd (1989) on Horace, Lowrie (2009: 57-8) with references, Habinek (2005: 8-33, 263), Miller (2014). **altaria circum:** anastrophe of the preposition, so that it follows the noun.

286. **populeis...ramis:** for the poplar, see 276 n. **adsunt:** construe with *ad cantus* 285 which expresses purpose. **tempora:** retained accusative after the middle *evincti*; cf. 265 n.

hic iuvenum chorus, ille senum, qui carmine laudes
Herculeas et facta ferunt: ut prima novercae
monstra manu geminosque premens eliserit anguis,
ut bello egregias idem disiecerit urbes,   290
Troiamque Oechaliamque, ut duros mille labores
rege sub Eurystheo fatis Iunonis iniquae

[handwritten marginal note: theme & variation]

288-9. facta ferunt: ut...: "tell of his deeds, how..." An *ut*-clause after a verb of speaking
introduces what is probably an indirect question, as at 7.205-7 *memini...* | *Auruncos ita
ferre senes, his ortus ut agris* | *Dardanus Idaeas Phrygiae penetrarit ad urbes*, Cat. 64.117-20
commemorem, ut... | *omnibus his Thesei dulcem praeoptarit amorem*, Hor. *Serm.* 2.3.315-16
matri denarrat, ut ingens | *belua cognatos eliserit*, and cf. *OLD* s.v. *ut* A.1.c. But the usage is
rare in prose, and possibly the Greek use of ὡς in indirect statement may also be a factor, as in
Cic. *ND* 1.63 *de dis neque ut sint neque ut non sint habeo dicere*, where he is translating a Greek
dictum like that at Diog. Laertius 9.51, as Pease (1979) on Cic. notes, with further references.
novercae: used loosely of Juno, his father's wife. Juno sent snakes to kill baby Hercules; cf.
Pind. *Nem.* 1 and Theoc. *Id.* 24, and cf. 697 n. for other twin snakes in the *Aeneid*. **monstra...
geminosque...anguis:** can be seen as hendiadys*, or *–que* can introduce a more specific term
after the general *monstra*; cf. 330 *reges asperque...Thybris* and 330 n. **eliserit:** cf. *elisos* at 261.
There are a number of similarities between the Hercules-Cacus story and the hymn; see Hardie
(1986: 111 n. 68) and Secci (2013: 209-13), who thinks the resemblances suggest that Evander
is inventing or embellishing the Hercules-Cacus story.

290. idem: meter shows this must be nom. sing. masc., referring to Hercules.

291. Troiamque: for Hercules' sack of Troy, see 157-9 n., *Il.* 5.638-51, Gantz (1993: 400-2),
and Vergil's allusions to this event at *Aen.* 2.643, 11.402. Somewhat embarrassingly, Aeneas
is listening to a hymn praising Hercules for sacking his city, but Evander must view both
Troy and Oechalia (see next sentence) as having been justly punished (cf. 196 n., 201 n.; at 3.2
Aeneas naturally describes Troy as not deserving its fate: *immeritam*). **Oechaliamque:** city
whose king promised his daughter Iole to Hercules, and then refused her to him; sources in
Gantz (1993: 434-7)—Soph. *Trach.* 351-74 omits the promise. Hercules' anger over a bride
denied to him prefigures the positions in *Aen.* 7-12 of both Turnus (cf. 9.138 *coniuge praerepta*)
and Aeneas (see also 635 n. on the Sabine women on the shield of Aeneas). Cf. Buchheit (1963:
123) (in German, stressing the tie to Aeneas), Fratantuono (2007: 240). **labores:** see next note.
The word links Hercules with Aeneas whose struggles are often called *labores*; cf. 1.10 *insignem
pietate virum, tot adire labores*, 7.117-18 *ea vox audita laborum* | *prima tulit finem*, and Aeneas'
words to his son at 12.435 *disce, puer, virtutem ex me verumque laborem*.

292. Eurystheo: scans as three syllables by synizesis (see Appendix A on meter). Juno arranged
for Hercules to be obligated to perform his famous labors for Eurystheus; cf. *Il.* 8.362-9, Gantz
(1993: 374, 381-416). **fatis Iunonis iniquae:** could mean "destiny imposed on him by Juno,"
but also suggests, more than most parts of the *Aeneid*, that Juno has some control over fate.
The links between Hercules and Aeneas continue: cf. the similar phrase *odiis Iunonis acerbae*
(1.668, Venus talking about Aeneas) and Juno's general persecution of Aeneas throughout the
epic (cf. 40-1 n.).

pertulerit. "tu nubigenas, invicte, bimembris,
Hylaeumque Pholumque, manu, tu Cresia mactas
prodigia et vastum Nemeae sub rupe leonem.   295
te Stygii tremuere lacus, te ianitor Orci
ossa super recubans antro semesa cruento;

---

293. **tu:** the anaphora* of *tu-tu-te-te* in 293-6 is common in hymns (Fordyce here, Nisbet and
Hubbard (1970) on Hor. *Carm* 1.10.9, with references). **nubigenas, invicte, bimembris:** three
compounds in a row only here in Vergil; Aristotle *Poet.* 1459a associates compounds above
all with the frenzied type of hymn known as dithyramb and they suit this enthusiastic hymn
as well. *Nubigenas* is used at 7.674; *invicte* points to the cult-title Invictus found often in
inscriptions (cf. the later *CIL* 6, 312-27) and associated with the Ara Maxima (often called
Ara Maxima Herculis Invicti); and *bimembris* was coined, Macrob. *Sat.* 6.5 says, by the
Catullan-era poet Cornificius (fr. 2 Courtney). The switch from third-person summary of
the hymn in 288-93a to direct quotation of its second-person address here, the elegance
of which is admired by Macrob. *Sat.* 6.6.14, imitates the switch in Orpheus' hymn at Apoll.
Rhod. *Arg.* 2.705-13.

294-5. **Hylaeumque Pholumque:** this strange version of the killing of these Centaurs is further
evidence of Evander and the Arcadians' love for slaughter (cf. 280-305 n.). Vergil at *Geo.* 2.455-
7 innovatively (see the note of Thomas (1988)) links Hylaeus and Pholus to the drunken battle
of Lapiths and Centaurs, and Hercules is often said to be involved in that conflict but is not
linked to their deaths in it. Servius says that Theseus killed Hylaeus (other versions name other
killers). For Pholus, Servius mentions the myth told at Apollod. 2.5.4 (see Gantz (1993: 390-
1), Diod. Sic. 4.12.3-8), in which Pholus is Hercules' host but mortally wounds himself by
touching the poisoned arrow (contrast Vergil's *manu...mactas*) with which Hercules has
accidentally wounded the wise old Chiron, leading to Chiron's death as well. Fordyce: "not
a very creditable exploit." Cf. also Parkes (2009) on Hercules and Centaurs in Vergil and
Statius. **Cresia mactas | prodigia:** the vivid pres. tense suggests "you are the killer of" the
Centaurs and the Cretan bull. The bull is described in a poetic plural or encomiastic exaggeration, and with continued Arcadian delight in slaughter (cf. 280-305 n.) is said to be killed
by Hercules even though every other version has it brought alive to Eurystheus; cf. Gantz
(1993: 394-5). **leonem:** for the Nemean lion, see Gantz (1993: 383-4). Papyrus finds mean
that we now know that Callimachus' *Victoria Berenices* at the start of *Aetia* 3 treated the
founding of the Nemean games after the killing of the lion; cf. Thomas (1999: esp. 72), and
for a translation, see not the Loeb but Nisetich (2001) or Harder (2012: 198-223). [Theoc.] 25
tells the story at length.

296-7. **ianitor Orci:** the watchdog Cerberus, met by Aeneas at 6.417-23, whom Hercules had
to bring up from hell (cf. Hom. *Il.* 8.366-9, *Aen.* 6.395-6, and Hor. *Carm.* 3.11.16). **ossa...
antro semesa cruento:** again the hymn dwells on the gruesome and bloody (cf. 196 n., 280-
305 n.), even implausibly, because as Henry (1889: vol. 3, 690-1) notes there is traditionally
little of flesh and bone in the underworld for Cerberus to gnaw on: the gore here makes his
cave like that of Cacus (195-7).

nec te ullae facies, non terruit ipse Typhoeus
arduus arma tenens; non te rationis egentem
Lernaeus turba capitum circumstetit anguis.   300
salve, vera Iovis proles, decus addite divis,
et nos et tua dexter adi pede sacra secundo."
talia carminibus celebrant; super omnia Caci

[handwritten annotations: "abl of means" under "carminibus"; "modifies Hercules (subject)" pointing to "dexter"]

---

298. **Typhoeus**: fiery hundred-headed giant who fought against the gods (cf. *Aen*. 1.665 *tela Typhoea*, Hesiod, *Theog*. 820-68, Gantz (1993: vol. 1, 48-51)), as Vergil again suggests the theme of gigantomachy (cf. 184-279 n.). Hercules helped the gods in some versions; Eurip. *Hercules* 1271-3 has him battling Typhoeus. The reader is perhaps allowed to think that after the mention of Cerberus, the hymn implies that Hercules meets Typhoeus in the underworld (with *facies* referring to shades), but the Hydra in the next phrase seems real enough (though it is also mentioned at *Aen*. 6.287ff.); cf. Miller (2014: 444-5). Hardie (1986: 110-18) discusses ways in which the Hercules-Cacus story resembles the myth of Typhoeus, as part of his larger discussion of gigantomachy in the poem (cf. 184-279 n.), and notes that Ovid *Fasti* 1.571-4 makes the similarity explicit.

299-300. **arduus arma tenens**: double adjective in asyndeton*, often used when one adjective is a participle or has adverbial force, and often with *arduus* (cf. 683 *arduus agmen agens*, 5.278, 5.567, 11.755). **rationis egentem**: from Lucr. 4.502 where it refers to inability to explain a phenomenon; here *ratio* = "calm resourcefulness" (cf. *OLD* 7 and 10). When fighting against a multi-headed snake who replaces every head you cut off with more (*anguis* = the Hydra, from Lerna; cf. 6.287, 803, and 7.658 on the shield of Hercules' son Aventinus), you need the cool ability to think of a plan: Hercules cleverly cauterized each stump after cutting off its head. Petrini (1997: 64) contrasts Evander's hero with the Hercules who is helpless to help Pallas at 10.464-5: "the storybook hero of Evander's tale [is] a hero never without resource: the slayer of Cacus in Book 8 is out of proportion to real life, a fiction for old men and children; the character that Vergil shows us in the tenth book is feeling and vulnerable, subject to the same helplessness that afflicts the world at large. The world that Pallas will enter and in which Aeneas must strive and act...is more complex than anything Evander's stories suggest, and more painfully and markedly human." Cf. too Gotoff (1984: 184 n. 11): "It should be noticed that Virgil's Cacus is more monstrous than Livy's. In Virgil, Hercules' victory does represent the triumph of good over evil. But the story appears in Evander's legendary narrative; in the 'real' world of Aeneas, distinctions will not be so simple."

301. **vera**: because his deeds prove his descent from Jupiter (cf. 4.12-13, 6.322). **addite**: vocative; cf. 304 n., *Ecl*. 4.49 *magnum Iovis incrementum*, Hor. *Carm*. 2.19.13-14, *beatae coniugis additum | stellis honorem*.

302. **dexter...pede...secundo**: religious-sounding language for a god's favorable presence (cf. 10.255 *adsis pede, diva, secundo*), but "Vergil is the first Latin author to use *dexter* with the meaning 'propitious' concerning a deity" and the only author to use *secundus* in a prayer, although *secundus* is used at times to describe the gods or in divination; Hickson (1993: 57, 60); cf. too Harrison (1991) on 10.255.

303. **super omnia**: "above all," "more than anything."

speluncam adiciunt spirantemque ignibus ipsum.
consonat omne nemus strepitu collesque resultant.   305
Exim se cuncti divinis rebus ad urbem

---

304. **adiciunt:** the "adding" of the Cacus story to the Salian hymn and the word *addite* in 301
may evoke the way that by a vote of the Senate Augustus' name was added to the *Saliare
Carmen*; cf. *Res Gestae* 10.1 *Nomen meum senatus consulto inclusum est in saliare carmen*,
Miller (2014: 457-9). **spirantemque ignibus ipsum:** the phrase echoes Lucretius' reference
to a feature of one of Hercules' labors not mentioned by Vergil, Diomedes' man-eating horses:
DRN 5.30 *spirantes naribus ignem*; Miller (2014: 447).

305. **consonat omne nemus strepitu collesque resultant:** cf. 5.149-50, *consonat omne nemus,
vocemque inclusa volutant | litora, pulsati colles clamore resultant*.

306-69. Evander tells Aeneas about the past of Latium and points out landmarks on the future
site of Rome (see map 1).

By having Aeneas visit Evander here, Vergil is able to present what to Romans must have
been a fascinating glimpse of their city's primitive state. As they walk from the Ara Maxima
to Evander's home on the Palatine, Evander first tells Aeneas about the earlier history of
Latium and Italy, in a way that interacts interestingly with other passages in the poem and
with recurrent themes about history, war, immigration, and decline from an earlier Golden
Age (306-36 n., 324-5 n.). Then he points out landmarks they are passing as they walk through
what will later be the Roman Forum. Evander's history of Latium contrasts with the narrator's
statement, when introducing Latinus and the Latins in Book 7, that Latinus, descended from
Saturn, rules over a people long at peace (7.45-6 and note, 8.324-5 n.); Latinus also told
Aeneas' representative that the Latins are the people of Saturn (7.202-4). Evander tells how
Saturn came to Italy after being driven from heaven by Jupiter, in lines evocative of the way
that Jupiter in Vergil's *Georgics* ended Saturn's Golden Age (cf. 324-5 n.). Saturn, he says,
gathered and taught laws to the people scattered on the local hills and ruled over a Golden
Age, but then that age yielded to ages of baser metals with the arrival of waves of immigrants,
the rage of war, and desire for wealth. Evander briefly tells his own history: he was driven
from his homeland in Greek Arcadia and brought to Italy by the direction of his prophetic
mother and (like Aeneas) Apollo. As they walk on, either Evander or the narrator comments
on various sites they pass, including the Carmental Gate, the asylum of Romulus, the Lupercal,
Argiletum, Tarpeian rock, and the Capitolium, as well as ruins left by Saturn and Janus, the
Forum itself, and the Carinae neighborhood (337-69; see map 1). Because Evander speaks
both about his present and the past life of the site of Rome and Latium, and the narrator at
times looks forward to the status in the Augustan age of the sites, the reader is presented with
periods of Roman history overlaid upon one another like the writing of a palimpsest (the
image is Freud's, for the nineteenth-century visitor to Rome—cf. Edwards cited 337-69 n.,
and above, Introduction to Book 8).

*306-36. Evander tells Aeneas a version of the history of Italy, including the golden rule of Saturn, the
gradual decay which followed, and his own coming to Italy in obedience to his mother Carmentis.*

For Evander's account of previous settlements on the site of Rome, Vergil draws on a tradition
that includes ethnographic writing on primitive people, Lucretius' history of human development in *DRN* 5, his own explanation in *Geo.* 1.118-59 of how and why Jupiter made life

perfectis referunt. ibat rex obsitus aevo,
⌐et comitem Aenean iuxta natumque tenebat
⌐ingrediens varioque viam sermone levabat.
miratur facilisque oculos fert omnia circum   310
Aeneas, capiturque locis et singula laetus
exquiritque auditque virum monimenta priorum.
tum rex Evandrus Romanae conditor arcis:

---

less easy for mankind, and the Golden Age in authors including Hesiod, Aratus, and his own *Ecl.* 4 and *Georgics.* Vergil combines a harsh primitivism, in which the earliest age is rough and brutish (cf. Taylor (1955), Ross (2007: 57-9), Farrell (1994) on Lucretius), with the notion of a Golden Age, which in most texts involves a life of ease with no need for laws (as in Latinus' words in 7.45-6). Saturn is instead a "culture-hero" who gives laws to the people scattered on Rome's hills and so prefigures the position of Evander and later Aeneas and Augustus. Casali (2010: 39) notes that Evander is, after Aeneas, "the character who speaks the most in the *Aeneid,*" and that he is "a symbol of the way in which the Romans...have learned their own past from the Greeks and from a Greek point of view"; cf. too Papaioannou (2003). Cf. Taylor (1955), Horsfall (1971), Wiesen (1973), Thomas (1982: 96-7; 2004-5: 138-9), Wallace-Hadrill (1982: 19-36), Perkell (2002), O'Hara (2007: 100-1), Feeney (2007: 108-39), Lowrie (2010: 392-5), and Wimperis (2017). Campbell (2003: 336-53) offers a "Table of Themes in Pre-histories and Accounts of the Golden Age."

307. **obsitus aevo:** "overgrown with age" <-*sero*; cf. Ter. *Eun.* 236 *pannis annisque obsitum.*

308. **iuxta:** adverb.

310. **miratur:** we will see the site of Rome through Aeneas' marveling eyes (cf. 91-2 n., and 1.456 *miratur,* of Aeneas gazing at Dido's murals). **facilisque:** "ready," "eager." **omnia circum:** anastrophe; cf. 286 n.

312. **virum monimenta priorum:** the motto, since the late nineteenth century, of the Archaeological Institute of America. Cf. 356 *veterum...monimenta virorum,* but at 3.102 *veterum voluens monimenta virorum* refers not to material culture but to remembered tradition. A *monimentum* is anything that reminds, so called *ab eo quod moneat mentem* (Servius on *Aen.* 6.512). Lowrie (2009: 117-22) discusses how the word is used at Hor. *Carm.* 3.30.1 *exegi monumentum* as an explicit metaphor for a literary work and in Livy's *Pref.* 10 as an implied metaphor for his history: *Hoc illud est praecipue in cognitione rerum salubre ac frugiferum, omnis te exempli documenta in inlustri posita monumento intueri* (Livy's early books of course share both material and attitude with much of *Aen.* 8). Lowrie notes (143) that "Vergil is coy about characterizing his work this way," but such a usage may be implied here in 8 as Evander speaks to Aeneas and Vergil to the Romans.

313. **Romanae conditor arcis:** proleptic reference to Evander's settlement of Pallanteum on the Palatine as the *Romana arx,* even though the later *arx* was on the Capitoline (see map 1).

acc. pl.   *nom. pl.*
"haec nemora indigenae Fauni Nymphaeque tenebant
gensque virum truncis et duro robore nata,   315
quis neque mos neque cultus erat, nec iungere tauros
aut componere opes norant aut parcere parto, *dative*
sed rami atque asper victu venatus alebat. *abl. of supine*
primus ab aetherio venit Saturnus Olympo *abl. of respect*
arma Iovis fugiens et regnis exsul ademptis.   320
is genus indocile ac dispersum montibus altis *abl. absolute*
composuit legesque dedit, Latiumque vocari
maluit, his quoniam latuisset tutus in oris.

↳ with subj gives an alleged reason

314. **indigenae:** masculine. **Fauni Nymphaeque:** Fordyce: "The multiplicity of Fauni is inconsistent with the place which Virgil has given to a singular Faunus in his pedigree of the Latin kings"
in 7.47-9. Vergil stresses details that make Evander's conception of Italian history different
from that of Latinus; this one also recalls stories Lucretius labels false at 4.580-1 (of echoing
places) *haec loca capripedes satyros nymphasque tenere | finitimi fingunt et Faunos esse loquuntur.*

315. **truncis...:** the legend of men springing from stones and trees is so well known that Penelope
can joke at *Od.* 19.163 that the disguised Odysseus was "not born from the fabled oak or rock";
cf. too Hesiod, *Op.* 147, Juv. 6.12 *homines...rupto robore nati.* **duro:** those born from the "hard
oak" were "hardy." Cf. *Geo.* 1.63-4 *lapides... | unde homines nati, durum genus* with the note of
Thomas (1988), 9.603 where Numanus says the Italians are a *durum a stirpe genus* (*stirpe* there
means "stock," "descent" but evokes the idea behind 8.315), and Lucr. 5.925-6 *genus humanum
multo fuit illud in arvis | durius, ut decuit, tellus quod dura creasset.*

316-17. **quis:** dative = *quibus.* **mos:** the rule or principle of which *cultus* is the visible manifes-
tation; cf. 1.264 *moresque viris et moenia ponet,* 6.852 *pacique imponere morem.* **tauros:** for
farming; cf. Mynors (1990) on *Geo.* 1.45. **componere...parcere:** theme and variation* to
describe saving provisions for the future; cf. Tib. 1.1.77-8 *composito securus acervo | despiciam
dites,* Hor. *Epist.* 1.1.12 *condo et compono quae mox depromere possim.*

318. **rami...venatus:** compound subject of closely linked things with a singular verb (AG §317b).
They lived as hunter-gatherers on berries or acorns from tree-branches and on the meat from
hunting; for primitive diets in classical texts cf. the charts at Campbell (2003: 341-5). **victu:**
abl. of specification, cf. 1.445 *facilem victu...gentem.*

319-20. **Saturnus:** Latin god of "sowing" (*sero*) but, as at the heart of Vergil's *Georgics,* identified
here with the Greek Kronos driven out by Zeus, and associated in both *Geo.* and *Aen.* with the
Golden Age replaced by Jupiter's reign (324-5 n.). Ennius dealt with this story in *Euhemerus*
p. 422 W, and probably *Ann.* frags. 20-5 Sk., 24-9 W. Saturn's exile is like that of Evander
(333 n.) or Mezentius (481 n.) and to a lesser extent that of Aeneas and Dido.

321. **indocile:** usually "unteachable," here "untaught," as Servius notes.

322-3. **composuit:** "brought together," and also suggesting the idea of "brought to order."
legesque dedit: laws are an unusual feature for a Golden Age (306-36 n., 324-5 n., Campbell
(2003: 348-9)); for lawgivers in the poem, cf. 666-70 n. on *his dantem iura Catonem.*
Latiumque... | latuisset: an etymology for the name Latium, as at Ovid, *F.* 1.237-8 *inde*

aurea quae perhibent illo sub rege fuere
saecula: sic placida populos in pace regebat,   325
deterior donec paulatim ac decolor aetas
et belli rabies et amor successit habendi.
tum manus Ausonia et gentes venere Sicanae,

---

diu genti mansit Saturnia nomen; | *dicta quoque est Latium terra latente deo.* Varro (fr. 394,
GRF p. 350) cited instead its position "hiding" between the Alps and Appenines; cf. O'Hara
(2017: 207-8). *Latuisset* is subjunctive because Evander gives Saturnus' reasoning; cf. 129 n.,
AG §592. **maluit:** i.e., that it should be called *Latium* rather than *Saturnia* (329); the word
also is an anagram of *Latium.*

324-5. **aurea quae perhibent:** cf. Enn. *Ann.* 20 Sk = 24 W *est locus Hesperiam quam mortales
perhibebant;* Vergil has already borrowed *est locus Hesperiam* at 1.530 and 3.163. **placida populos in pace regebat:** precise recall and contradiction of the narrator's words at 7.45-6 *rex arua
Latinus et urbes* | *...longa placidas in pace regebat.* The earlier passage associates Latinus' people
with Golden Age peace, as does Latinus' claim that they are the people of Saturn, just not by
the compulsion of law (cf. 322-3 n.), but on their own (7.202-4, quoted 329 n.); Evander puts
the Golden Age in the past. On the inconsistency as part of deliberate ambiguity about the
Italians, see O'Hara (2007: 96-101). The Golden Age is a major theme in all of Vergil's works,
developed from treatments in Hesiod *Opera et Dies* 106-201 and Aratus *Phaenomena* 96-136.
Vergil's *Fourth Eclogue* tells how after the birth of a child the Golden Race will return: *Ecl.* 4.8-
9 *ferrea primum* | *desinet ac toto surget gens aurea mundo.* The *Georgics,* like Evander here, put
the Golden Age in the past: *Geo.* 1.121-46 tells how Jupiter wanted the farmer's life not to
be as easy as before; cf. *Geo.* 2.538 *aureus hanc vitam in terris Saturnus agebat.* Jupiter in *Aen.*
1.291 says that under Aeneas' descendant *Iulius Caesar,* the age will grow gentler (see 326 n.),
while Anchises in the underworld says that Augustus will restore Saturn's Golden Age: *Aen.*
6.792-4 *Augustus Caesar, divi genus, aurea condet* | *saecula qui rursus Latio regnata per arva* |
Saturno quondam. On the Golden Age, cf. Wiesen (1973: esp. 754-6, 762-3), Thomas (2001:
1-7; 2004-5), Perkell (2002), and (with a broader focus) Wallace-Hadrill (1982), Zanker (1988:
167-92), Galinsky (1996: 91-121), Campbell (2003: 336-53).

326. **decolor:** "dimmer," "of an inferior color" rather than gold (324); bronze and iron are duller
than gold in appearance. The opposite process, a return to a better age, is predicted for the
Augustan future by Jupiter at 1.291 *aspera tum positis mitescent saecula bellis.*

327. **amor...habendi:** "passion for possessions"; at *Geo.* 4.177 *amor habendi* is what drives the
bees. Cf. Ovid, *Met.* 1.130 *amor sceleratus habendi,* of his Iron Age, *Ars* 3.541 *nec amor nos
tangit habendi;* Hor. *Epist* 1.7.85 *amore senescit habendi.* For the thought, cf. Sallust *Cat.* 2.2.1
on early human history: *tum vita hominum sine cupiditate agitabatur; sua quoique satis
placebant.*

328. **Ausonia:** "'learned' or romantic name for Italy" in the Hellenistic poets (Fordyce, citing
Apoll. Rhod. *Arg.* 4.660 on the "Ausonian sea" and "Tyrrhenian shore"). **Sicanae:** a Sicilian
tribe regarded as Iberian or Italian in origin, often by synecdoche* denoting all inhabitants of
Sicily. Dion. Hal. *Rom. Ant.* 1.60 lists a long succession of immigrants to Italy before Aeneas;
see also next note on *metonomasia.*

saepius et nomen posuit Saturnia tellus; *abl. description*
tum reges asperque immani corpore Thybris,   330
a quo post Itali fluvium cognomine Thybrim
diximus; amisit verum vetus Albula nomen.
me pulsum patria pelagique extrema sequentem
Fortuna omnipotens et ineluctabile fatum

obj. of sentence   *abl of separation*

theme in variation

329. **posuit:** "lay aside" an old name for a new one (*OLD* 10); cf. 1.530-3 = 3.163-6, where *Hesperia, Oenotria*, and *Italia* are all mentioned. Vergil's interest in changes of names (*metonomasia*) recalls that of Callimachus, who wrote the treatises *Local Nomenclature* and *Foundations of Cities and Islands and Their Changes of Names*; cf. 1.267-8 on Ascanius, 3.693-4 on Plemyrium, 7.774-7 on Virbius, 8.322-3, and O'Hara (2017: 88-91). **Saturnia tellus:** Ennius (319-20 n.) called Italy *Saturnia terra* (*Ann.* 21 Sk. = 26 W), and Vergil uses *Saturnia tellus* in an idealized passage at *Geo.* 2.173 for fertile Italy, though most of that poem treats Jupiter's harsh Iron Age. With Evander's account contrast Latinus' claim at 7.203-4 that the Latins are Saturn's people: *Saturni gentem haud vinclo nec legibus aequam, | sponte sua veterisque dei se more tenentem*, and Diomedes at 11.252 on the Latins as *fortunatae gentes, Saturnia regna*.

330. **reges asperque...Thybris:** *-que* introduces a particular name after the general *reges*, as at 7.535 *corpora multa virum circa seniorque Galaesus*. Servius' several stories about Thybris suggest he was an Etruscan king who committed banditry and/or died fighting by the Tiber; cf. also next note. **asperque immani corpore:** cf. Lucr. 5.33, *asper, acerba tuens, immani corpore serpens*, which Vergil also imitates at 9.794 *asper, acerba tuens* (Turnus) and adapts at *Geo.* 3.149 *asper, acerba sonans* (the gadfly).

331. **Itali:** the immigrant Evander is the only individual in the poem to refer to himself as "Italian"; cf. Wimperis (2017). Ethnic identity, whether of Trojan, Greek, Italian, Etruscan, and eventually Roman, is a key issue in the poem. **cognomine:** "as a (significant) name" (cf. 31 n.). For the Tiber's names cf. 72 n. Servius reports numerous derivations, Livy 1.3 names it for a Tiberinus descended from Aeneas who was a king of Alba Longa, Varro, *LL* 5.30 for Thebris, an Etruscan king of Veii.

333. **pulsum patria:** Evander does not say why he was exiled. Servius reports a story that he murdered his father at the instigation of his mother, Servius *auctus* that he killed his mother. Dion. Hal. *Rom. Ant.* 1.31 says that after factional strife, Evander's defeated party chose to emigrate; cf. Evander's story of Mezentius at 481-95, and in this poem Aeneas, Dido, and Saturn (319-20) are also exiles. Ovid *F.* 1.481-4 has Evander's mother say vaguely that it was not his *culpa* that exiled them, but an offended god, probably reflecting Ovid's exile by Augustus; cf. Green (2004) on *F.* 1.479-96. **pelagique...:** "and seeking the ends of the sea," i.e., a refuge on some remote shore.

334. **Fortuna...fatum:** cf. 6.683 *fataque fortunasque virum*. Scholars disagree over whether Vergil sees both terms as similar in meaning or views fortune as random and fate as fixed by the gods; see Nicoll (1988: 463), Kristol (1990: 181-91), *VE* pp. 474-5, 497-8. **ineluctabile:** Aeneas' narration at 2.324 quotes a Trojan who uses this sonorous word, probably invented by Vergil, of their city's fall.

his posuere locis, matrisque egere tremenda   335
Carmentis nymphae monita et deus auctor Apollo."
Vix ea dicta, dehinc progressus monstrat et aram
et Carmentalem Romani nomine portam

[handwritten: mother is the hinge between 2 sections]

---

336. **Carmentis:** or Carmenta (Livy has both forms), an Italian deity associated with prophecy because of her name (Ovid, *F.* 1.467 *quae nomen habes a carmine*). Cf. also next note. **Apollo:** also led Aeneas, especially in Books 3 and 6 (cf. 3.73-83), and will help Augustus at Actium (704 and n.).

337-69. Evander as they walk gives Aeneas a tour of the future site of Rome, and he or the narrator points out various places that the Roman reader would recognize. Finally, he brings Aeneas to his own dwelling, reminding him that, though poor, it had once welcomed the god Hercules.

The tour of the site of Rome must have been of special interest to the Roman reader, and of course the modern tourist can see some of the same sites, though of some places named there is no trace today (see map 1). It was noted above (306-69 n.) that this whole section of Book 8 presents the history of Rome in layers as in a palimpsest. The tour also complements the shield of Aeneas at the end of Book 8, which itself features several topological features of the city. Evander and Aeneas pass the altar and gate named after Evander's prophetic mother Carmenta (337-41); the grove that Romulus will later make his Asylum (342-3); the Lupercal, which is given different associations than will be seen on Aeneas' shield (343-4); the Argiletum, named for a guest of Evander who was killed (345-6); the Tarpeian Rock (347); and the Capitol, where the temple of Jupiter Optimus Maximus would later stand and whose grove now frightens locals who claim to have seen Jupiter there (347-54). From near the Capitol he points to the Janiculum and to ruins of Janus there and Saturn on the Capitol (355-8). When they arrive at Evander's house, apparently on the Palatine near where Augustus had his home, they can see cattle grazing in what would be the Roman Forum and the elegant Carinae region (359-61). The passage alternates between the perspective of Evander and that of the modern narrator and reader, and contrasts the rustic primitiveness of the region and its inhabitants and their beliefs with the wealth and elegance of the modern city (cf. 98-100 n.).

For the sites mentioned, cf. Richardson (1992), and the guidebooks Coarelli (2008) and Claridge (2010). On the tour, cf. Fowler (1917: 71-8), McKay (1970: 122-33), Wiseman (2009: 390-5, orig. 1984), White (1993: 182-90) (also on prehistoric Rome in Tib. 2.5 and Prop. 4), Edwards (1996: 27-8) (quoting Freud), Edmunds (2001: xiv-xv), Klodt (2001: 11-36) (in German), Milnor (2005: 8-10), Feeney (2007: 161-6), Lowrie (2009: 168-72), Kondratieff (2014: 196-9) (with map p. 218), as well as my map 1. Later authors play intertextually with this passage: see Huskey (2002) on Ovid *Tr.* 3.1; Martindale (1993: 48-53) and Johnson (1987: 118-21) on Lucan *BC* 9.961-99; Hui (2011) on Freud, Vergil, Lucan, and Petrarch's *Africa*; and Foster (2013) on Servius and the poet Claudian.

337-8. Carmenta had an altar south of the Capitoline Hill, near the gate named for her, which is usually thought to be part of the wall built by Servius Tullius (see map 1); cf. Dion. Hal. *Rom. Ant.* 1.32, Richardson (1992: 301). Again Vergil is backdating features of later Roman history into the time of Aeneas and Evander (cf. 285 n.).

gen.

quam memorant, nymphae priscum Carmentis honorem,
vatis fatidicae, cecinit quae prima futuros   340
Aeneadas magnos et nobile Pallanteum.
hinc lucum ingentem, quem Romulus acer asylum
rettulit, et gelida monstrat sub rupe Lupercal
Parrhasio dictum Panos de more Lycaei.
nec non et sacri monstrat nemus Argileti   345
testaturque locum et letum docet hospitis Argi.

---

339. **honorem:** probably in apposition to *portam*, possibly to the whole idea of naming the gate for her (for apposition cf. 387 n., 683-4 n.).

341. **Aeneadas magnos et nobile Pallanteum:** spondaic line, like 54, as well as a four-word hexameter (ignoring the *et*), for which cf. 103 n. Carmenta's prophecy is precisely true: Aeneas' race (*Aeneadae*), but only Evander's city (*Pallanteum*), which is named for his ancestor but reminds us of the younger Pallas, are destined for greatness. The line of Evander is to be wiped out. Cf. O'Hara (1990: 48).

343-4. **rettulit:** usually means "restore" or "reproduce from a model" as in 5.598, but here must mean "turn into" or "establish as"; cf. Adkin (2001). The perfect tense represents the point of view of Vergil and his readers. For Romulus' Asylum, between the two peaks of the Capitoline, where he welcomed inhabitants from other cities in order to increase Rome's population, see Livy 1.8 and my map 1. **Lupercal:** a cave either on the southwest side of the Palatine, or a short distance from the Palatine closer to the later Circus Maximus; see Richardson (1992: 238-9), and my map 1. Evander and Aeneas seem to be walking between the Capitolium on their left and the Palatine on their right, which they will ascend on its north side. The Lupercal was restored by Augustus (*Res Gestae* 19, Suet. *Aug.* 31), and connected by Evander (and Livy 1.5) with *Pan* as known on Mount Lycaeus in Evander's Arcadia, based on a derivation of Lupercal and Lycaeus from Roman (*lupus*) and Greek (*lukos*) words for "wolf"; cf. Maltby (1991) for both words. Romans often attributed the cave's name instead to the wolf that suckled Romulus and Remus, a derivation implied on Aeneas' shield (630-1 n.). Goldschmidt (2013: 53-4, 90-100) argues that with features like this that backdate material found in Ennius (or, we might add, Livy; see also 285 n. and 663-5 n. on the Salii), Vergil "sets up the *Aeneid* as the Ur-Epos, a Roman epic to replace the *Annales* that is in some ways 'older' than Ennius ever was" (p. 54). **Parrhasio:** "Arcadian," after a town in Arcadia; Evander is *Parrhasius* at 11.31. **Panos:** Greek genitive.

345-6. **sacri:** "accursed" or "consecrated." **Argileti:** another spondaic line, produced as often by a four-syllable word (see Appendix A on meter and 54 n.). In Augustan times the Argiletum was a street northwest of the Forum; the area would be in front of Aeneas and Evander as they walk and if thought of as extending far enough away would include the future site of the Forum of Augustus (see map 1). Evander attributes its name to the death of a guest named

hinc ad Tarpeiam sedem et Capitolia ducit
aurea nunc, olim silvestribus horrida dumis.] *adj of means*
iam tum religio pavidos terrebat agrestis
dira loci, iam tum silvam saxumque tremebant.   350
"hoc nemus, hunc" inquit "frondoso vertice collem
(quis deus incertum est) habitat deus; Arcades ipsum
credunt se vidisse Iovem, cum saepe nigrantem

Indirect Statement

Argus; Servius and Servius *auctus* say that he plotted to kill his host Evander and become king, and was killed either by Evander's men without his knowledge or by Evander himself. Servius and Varro *LL* 5.157 also mention a derivation from a word for potter's clay. On Evander's fondness for killing, cf. 196 n.; is Evander giving his current guest a lesson on what happens to guests who cause trouble?

347. **ad Tarpeiam sedem:** the Tarpeian rock that was probably on the southwest face of the Capitoline (see map 1), so called from Tarpeia who (in the time of Romulus) betrayed the citadel to the Sabines. Cf. 652 *Tarpeiae...arcis*, Varro *LL* 5.41, Livy 1.11, Prop. 4.4. **Capitolia:** poetic plural. **ducit:** Evander presumably "led" Aeneas to the foot of the hill, not up the hill as a younger tour guide would do.

348. **aurea:** the roof of the temple of Jupiter Optimus Maximus (see map 1) was gilded when it was rebuilt after a fire in 83 BCE; the ceilings had been gilded after the fall of Carthage in 146. Plin. *NH* 33.57 reports that not all approved of the gilding; cf. Sen. *Contr.* 1.6.4, 2.1.1 (associating such luxury with civil wars) and Prop. 4.1.5 (in a similar contrast) *fictilibus crevere deis haec aurea templa.* For the contrast between Evander's poverty and Augustan wealth, cf. 98-100 n. **olim:** literally must refer from Vergil's perspective to the past but, as Zetzel notes, can evoke a possible future in which the Capitolium will be rustic again. See 360-1 n., Zetzel (1994: 21), Edwards (1996: 31), Feeney (2007: 165).

349-50. **iam tum...iam tum:** "even then...even then": emphatic. **religio...dira:** "frightful awe." *Religio* is Lucretius' main target of criticism; Hardie (1986: 218) notes that Lucretius would not dissent from this passage's suggestion that (in Hardie's words) "*religio* arises among the primitive people as a result of an uncomprehending dread of Nature," especially the storms to be described in 352-4, and that it is curious to have this "rather dubious religious emotion" lie "at the heart of the very being of Rome."

352-3. **quis deus incertum est:** parenthetical—"what god we know not"; Romans knew that here stood their temple to Jupiter Optimus Maximus (see map 1), and a smaller temple to *Iuppiter Tonans* dedicated by Augustus in 22 BCE (to which the reference to weather in 353-4 may allude). **ipsum:** "in visible presence"; cf. 31 n. **cum saepe...:** "when, as often," cf. 1.148, 10.723 *ceu saepe*, 5.273 *qualis saepe*, Lucr. 4.34 *cum saepe.*

abl. of means

abl. of description or
abl. absolute

aegida concuteret dextra nimbosque cieret. /
haec duo praeterea disiectis oppida muris,   355
reliquias veterumque vides monimenta virorum.   *etymology*
hanc Ianus pater, hanc Saturnus condidit arcem;
Ianiculum huic, illi fuerat Saturnia nomen."
talibus inter se dictis ad tecta subibant
pauperis Evandri, passimque armenta videbant ⎤   360
Romanoque foro et lautis mugire Carinis.   ⎦ *indirect statement*

---

354. **aegida:** Gr. acc. Zeus brandishes the *aegis*, a shield covered by a goatskin (Gr. *aix, aigos*), to create storms and strike terror: cf. Hom. *Il.* 4.166-8 "Zeus son of Kronos from his high throne will overshadow them with his awful *aegis* in punishment of this treachery," and 17.593, where Zeus uses the *aegis* to cover Ida in mist, and see Nisbet and Rudd on Horace *Carm.* 3.4.57. The word *dextra* shows that it is not here a defensive shield which would be on the left hand. For the *aegis* as worn by Pallas, see 435 n. **nimbosque cieret:** represents Homer's epithet for Zeus "cloud-gatherer," *Il.* 1.511, *Od.* 1.63, etc. Vergil at times avoids a Greek compound, e.g., 1.85 where Africus is "packed with storms" (*creberque procellis*) rather than "storm-packed" (Austin (1971) ad loc.), 7.651, where Homer's "horse-breaker" becomes *equum domitor* "breaker of horses" (Horsfall (2000) ad loc.), and below 434 and note. For weather, see 349-50 n., 352-3 n.

355-8. Evander apparently points to ruins on the Janiculum west of the Tiber (see map 1), though some have suggested these lines make better sense if they refer to a settlement called Ianiculum that was also on the Capital. Janus and Saturn are depicted as sharing power peacefully in Varro, as quoted in Augustine, *Civ.* 7.4; Ovid, *F.* 1.235-46; Macrob. *Sat.* 1.7.19-26. There may be a point in that the name Ianiculum survives as the name of the hill, while Saturnia does not. Varro *LL* 5.42 said that *Saturnia* was on the Capitoline: thus Vergil subtly alludes to the way in which Saturn was supplanted by Jupiter, again pointing to the end of the Saturnian and beginning of the Jovian age. On the sites, cf. Kondratieff (2014: 198-9). **fuerat:** the tense alludes to the change of name.

360-1. **pauperis Evandri:** cf. 98-100 n. **lautis:** < *lavo,* "wash," "clean," and so "spiffed up," "luxurious," "posh," in contrast to the home of *pauper Evander* (360); the adjective does not appear elsewhere in epic or lyric and may be sarcastic. **mugire:** Feeney (2007: 164) notes that Vergil puns on the name of the nearby Porta Mugonia ("Moo-Gate"; cf. Varro *LL* 5.164, map 1), and observes that "the Roman Forum in medieval times returned to the time of Evander and was for centuries yet again a place for cows to graze, 'Campo Vaccino.'" **Carinis:** Carinae was a fashionable district on the slopes of the Esquiline (see map 1), where Pompey, Cicero, and later Tiberius lived, and Servius says that Augustus was brought up there; on the area, cf. Coarelli (2007: 178-9), and, on Servius, Timpanaro (1967).

impersonal passive

ut ventum ad sedes, "haec" inquit "limina victor
Alcides subiit, haec illum regia cepit.
aude, hospes, contemnere opes et te quoque dignum
finge deo, rebusque veni non asper egenis."   365
dixit, et angusti subter fastigia tecti
ingentem Aenean duxit stratisque locavit
effultum foliis et pelle Libystidis ursae:
nox ruit et fuscis tellurem amplectitur alis.

abl.

takes the ablative: "deo"

word picture

---

362. They seem to have climbed to Evander's home on the Palatine, where Augustus' house
would later be; see map 1. Recent excavations have taught us much about Augustus' house:
cf. McKay (1970: 133-5), Richardson (1992: 117-18), Coarelli (2007: 131-5), Miller (2009:
186). Rees (1996) argues instead that readers should think of the Regia in the Forum at
the foot of the Palatine inhabited first by Roman kings then by the Pontifex Maximus. On
Evander's simple house as prefiguring that of Augustus, see Milnor (2005: 8-10), Miller (2009:
213-14).

363. **subiit:** the last syllable is lengthened in arsis (see Appendix A on meter). **regia:** see previous
note. **cepit:** "had room enough for him," was large enough to entertain him though he was so
great; cf. 9.644 *nec te Troia capit* (of Ascanius); Juv. 10.148 *hic est, quem non capit Africa*, of
Hannibal.

364-5. Famous lines even in antiquity, twice quoted by Seneca to support his Stoic arguments
(*Ep. Mor.* 18.12, 31.11); cf. Juv. 11.60-1 *nam cum sis conviva mihi promissus, habebis | Evandrum,
venies Tirynthius*. Heracles was a distinctly Stoic hero in the first century CE and later, but it
is unclear how early his close association with Stoicism developed; Sedley (1998: 75 n. 62) is
skeptical. **te quoque dignum | finge deo:** ambiguous: Evander apparently urges Aeneas to
emulate Hercules, who has become a god, but the words could also suggest being worthy of
becoming a god or of Aeneas' divine descent.

366. **angusti...tecti:** the proximity of Evander's house to that of Augustus (see map 1) allows us
to hear a pun between *angustus* and *Augustus*, and thus a contrast between Evander's poverty
and Augustan wealth (cf. 98-100 n.). Late republican and early imperial moralizing about
wealth often focused on the building of extravagant private homes; cf. Hor. *Carm.* 2.15 with
Nisbet and Hubbard (1978), Edwards (1993: 137-72).

368. The couch was composed of leaves covered with a bearskin. **Libystidis:** at 5.37 and here
Vergil uses an adjective found previously only in Callim. fr. 676 and Apoll. Rhod. *Arg.* 4.1753.
It is not clear why, except for literary reasons, an Arcadian would have a Libyan fur; cf. Fordyce
here, Clausen (2002: 167-8), and Secci (2014) who argues that allusion to Apollonius suggests
"the creation of a new homeland within a foreign territory."

369. **ruit:** not our "falls" (e.g., in "nightfall"), but "comes on quickly"; cf. 2.250 *ruit Oceano nox*
"rises (quickly) from Ocean." **nox ruit et fuscis tellurem amplectitur alis.** Dainotti (2015: 16)
notes how the words *fuscis...alis* surround and "embrace" *tellurem amplectitur*.

At Venus haud animo nequiquam exterrita mater   370
Laurentumque minis et duro mota tumultu

370-453. Venus asks Vulcan for weapons for Aeneas, in a seduction scene in which the goddess
of sexual desire asks her much-neglected husband to help her son by a mortal father (370-406).
After their embraces and a night of sleep, Vulcan arises early for work, like a wife or widow
working to preserve her chastity and raise her children. He goes to his workship, where the
Cyclopes are working on projects for various gods, which he tells them to put aside to make
"arms for a keen man," and they all begin melting the metals needed (407-53).

The scene is modeled on Hom. *Il.* 18.428-67, where Thetis asks Hephaestus (= Vulcan)
to forge arms for her son Achilles (see 383 n. on Venus' citation of her literary model), as well
as the "deception of Zeus" in *Il.* 14.159-353, where Hera uses the girdle of Aphrodite/Venus
to seduce Zeus. There are also echoes of Lucretius' description of Venus' overcoming Mars at
DRN 1.31-40 and of other intertexts. Rhetorically, as Servius notes, the scene depicts a highly
effective *suasio*, but it is interesting to see that the shield of Aeneas is produced as a result of
sexual bribery by an unfaithful spouse (cf. also 407-53 n. on the comparison of Vulcan to a
chaste widow or wife). Several aspects of the scene scandalized critics (381-2 n., 405 n.); more
positive was the response in the sixteenth century of Montaigne, who was inspired by 387-406
and its reworking of Lucretius to write in old age an essay on love and sexuality (*Essais* 3.5,
"Sur des vers de Virgile" or "Upon some verses of Virgil"). Cf. Milnor (2005: 5-10), Lada-
Richards (2006), especially on intertexts (including the *Homeric Hymn to Aphrodite* in which
the goddess seduces Aeneas' father Anchises) and gender issues; Casali (2006; 2010) on intertexts such as Lucretius and on potential parallels between Vergil as artist producing the *Aeneid*
for Augustus and Vulcan producing the shield under compulsion from Venus; Hardie (1986:
104-5) on connections between this scene and Juno's bribery of Aeolus in 1.50-80; Lyne (1987:
35-44); Leach (1997) on Venus, Thetis, and the Roman mother; Nelis (2001: 339-48) on
models in Homer and Apollonius; Smolenaars (2004), Putnam (1998: 167-80), and McCarter
(2012) on borrowings from Callimachus' *Hymn to Artemis*. Lyne (1987: 36-7) notes the
juxtaposition between Evander's telling Aeneas to scorn wealth and make himself worthy of
a god (364-5) and the sensuality of the Vulcan-Venus seduction scene that follows it (370-
406).

370-406. *Venus, frightened for Aeneas, appeals to her husband Vulcan, reminding him that during
the Trojan War she had not asked for arms for him, as the mothers of Achilles and Memnon had.
She embraces and caresses him, and excites his passion, and he tells her that he will do anything he
can, and they sleep together.*

370-1. **haud...nequiquam:** "not without reason." **mater:** emphatic by position: as a mother she is
frightened for her son. **tumultu:** cf. 4 and n.

Volcanum adloquitur, thalamoque haec coniugis aureo
incipit et dictis divinum aspirat amorem:
"dum bello Argolici vastabant Pergama reges
debita casurasque inimicis ignibus arces,   375
non ullum auxilium miseris, non arma rogavi
artis opisque tuae, nec te, carissime coniunx,
incassumve tuos volui exercere labores,
quamvis et Priami deberem plurima natis,
et durum Aeneae flevissem saepe laborem.   380

---

372. **coniugis:** some say this refers to her bedroom, which her husband Vulcan had made, but it must be his own chambers. **aureo:** two syllables by synizesis, as often with this word; see Appendix A on meter.

373. **et dictis...:** as Venus breathes love into her words in a line full of assonance* (seven *i*-sounds, followed by three *a*'s) and alliteration*, Vergil blends two passages from Lucretius' proem to Venus: the request for inspiration at 1.28 *quo magis aeternum da dictis, diva, leporem*, and the request in 38-40 that she sweet-talk Mars: *hunc tu, diva, tuo recubantem corpore sancto | circumfusa super, suavis ex ore loquelas | funde*. Casali (2006: 189-90) notes that in Lucretius the poet asks Venus to create peace, and to add charm to his words, while in Vergil she adds *amor* to her own words as she seeks weapons for war.

374-5. **Pergama:** poetic plural = Troy. **debita:** "doomed" or owed by destiny to its destroyers; cf. 9.107-8 *tempora Parcae | debita complerant*, Livy 24.25.3 *debitos iam morti destinatosque*. **casuras:** "about to/destined to fall."

376-7. **arma...| artis opisve tuae:** at 1.600-1 *grates persolvere dignas | non opis est nostrae*, Aeneas uses a predicate genitive to say it is "not within our power/resources" to thank you (Dido) properly. Here in a similar but compressed expression Venus says she did not ask Vulcan for arms (that were) "within your skill (*artis*) and your power/resources (*opis*)," implying that he alone could make them. **nec te...:** "nor in a lost cause (*incassum*, lit. 'in vain') to busy you and/or your labors." The *-ve* of *incassumve* means that *te* cannot be the subject of *exercere*, so both *te* and *tuos labores* are direct object. For *exercere* of setting a person to work, cf. 1.430-1 *apes... | exercet sub sole labor*. **carissime coniunx:** common in Latin inscriptions but also occurs in this or a similar form at Ovid *Met.* 11.727, *Trist.* 3.4.53, and Stat. *Silv.* 3.5.110.

379-80. **Priami...natis:** Venus' debt to "the sons of Priam" was mainly to Paris, who had awarded her the golden apple in the famous beauty contest, but the phrase is also Homeric to refer to some or all of Priam's many sons (*Il.* 1.255, 4.35, 5.463-4, 21.105). **deberem... | ...flevissem:** the imperfect refers to a continuing obligation, the plup. to prior behavior even though repeated (*saepe*).

nunc Iovis imperiis Rutulorum constitit oris:
ergo eadem supplex venio et sanctum mihi numen
arma rogo, genetrix nato. te filia Nerei,
te potuit lacrimis Tithonia flectere coniunx.
aspice qui coeant populi, quae moenia clausis   385
ferrum acuant portis in me excidiumque meorum."
dixerat et niveis hinc atque hinc diva lacertis
cunctantem amplexu molli fovet. ille repente

381-2. **nunc... | eadem:** "I, (though I am) the same person who before had not..., now do...";
idem often points out a contrast in a person's attitudes or actions at different times. **sanctum
mihi numen:** both meter and content are striking. The three final two-syllable words produce
a harsh clash of ictus and accent (see Appendix A on meter), and Venus' claim that Vulcan's
divinity is "sacred to me," as she asks him to help the son she had by her mortal lover
Anchises, has startled critics for ages. Servius, who notes that she is *petitura pro filio de
adulterio procreato* (see his whole note on 373), wanted to punctuate after *rogo* so that *genetrix
nato* would refer to Aurora and her son. Macrob. *Sat.* 1.24.6-8 has a scholar say that the
passage is embarrassing enough for Vergil to have wanted to burn the poem, and his friends
shudder in response (*omnes exhorruissent*). For Roman awareness of the adulterous nature
of Aeneas' birth, cf. Ovid's defense of himself from a charge of having promoted adultery at
Tristia 2.261-2: *sumpserit "Aeneadum genetrix"* [i.e., Lucretius' poem] *ubi prima, requiret, |
Aeneadum genetrix unde sit alma Venus.* Cf. Lyne (1987: 35-44), Casali (2006: 189-91).

383-4. **filia Nerei:** Thetis (370-453 n.); Venus cites both precedent, and (strikingly) also her own
literary models. In Vergil the genitive of Greek proper names in *-eus* is always monosyllabic *-ei*.
Tithonia...coniunx: *Eos* or *Aurora*, the Dawn, married to Tithonus; her son was Memnon,
the Ethiopian prince for whom Vulcan also made arms when he fought at Troy. His story was
told in the *Aethiopis*, a lost poem of the Epic cycle; cf. Kopff (1981), Horsfall (2003: 465-72),
Casali (2006: 188). Aeneas sees the arms of Memnon depicted on Dido's temple, and Dido
later asks Aeneas about them (1.489, 751).

385-6. **moenia...acuant:** the personification* is "two removes from prosaic expression, 'city walls'
for 'cities' for 'citizens'; cf. 7.629f. *urbes | tela novant*" (Eden).

387-8. **niveis...lacertis:** it is the Iliadic Hera whose usual epithet is "white-armed." **cunctantem:**
this form of this word appears in several crucial passages, describing Dido before the hunt
(4.133), Aeneas as Dido leaves his presence (390), the Golden Bough as Aeneas snatches it
(6.211), Turnus before Allecto enflames him (7.449), Vulcan here, and finally Aeneas thinking
whether to spare Turnus (12.940). Casali (2006: 388) suggests Vulcan's acquiescence after
hesitation comments on the position of an artist pressured to produce a work of art. Lada-
Richards (2006) likens him to the elegiac lover who is not in control of his desires as a proper
Roman man should be (cf. also 370-453 n.). **repente:** in strong antithesis to *cunctantem*. Her
words left him "hesitating"; the effect of her caresses is rapid as lightning.

accepit solitam flammam, notusque medullas
intravit calor et labefacta per ossa cucurrit,   390
non secus atque olim tonitru cum rupta corusco
ignea rima micans percurrit lumine nimbos.
sensit laeta dolis et formae conscia coniunx.
tum pater aeterno fatur devinctus amore:
"quid causas petis ex alto? fiducia cessit   395
quo tibi, diva, mei? similis si cura fuisset,

389-90. **solitam flammam:** his customary response to his wife, or the fire with which the smith god works daily? **medullas | ...ossa:** fire in the marrow within the bones is often the site of erotic passion in love poetry; cf. 4.66 *est mollis flamma medullas*, 7.355, Cat. 64.92-3 *concepit corpore flammam | funditus atque imis exarsit tota medullis*, Rosenmeyer (1999). **labefacta:** "tottering, weakening" (in constrast to *cunctantem*), a Lucretian word (eight times, including the erotic 4.1114 *membra voluptatis dum vi labefacta liquescunt*) also used often by Cicero; in Vergil, cf. 4.395 *animum labefactus amore*, of Aeneas almost losing his resolve with Dido. **per ossa cucurrit:** cf., in non-erotic contexts, *gelidusque per ima cucurrit | ossa tremor* 2.120-1 and similar phrases at 6.54-5, 12.447-8, as well as 12.66 *calefacta per ora cucurrit*, of Lavinia's erotically charged blush.

391-2. **non secus atque:** the simile* compares to rolling thunder and lightning the fires of the stirring passion of the god whose job it is to make lightning bolts; see West (1990a) for "irrational correspondence" in similes. **olim:** "as often happens," "at times" (*OLD* 4). **corusco:** to anyone encountering 391 and the first three feet of 392, this word must seem to modify *tonitru*, and although it usually describes flashing light, it must challengingly suggest "quivering thunder," as Page suggests. But then *lumine* in 392 provides an easier word for it to modify. Cf. Lucr. 6.282-4, which Vergil may be recalling: *maturum tum quasi fulmen | perscindit subito nubem, coruscis | omnia luminibus lustrans loca percitus ardor.*

393. **sensit:** used absolutely. Venus "felt," "recognized," the result at once. **laeta dolis:** Hera in the model at *Il.* 14.329 is *dolophroneousa*, "planning tricks." Vergil probably alluded to that passage already at *Aen.* 4.128, *dolis risit...repertis* (Venus "smiled at the discovery of (Juno's) trickery"). Venus or Aphrodite is "laughter-loving" in many texts, including *Il.* 14.211. Note the coincidence of ictus and accent (see Appendix A on meter) in all but one foot in this line.

394. **pater:** a term of respect applied to all deities, but here used with clear irony: Vulcan never became a father with his wife, but has been asked to help her son. **aeterno...devinctus amore:** slight alteration of Lucretius' description of Venus' "conquest" of Mars, who is *aeterno devictus* ("defeated, subdued") *vulnere amoris* (*DRN* 1.34). The change may allude to the song sung by Demodocus (*Od.* 8.266-366) in which Hephaestus "bound" Ares and Aphrodite in a high-tech trap when she was cheating on him. Cf. Kraggerud (1997), Smolenaars (2004), Casali (2006: 191-2).

395-6. **quid:** "why?" **ex alto:** i.e., going far back to find reasons; cf. Cic. *ad Fam.* 3.5 *quae... scripserim...quoniam ex alto repetita sint, non necessaria te putasse.* **quo:** "where, to what place," cf. 2.595 *quonam nostri tibi cura recessit? Geo.* 4.324-5 *quo tibi nostri | pulsus amor?* and the Supremes' 1964 "Where Did Our Love Go?" **mei:** gen. with *fiducia.*

tum quoque fas nobis Teucros armare fuisset;
nec pater omnipotens Troiam nec fata vetabant
stare decemque alios Priamum superesse per annos.
et nunc, si bellare paras atque haec tibi mens est,   400
quidquid in arte mea possum promittere curae,
quod fieri ferro liquidove potest electro,
quantum ignes animaeque valent, absiste precando
viribus indubitare tuis." ea verba locutus
optatos dedit amplexus placidumque petivit   405
coniugis infusus gremio per membra soporem.

396-9. **cura:** "concern," "worry," for Aeneas or perhaps even "love" for Vulcan her husband, i.e., "if you had shown this kind of concern then...." Elsewhere Vergil alludes to the etymology *cura quod cor urit* (cf. O'Hara (2011) on 4.2 and (2017: 119)); does he here for the fire-god? **fuisset...fuisset:** the identical endings mark how exactly his service would have corresponded to her desire. This condition is slightly compressed and illogical: "if you had shown similar *cura*, [I could have taken action because] it would have been permissable...." Some parts of the poem suggest that fate is fixed, but that its action may be delayed (cf. 7.315 *at trahere atque moras tantis licet addere rebus*) or that certain details are flexible (12.819-20 *illud te, nulla fati quod lege tenetur,* | *pro Latio obtestor*). But what an oft-cuckolded god says to his wife, the goddess of sex, when she caresses his arms is not a good source of philosophical doctrine about the nature of fate.

401-3. **quidquid...quod...quantum:** the tricolon* with alliteration* marks the vehemence of Vulcan's promise, and his impatience produces the vigorous anacoluthon* after *valent*: "whatever can be done—stop doubting...." **potest electro:** the Greek word produces a spondaic line with clash of ictus and accent in the fifth foot (cf. 54 n. and Appendix A on meter). **animaeque:** i.e., the wind of the bellows. Vergil puns on *animae*, "breath (of the bellows)," and Greek *anemos*, "wind"; cf. 1.56-7 *celsa sedet Aeolus arce* | *sceptra tenens mollitque animos* (i.e., of the winds) *et temperat iras*.

405. **optatos...amplexus:** cf. Cat. 64.372 *optatos animi coniungite amores*, in the wedding song for Peleus and Thetis.

406. **coniugis infusus gremio per membra:** can be read as a simple picture of Vulcan collapsed in Venus' lap, in a further echo of Lucretius' proem (373 n., 394 n.); cf. too *Aen.* 8.30 (Aeneas) *dedit per membra quietem*. But the words can be and in antiquity were read as a shockingly clear description of sexual intercourse: cf. *profundant* at Lucr. 4.1035, for *gremium* and *membra* see the index to Adams (1982), and for ancient discussion by Valerius Probus, Annaeus Cornutus, and others, see Servius here, Aulus Gellius *NA* 9.10, Casali (2006: 193), and Eden ad loc.

Inde ubi prima quies medio iam noctis abactae
curriculo expulerat somnum, cum femina primum,
cui tolerare colo vitam tenuique Minerva
impositum, cinerem et sopitos suscitat ignis 410
noctem addens operi, famulasque ad lumina longo
exercet penso, castum ut servare cubile

407-53. Vulcan rises long before dawn, like a wife or widow rising early to do woolwork to support her childen, and hurries to his workshop, where he finds his workmen, the Cyclopes, at work on various tasks for other gods, which he tells them to put aside in order to devote themselves to making arms for one man, and they quickly begin to work on Aeneas' shield.

The implied simile* of a woman rising early to weave wool to support her children builds upon three similes in Greek epic: in *Il.* 12.433-5, a woman weaves "to gain for her children a meager wage"; in Apoll. Rhod. *Arg.* 3.291-7, the fire in Medea's heart is like that kindled by a woman to weave at night; and in 4.1060-7, Medea's tears are like those of a widow who weaves all night to support her children. The lines literally serve to mark how early Vulcan arises to work, but several other aspects of them are interesting and challenging. The emphasis on the woman's chastity well suits an Augustan context in which the princeps promoted both moral reform and the anti-adultery marriage legislation to come in 18-17 BCE, around the time of the publication of the *Aeneid*. The association of weaving with chastity is like that of Livy's story of Lucretia (1.57), and the emperor's insistence that women in his own (fabulously wealthy) family should weave clothing; Suet. *Aug.* 64; Milnor (2005: 83-5). It is strikingly bizarre, however, to compare to a chaste widow or matron the god Vulcan as he rises from bed after having been sexually bribed by his wife, the goddess of sex, to make weapons for her son conceived in an adulterous relationship with a mortal (see 370-453 n., 381-2 n.). There may also be a connection between the woman and Vulcan (and perhaps even Vergil, Casali (2006) suggests) as craftspersons working for hire under duress. Cf. Lada-Richards (2006) and G. Williams (1983: 126-8) on how the simile continues the reversals of gender and power seen in Venus' seduction on Vulcan in 370-406; cf. 387-8 n., and on gender in the simile also Milnor (2005: 5-10).

407-8. **abactae:** < *abigo*, "having been driven away" but almost with a present sense, based on the idea of night driving in a chariot. **curriculo:** the word can mean "chariot," but here must primarily mean night's "course," as often with heavenly bodies; night is halfway through either her whole route or the part in which she is departing, i.e., between midnight and dawn.

409. **tolerare:** subject of *impositum* (*est*); cf. Lucr. 2.1171 *tolerarit...aevom*. **colo:** the distaff, the stick or spindle onto which wool is wound for spinning. **tenuique Minerva:** the goddess' name used in metonymy* for the wool-weaving or other small crafts with which the woman supports her family (cf. 7.805). The adjective must primarily mean "humble," but elsewhere when applied to weaving it means "fine," "delicate" (cf. 7.14), at times as an important metaphor for Callimachean-style poetry; cf. Casali (2006), Clausen (1994: 175) on *Ecl.* 6.8 *tenui... harundine*. See 625 n. for the shield as *textum*.

412. **castum:** wool-making might save her from earning money through prostitution, or if her husband is dead perhaps to avoid remarriage and remain *univira*, a woman who had only one husband for her entire life; cf. O'Hara (2011) on *Aen.* 4.27.

coniugis et possit parvos educere natos:
haud secus ignipotens nec tempore segnior illo
mollibus e stratis opera ad fabrilia surgit.   415
insula Sicanium iuxta latus Aeoliamque
erigitur Liparen fumantibus ardua saxis,
quam subter specus et Cyclopum exesa caminis
antra Aetnaea tonant, validique incudibus ictus
auditi referunt gemitus, striduntque cavernis   420
stricturae Chalybum et fornacibus ignis anhelat,
Volcani domus et Volcania nomine tellus.
hoc tunc ignipotens caelo descendit ab alto.

---

413. **et possit...**: cf. *Il.* 12.433-5 cited above 407-53 n. **educere:** "bring up"; *ēdūcere*, literally "lead out," is used as a synonym of *ēdūcāre*, most of whose forms do not fit the hexameter (*educat* at 10.518 is the exception).

416-17. **insula...**: Vergil in saying that Vulcan's workshop is under an island next to Aeolian Lipare comments on a scholarly dispute. Callimachus and Apollonius, as their scholiasts noticed, disagreed about where the workshop was, with Callimachus putting it under Lipare (*Hymn* 3.47, *Aetia* frag. 115.11-21), while Vergil sides with Apollonius, who said it was Hiera. Vergil glosses Hiera's Latin name *Vulcano* in 421, though in *Geo.* 4.170-5 the Cyclopes toil under Mount Etna in Sicily, and below he will speak of *antra Aetnaea* (419) and *Aetnaei Cyclopes* (440). Cf. Hardie (1986: 105-6), Johnston (1996), O'Hara (2001: 373-6).

418. **caminis:** probably dat., "for the forges," though Servius asks whether it is (dat.) "for" or (abl.) "by" them. This Greek word appears in the dat. pl. (Greek of course has no abl.) at line-end, as here, referring to Vulcan's workshop at Callim. *Aet.* fr. 115.11.

419. **incudibus ictus:** local abl. attached to a noun.

420-1. The alliteration* of *s* suggests the sound of the hissing metal. **stricturae:** the "lumps" or "smeltings" of iron ore. **Chalybum:** famous workers in iron; cf. 10.174, *Geo.* 1.58 *at Chalybes nudi ferrum* (*mittunt*); Aesch. *Septem* 728, Apoll. Rhod. *Arg.* 2.1001-8, Cat. 66.48 translating Callim. *Aetia* fr. 110. Below in *446 Chalybs* = "iron." **anhelat:** the flame "pants" at each blast of the bellows.

422. Vergil explains that the island is named for the smith-god (cf. 416-17 n.); the whole line is in apposition to 416 *insula*.

423. **hoc:** archaic* for *huc,* as at Plaut. *Amph.* 165.

Ferrum exercebant vasto Cyclopes in antro,
Brontesque Steropesque et nudus membra Pyracmon.   425
his informatum manibus iam parte polita
fulmen erat, toto genitor quae plurima caelo
deicit in terras, pars imperfecta manebat.
tris imbris torti radios, tris nubis aquosae
addiderant, rutuli tris ignis et alitis Austri.   430
fulgores nunc terrificos sonitumque metumque
miscebant operi flammisque sequacibus iras.

424-53. Gransden quotes Burke (1958: 170-1), written in 1757: "There is not perhaps in the whole *Aeneid* a more grand and laboured passage than the description of Vulcan's cavern in Etna, and the works that are there carried on." Note that these Cyclopes have little in common with the wild monsters of *Aen.* 3.588-681. For intertexts in Callimachus, Apollonius, and the *Georgics*, see 425 n., 426-8 n., 449-53 n.

424-5. **Cyclōpĕs:** Gk. nom. pl. **Brontesque Steropesque...Pyracmon:** as Servius notes, the Cyclopes are named for their work: Brontes, "thunder"; Steropes, "lightning," and Pyracmon "fire" + "anvil" (note *incudibus*, "anvils" in 419). The first two are from Hes. *Theog.* 140 and are mentioned in Callim. *Hymn to Artemis* 68, 75; Apoll. Rhod. *Arg.* 1.511 has the collocation βροντῇ τε στεροπῇ τε as common nouns in a discussion of Cyclopes. Ovid *F.* 4.288 puts Brontes and Steropes in a line with Acmonides, "son of Anvil," found in Callim. fr. 498 Pf. Cf. O'Hara (2017: 213; 2001: 388-9).

426-8. The formation of the thunderbolt owes much to Apoll. Rhod. *Arg.* 1.730-4, the depiction on Jason's cloak of the Cyclopes working on a bolt that is almost finished. For Jason's cloak as a model for Aeneas' shield, cf. 625 n., 626-731 n. **his... | erat:** *his* is dat.: "they had," while *manibus* is abl. **informatum:** "roughly shaped"; *informare* means to shape in outline. **fulmen:** "thunderbolt," while the *fulgores* of 431 are flashes of lightning; Eden cites Seneca *N.Q.* 2.57, Ovid *Met.* 1.56, Lucan 4.77-8. **quae plurima:** "which in great numbers," "one of the many which." **pars...manebat:** balances *iam parte polita* but is added irregularly in asyndeton* as an independent clause.

429. **imbris torti:** Servius says twisted rain is "hail," but *torti* may also suggest "hurled rain"; cf. 4.208 *fulmina torques*, 9.671 *torquet aquosam hiemem*. **radios:** the thunderbolt is depicted on ancient coins not with our modern zigzag (as in Harry Potter's scar, or on our warning signs for high voltage) but as a bundle of rays, like the arrows grasped by the eagle on the back of the U.S. dollar bill. The twelve rays are formed with "rain," "cloud," "fire," and "wind," because these are ordinary accompaniments of a thunderstorm.

432. **flammisque...:** abl. of description with *iras*; they add both physical (flash, sound, flame) and abstract (fear, anger) qualities to the bolt. Lines 431-8 crackle with thirteen *q* sounds.

parte alia Marti currumque rotasque volucris
instabant, quibus ille viros, quibus excitat urbes;
aegidaque horriferam, turbatae Palladis arma,   435
certatim squamis serpentum auroque polibant
conexosque anguis ipsamque in pectore divae
Gorgona desecto vertentem lumina collo.
"tollite cuncta" inquit "coeptosque auferte labores,
Aetnaei Cyclopes, et huc advertite mentem: 440
arma acri facienda viro. nunc viribus usus,
nunc manibus rapidis, omni nunc arte magistra.
praecipitate moras." nec plura effatus, at illi
ocius incubuere omnes pariterque laborem
sortiti. fluit aes rivis aurique metallum   445

---

434. **instabant:** usually intransitive, but here = "work eagerly on." Mars fights on chariot in the simile at 12.331-6; cf. *Il.* 5.359-66, [Hes.] *Scutum* 61, 195, *HH8Ares* 1. **ille viros...excitat urbes:** = one Iliadic epithet for Ares, *Il.* 17.398 λαοσσόος ("rouser of hosts"); cf. 354 n.

435. **aegida:** Gr. acc. Evander mentions the *aegis* of Jupiter in 354 (see note). In Homer Zeus lends it to Athena (*Il.* 5.738-42), and Horace (*Carm.* 3.4.57 *sonantem Palladis aegida*) represents her as using the *aegis* as a shield in battle, but here it seems to be a breastplate (*pectore*, 437). **turbatae:** i.e., when roused to war; cf. 8.4, Fordyce's survey here of uses of the word, and on Pallas here Panoussi (2009: 111).

436. **squamis serpentum auroque:** "with serpent scales of gold"; hendiadys*. **polibant:** archaic* form of *poliebant*, used in part to fit the hexameter (*VE*, pp. 846-7). The word means not "polish" but "adorn" as in Catullus 64.48 *Indo...dente politum*, "decorated with ivory."

437-8. **Gorgona:** Gk. acc. Medusa the Gorgon, depicted on Athena's aegis, has snakes for hair (cf. Allecto 7.346, 450), and even after Perseus cuts her head off, her gaze can still turn men to stone. **vertentem lumina:** Vulcan's skill may have given the Gorgon's head movable eyes, or eyes so life-like they appear to move (cf. 632-4 n.). Alternately Servius and Servius *auctus* suggest the verb means she "turns" onlookers to stone, or "turns (away) the eyes" of those seeking to avoid petrification.

441-2. **arma...viro:** an echo of 1.1 *arma virum*, one of eleven in the poem (cf. Hardie (1994) on 9.57); cf. also 12.425 *arma citi properate viro*. **acri:** dat. **viro...viribus:** distinguish *vir* from *vires*, but the verse also puns on the similar sounds. **usus:** supply *est*: "occasion" like *opus est* + abl. **nunc...nunc...nunc:** tricolon* with anaphora*. **arte magistra:** both nouns, not "master-craft" but your *ars* as your guide or master; also at 12.427.

443. **praecipitate moras:** "fling over (all) delay(s)"; cf. 12.699 (Aeneas) *praecipitatque moras omnis*.

445. **sortiti:** probably participle, and not *sortiti (sunt)*; *-que* links the adverb *ocius* and *pariter... laborem | sortiti*. In Homer Hephaestus works alone, with the help of his implements, while Vulcan runs a crew, in a scene that suits the later, Roman sense of how things are done. **aurique:** gen. of substance or material (AG §344); cf. *Geo.* 2.165 *aeris...metalla*.

vulnificusque chalybs vasta fornace liquescit.
ingentem clipeum informant, unum omnia contra
tela Latinorum, septenosque orbibus orbis
impediunt. alii ventosis follibus auras
accipiunt redduntque, alii stridentia tingunt   450
aera lacu; gemit impositis incudibus antrum;
illi inter sese multa vi bracchia tollunt
in numerum, versantque tenaci forcipe massam.

---

446. **vulnificus:** a compound first found here, but perhaps borrowed from an earlier author like Ennius; cf. Horsfall (2000) on 7.324 *luctificam*. **chalybs:** cf. 420-1 n.

448. **septenosque...:** "and weld circle upon circle sevenfold," with a bold use of *impediunt*. **orbis:** circular plates of metal welded one upon another. The shield of Turnus is *septemplex* (12.925), that of Mezentius has many layers of brass, linen, and hide (10.784). The epic model is the shield of Ajax at *Il.* 7.245-8, which has seven layers of ox-hide and one of bronze.

449-53. Repeated from *Geo.* 4.171-5, where the bees are compared to Cyclopes, but with four words changed (*ventosis* for *taurinis*, *antrum* for *Aetnam*, *multa* for *magna*, and *massam* for *ferrum*). Vergil more frequently uses material from narrative in the *Georgics*, rather than similes, for similes in the *Aen.*, e.g., *Geo.* 3.232-4 and *Aen.* 12.103-6. See Eden here, Briggs (1980). Further intertextual complexity: Farrell (1991: 243-5) notes that the *Georgics* simile imitates the Cyclopes scene at Callim. *Hymn* 3.46-61, but *stridentia tingunt | aera lacu* in *Geo.* 4.172-3 (= *Aen.* 8.450-1) acknowledges Callimachus' allusion to the metalworking simile used at *Od.* 9.389-94 as Odysseus drives the stake into the Cyclops' hissing eye. On intertextuality with Callimachus and Apollonius, cf. too Casali (2006: 199), McCarter (2012).

451. **lacu:** the blacksmith's water tank. **impositis:** "set in position" on the cave's floor and so able to make the whole cave "groan" (with light personification* as well).

452-3. In lines adapted from Callim. *Hymn* 3.59-61 (cf. 449-53 n.), the rhythm conveys the sense of effort, with five spondees in 452, clash of ictus and accent in the middle of that line, then as the hammers find their rhythm, coincidence in the last two feet of 452 and the last four of 453 (cf. Appendix A on meter). **inter sese:** in alternation, taking turns. **in numerum:** "in cadence," cf. *Ecl.* 6.28 *in numerum Faunosque ferasque videres | ludere* and Lucr. 2.631, 637. For rhythm suggesting struggle, cf. *Geo.* 2.526 *inter se adversis luctantur cornibus haedi*, 3.220 *illi alternantes multa vi proelia miscent*, *Aen.* 10.146-7 *illi inter sese duri certamina belli | contulerant*, 12.720 *illi inter sese multa vi vulnera miscent*; and for spondees used to describe the Cyclops Polyphemus, cf. 3.658 *monstrum horrendum, informe, ingens, cui lumen ademptum*. Barchiesi (1997: 278-9) and Casali (2006: 203-4) note that *in numerum*, which could suggest poetic meter, furthers the parallel between Vulcan's craftwork and that of the poet Vergil (407-53 n.).

Haec pater Aeoliis properat dum Lemnius oris,
Evandrum ex humili tecto lux suscitat alma   455
et matutini volucrum sub culmine cantus.
consurgit senior tunicaque inducitur artus
et Tyrrhena pedum circumdat vincula plantis.
tum lateri atque umeris Tegeaeum subligat ensem
demissa ab laeva pantherae terga retorquens.   460

454-607. The next day Aeneas goes to Evander, who says he has few troops of his own, but tells Aeneas where to find an Etruscan army ready to fight their former king Mezentius. He also offers his son Pallas as a warrior (454-519). Omens in the sky frighten everyone else, but Aeneas claims that they are a sign that his mother Venus is bringing him weapons from Vulcan (520-53). As the Arcadians prepare to leave with Aeneas, Evander makes a tearful speech of farewell to his son (554-84). The soldiers gallop off and make camp near the Etruscans (585-607).

Vergil adapts *Od.* 3.404-86, with allusions to Telemachus' visit to Nestor: "At dawn guest (Telemachus, Aeneas) and host (Nestor, Evander) meet to confer; the host offers the escort of his son (Peisistratus, Pallas) to the place where help may be obtained (Sparta, the Etruscan camp)..." (Eden). Details are borrowed from other Odyssean scenes (see 457-60 n., 461-2 n., 514 n., 520-53 n.), and from the Iliadic Nestor (554-84 n., 563-6 n.). See Knauer (1964a: 254-5) (in German), Knauer (1990: 405-6) (in English), Eden on 254ff., Petrini (1997: 50-2).

At the same time, the offer of Pallas' help sets in motion the poem's Iliadic plot, in which Pallas will play the role of Achilles' friend Patroclus, who was killed by Hector.

454-519. Evander tells Aeneas that nearby Etruscans have driven out their king, who took refuge with Turnus. Seers have warned the Etruscans that to fight Mezentius they would need a foreign leader. Since Evander is too old, and Pallas is half-Italian, Evander urges Aeneas to become their leader, promising to send Pallas with him, so that Pallas can learn warfare under Aeneas' guidance.

454. **properat:** usually intransitive in prose (exceptions in Sallust and Tacitus); used in the same context at *Geo.* 4.170-1 *Cyclopes fulmina massis | cum properant*. **Lemnius:** after the Aegean island where Vulcan landed after being flung from heaven by Zeus (*Il.* 1.593), which became "dearest to him" (*Od.* 8.283-4), and where he received cult; cf. Burkert (1983: 190-6). His workshop was sometimes said to be there (Cic. *N.D.* 3.55 *Lemni fabricae traditur praefuisse*), but cf. 416-17 n.

457-60. Adapted from a Homeric formula for getting up and putting on clothes, shoes and sword: cf. Agamemnon at *Il.* 2.41-5 and 10.21-4, Telemachus at *Od.* 2.1-5, and Menelaus at *Od.* 4.306-10. **inducitur artus:** middle with direct object (cf. 265 n.). **Tegeaeum:** i.e., brought from Tegea in his native Arcadia (cf. 5.299, *Geo.* 3.18), though his sandals are Etruscan (458). **demissa:** proleptic; the hide is flung back to hang on the left. For *retorquens*, cf. 7.666 *tegimen torquens immane leonis* (Hercules' son Aventinus).

nec non et gemini custodes limine ab alto
praecedunt gressumque canes comitantur erilem.
hospitis Aeneae sedem et secreta petebat
sermonum memor et promissi muneris heros.
nec minus Aeneas se matutinus agebat.   465
filius huic Pallas, illi comes ibat Achates.
congressi iungunt dextras mediisque residunt
aedibus et licito tandem sermone fruuntur.
rex prior haec:
"maxime Teucrorum ductor, quo sospite numquam   470
res equidem Troiae victas aut regna fatebor,
nobis ad belli auxilium pro nomine tanto

461-2. limine ab alto: kings tend to have lofty dwellings (cf. 11.235 *alta...limina*, of Latinus' palace) but the humbleness of Evander's house has been stressed (363 n., *ex humili tecto* 455), so the conventional epithet is a little strong or possibly ironic here; cf. Yardley (1981). That Evander crosses a threshold to seek Aeneas suggests that we are to imagine a complex of small buildings. **custodes... | canes:** "watch-dogs"; in Homer Telemachus three times is accompanied by two dogs: *Od.* 2.11 (after the passage cited 457-60 n.), 17.62, 20.145. Petrini (1997: 52) argues that Vergil associates Evander with the boy Telemachus to suggest "the cultural innocence of Evander and...his vision of the heroic world." Yardley (1981) suggests that readers encountering *custodes* in 461 would assume they are human bodyguards or attendants, until *canes* specifies that they are humble dogs. **erilem:** a word rare in epic, which gives a colloquial touch here and in 7.490 *mensaeque adsuetus erili* (Silvia's pet stag).

463-4. sedem et secreta: hendiadys*. **petebat:** Evander is subject, as in 457-60, despite the intervening sentence about the dogs (461-2), as *heros* at the end of 464 makes clear.

466. huic...illi: "the former...the latter," the reverse of the usual idiom, probably because Evander has been the focus of the passage.

468. licito: allowed now that the festival is over.

469. For the half-line, see 41 n.; Goold (1990: 110) notes that a number of half-lines come at the start or end of speeches, suggesting that when Vergil died he had not yet completed all the transitions before or after speeches.

470. quo sospite: cf. *sospite...nato* 11.56-7, *te sospite* Hor. *Carm.*1.28.27, 1.37.13, Enn. *Ann.* 598 Sk. = W. p. 563.

471. victas: to be taken with both *res* and *regna*, as an adjective can modify two or more nouns of different genders; see AG §287.

472. pro nomine tanto: "in proportion to such a great name" (*OLD* 12); whether he refers to the Arcadians' fame or to Aeneas' is not clear: Pallas on hearing the Trojans' name is stunned (*obstipuit tanto percussus nomine* 121), but Aeneas says in 132 that he has come because of Evander's *fama*.

exiguae vires; hinc Tusco claudimur amni,
hinc Rutulus premit et murum circumsonat armis.
sed tibi ego ingentis populos opulentaque regnis   475
iungere castra paro, quam fors inopina salutem
ostentat: fatis huc te poscentibus adfers.
haud procul hinc saxo incolitur fundata vetusto
urbis Agyllinae sedes, ubi Lydia quondam
gens, bello praeclara, iugis insedit Etruscis.   480
hanc multos florentem annos rex deinde superbo

473-4. Tusco...amni: the Tiber; *amni* is abl. **hinc Rutulus premit...:** there is no reference elsewhere in the poem to Turnus and the Rutulians' harassing the Arcadians; Tiberinus does say the Arcadians are in constant war with the Latins (55 n.), while Allecto taunts Turnus for thanklessly protecting the Latins from the Etruscans (7.425-6).

475. opulentaque regnis: "rich in royal forces (lit. 'kingdoms')"; the Roman reader might think of the forces of the later twelve city-states of Etruria.

476. quam fors inopina salutem: "a way of salvation which (a) surprising/ unexpected (bit of) luck..."; cf. the Sibyl's reference to Evander's city at 6.96-7 *via prima salutis, | quod minime reris, Graia pandetur ab urbe.*

478. saxo...fundata vetusto: cf. 3.84 *templa dei saxo...structa vetusto.*

479. Agyllinae: cf. 7.652; the Romans called the city, thirty miles north of Rome, Caere (cf. 597). **Lydia:** for the Lydian origin of the Etruscans, cf. Herod. 1.94, *Aen.* 2.781-2 *Lydius...Thybris*; Cat. 31.13, Hor. *Serm.* 1.6.1. Modern archaeologists have long been skeptical (Barker and Rasmussen (1998: 43-4), Bonfante and Bonfante (2002: 49-52)), but some scientists have claimed that DNA analysis supports the idea of a Near Eastern origin. Cf. Perkins (2009) and Kron (2013); Perkins stresses that the science is inconclusive.

481. deinde: picking up *multos florentem annos:* when it had flourished long, "then" it came into the hands of Mezentius. The name Mezentius was once thought to be a literary invention but has now been found inscribed on early Etruscan artifacts; cf. Grandazzi (1997: 97), Bonfante and Bonfante (2002: 30), De Grummond (2006: 205-7), Horsfall (2000: 426). Aeneas will fight and kill Mezentius at 10.689-908; cf. also 8.6-7 n. The story of Mezentius in the *Aeneid* differs from other treatments, in which after the death/deification of Aeneas, Ascanius must fight and kill Mezentius. Cf. Harrison (1991: 236), Horsfall (2000: 424-5, with references).

Evander told a brief version of his own history without saying why he was driven into exile (333-6) and now offers a lurid version of Mezentius' exile. How would Aeneas or Roman readers have reacted to Evander's tales of Mezentius, or his laconic version of his own exile? Would they expect them to be accurate and true, or as exaggerated as the claims of Turnus' embassy to Diomedes (12 n., 13 n.) or Aeneas' own description of how he was treated by the Latins (118 n.)? Cf. also below 563-6 and note for Evander's story of his youthful exploits against a three-souled opponent, where Servius says he is laying claim to a feat of Hercules; and on Evander's credibility, see Secci (2013), O'Hara (n.d.).

imperio et saevis tenuit Mezentius armis.
quid memorem infandas caedes, quid facta tyranni
effera? di capiti ipsius generique reservent!
mortua quin etiam iungebat corpora vivis 485
componens manibusque manus atque oribus ora,
tormenti genus, et sanie taboque fluentis
complexu in misero longa sic morte necabat.
at fessi tandem cives infanda furentem
armati circumsistunt ipsumque domumque, 490
obtruncant socios, ignem ad fastigia iactant.
ille inter caedem Rutulorum elapsus in agros
confugere et Turni defendier hospitis armis.

---

483. quid memorem...: also at 6.601, and cf. Enn. *Ann.* 314 Sk. = 315 W *quid ego haec memoro.* This is the figure praeteritio*.

484. di capiti...: similar wishes at 2.190-1 *quod di prius omen in ipsum | convertant*; 6.529-30 *di talia Grais | instaurate.* **reservent**: "keep in store" similar suffering.

485. mortua...vivis: Evander's fondness for gore, evident in his story of Hercules and Cacus and the hymn to Hercules (196 n.), is again on view. He attributes to Mezentius a practice ascribed to Etruscan pirates in Cicero, *Hortensius* frag. 95 M: *qui quondam cum in praedonum Etruscorum manus incidissent, crudelitate excogitata necabantur, quorum corpora viva cum mortuis, adversa adversis accommodata, quam aptissime colligabantur.* Kronenberg (2005: 408-10) argues that the passage in Augustine quoting Aristotle and Cicero suggests that the torture can be interpreted philosophically as "a remythologization of the binding together of the soul to the body."

486. -que...atque: rare; cf. *Geo.* 1.182, 3.434; Lucr. 5.31.

487. genus: in apposition to the action described in 485-6 (cf. 683 *insigne* and 683-4 n.).

488. longa: "slow," "lingering."

489. infanda: neut. pl. adverbial acc.; cf. *insueta rudentem* 248, *vana tumentem* 11.854, *acerba fremens* 12.398. **furentem**: for *furor* in the *Aen.* cf. 184-279 n., 219-20 n.; for use of the word at Rome to describe one's political opponents cf. Cic. *Cat.* 2.1.1 *Tandem aliquando, Quirites, L. Catilinam, furentem audacia...eiecimus*, with Batstone (1994: 229).

490. armati...: see Dainotti (2015: 80) for the "menacing tramp of soldiers" in this heavily spondaic, four-word line.

491. ignem: they burn his palace; cf. *flammas ad culmina iactant* of Priam's palace at Troy at 2.478.

493. confugere...defendier: historic infinitives, the latter an archaic* form of the pass. inf. Mezentius' finding refuge with Turnus is a Vergilian invention that makes his story like that of Rome's last king Tarquinius Superbus, who is taken in by Lars Porsenna; cf. 8.646-8 on Aeneas' shield and note.

ergo omnis furiis surrexit Etruria iustis,
regem ad supplicium praesenti Marte reposcunt.   495
his ego te, Aenea, ductorem milibus addam.
toto namque fremunt condensae litore puppes
signaque ferre iubent, retinet longaevus haruspex
fata canens: "o Maeoniae delecta iuventus,
flos veterum virtusque virum, quos iustus in hostem   500
fert dolor et merita accendit Mezentius ira,
nulli fas Italo tantam subiungere gentem:

---

494. **omnis…Etruria:** Evander makes it seem as though Mezentius has slipped away (*elapsus* 492) alone and that Etruria is united in its opposition to him (cf. *omne…Latium* 4-5 and the *Res Gestae* quoted there), but in 7.651-3 Vergil has said that from Caere alone Mezentius' son Lausus leads a thousand men; Kronenberg (2005: 410), O'Hara (n.d.). Cf. also 679 n. on the number of Roman senators with Octavian and Antony. **furiis…iustis:** Evander's notion of the justified *furor* of Hercules against Cacus (implied at 219, 228), and of Mezentius' subjects against him (cf. also 500-1 n., and 291 n. on the justified punishment of Troy and Oechalia), dovetails with his influential call at 11.176-81 for Aeneas to avenge Pallas by killing Turnus, which Aeneas will do *furiis accensus* (12.946). Evander will soon quote a soothsayer speaking of righteous pain and deserved anger (500-1 and note).

495. **praesenti:** suggests both location and time: the army is both nearby and ready to start a war at once.

497. **fremunt…puppes:** by synecdoche*, the ships are said to do that which the soldiers on them do: they loudly insist on attacking (cf. 385 *moenia* and 385-6 n.).

499. **Maeoniae:** part of Asia Minor associated with the Lydians (cf. 4.216) and so with the Etruscans (479 n., 11.759). **iuventus:** cf. 4-6 n.

500-1. **flos veterum virtusque virum:** Servius calls this alliterative phrase "Ennian"; cf. Enn. *Ann.* 308 Sk. = 305 W *flos delibatus populi* ("picked flower"), and for *flos* of troops, cf. Aesch. *Ag.* 197, *Pers.* 59, Thuc. 4.133, Cic. *Phil.* 11.39 *tirones milites, flos Italiae.* On the frequent association of *virtus* and *vir*, see O'Hara (2017: 127-8) on *Aen.* 1.566 and O'Hara (2011) on *Aen.* 4.3 *viri virtus.* Cf. too *vivida virtus* at 5.754, 11.386. **iustus…dolor et merita…ira:** cf. 494 *furiis…iustis.* The oracle that Evander quotes shares his ideology and vocabulary, and takes eleven words to tell the Etruscans that their anger is justified: Evander is explaining the situation to Aeneas. At 10.714 the narrator uses similar language of the Etruscans: *iustae quibus est Mezentius irae.*

502. **subiungere:** "put under control, tame," used literally elsewhere of putting oxen under the same yoke; cf. *Ecl.* 5.29 *curru subiungere tigris.* The dat. *nulli* is probably to be taken with the compound *subiungere*, but a reader might well link it with *fas (est).*

externos optate duces." tum Etrusca resedit
hoc acies campo monitis exterrita divum.
ipse oratores ad me regnique coronam   505
cum sceptro misit mandatque insignia Tarchon,
succedam castris Tyrrhenaque regna capessam.
sed mihi tarda gelu saeclisque effeta senectus
invidet imperium seraeque ad fortia vires.
natum exhortarer, ni mixtus matre Sabella   510
hinc partem patriae traheret. tu, cuius et annis
et generi fatum indulget, quem numina poscunt,
ingredere, o Teucrum atque Italum fortissime ductor.

503-4. **externos optate duces:** an important theme, repeated in several passages: cf. the words
of the *vates* at 7.68-9 *externum cernimus... | adventare virum*, and of Faunus at 7.98 *externi
venient generi*. The three prophecies point toward the newcomer Aeneas, and at 10.155-6 the
Etruscans join Aeneas: *iussis gens Lydia diuum | externo commissa duci*; cf., in Italian, Horsfall
(1991), or briefly in English Horsfall (2000: 289-90), Toll (1997), Nakata (2012), Wimperis
(2017). **tum Etrusca:** unusual elision of *tum*, in the *Aeneid* only here and at 7.616, where it
follows two other monosyllables; cf. Soubiran (1966: 405-18). **resedit:** "settled down," i.e.,
leaving the ships and ceasing to urge immediate departure. **hoc...campo:** "on the plain here."
He speaks of the plain as close by, cf. 603 *haud procul hinc*. On the references to locations in
497-504, cf. Kinsey (1990).

505-6. **oratores:** ambassadors, as in 7.153; cf. *legatos* in 8.143. **misit mandatque:** the earlier
dispatch of ambassadors is described by a perfect tense, then a graphic present depicts the
"offer" or "handing over" of the badges of authority. **Tarchon:** the traditional eponymous
founder of Tarquinii, whose name is linked to that of the last two Roman kings; he agrees
at 10.146-54 to an alliance with Aeneas, and fights in Books 10-12. The riddling words
of Lycophron, *Alexandra* 1232-9 make Tarchon a son of Heracles who makes an alliance
with Aeneas. Dainotti (2015: 260) notes of *ipse...Tarchon* that "the hyperbaton* signals the
elevated tone."

507. **succedam...capessam:** jussive subjunctives after the request implied in *mandat insignia*.

508-9. **gelu:** cf. 5.395-6 *gelidus tardante senecta | sanguis hebet*, of an old boxer. **saeclis...effeta:**
"worn out by the (passing) generations"; cf. 7.440 *verique effeta* as well as *Il.* 1.250 where
Nestor (a model for Evander) is said to have outlived two generations. **seraeque:** usually "late,"
here "past its prime," "too far gone"; cf. Sil. Ital. *Pun.* 3.255 *consilio viridis sed belli serus*.

510-11. **mixtus matre Sabella:** Servius says this = *duplici genere natus*; in 6.762 Silvius, half-
Trojan and half-Italian, is *Italo commixtus sanguine*; cf. also 12.835-6 *commixti corpore
tantum | subsident Teucri* and 838 *hinc genus, Ausonio mixtum quod sanguine surget*. **hinc:**
from here, from Italy.

513. **ingredere:** a stately word, "advance," "enter on your task"; the same imperative is used at
Geo. 1.42, where the poet invokes Octavian/Augustus.

hunc tibi praeterea, spes et solacia nostri,
Pallanta adiungam; sub te tolerare magistro   515
militiam et grave Martis opus, tua cernere facta
adsuescat, primis et te miretur ab annis.
Arcadas huic equites bis centum, robora pubis
lecta dabo, totidemque suo tibi nomine Pallas."
     Vix ea fatus erat, defixique ora tenebant   520

---

514. **solacia:** Servius says Pallas is his sole consolation because his wife is dead; cf. Euryalus' mother: *tune ille senectae | sera meae requies* (9.481-2). Vergil draws inspiration from *Od.* 3.325-485, where Nestor entrusts his son Peisistratus to Telemachus, and from two heroes who send their sons with Jason in Apollonius, Lycus in 2.802, and Alcon in 1.95, "though he had no other sons to protect his old age and livelihood." Cf. Papanghelis (1993), Nelis (2001: 364), as well as Evander's farewell speech at 560-83.

516. **grave Martis opus:** Homer's "great work of Ares" (*Il.* 11.734). **tua cernere facta:** G. Williams (1983: 104) thinks of "the Roman practice of *contubernium*, whereby an aristocratic father would put his son in the care of an army commander on active service." Cf. 287-8 *laudes | Herculeas et facta ferunt, Ecl.* 4.26-7 (of the wonder child) *at simul heroum laudes et facta parentis | iam legere et quae sit poteris cognoscere virtus,* 12.435 (Aeneas to his son) *disce, puer, virtutem ex me verumque laborem.* Petrini (1997: 58-62) links the child in *Ecl.* 4 to what Evander says about Pallas here, and with the passage in *Aen.* 10.159-62 that shows Pallas sitting with Aeneas and asking him about war, the stars, and his experiences on land and sea.

517. **primis...ab annis:** as when used by Sinon in 2.87, these words refer not to childhood or the first years of a man's life, but to the first years of manhood or adult life; so Horsfall (2008), Henry (1889: 73-6). **miretur:** Servius suggests this means *imitetur,* citing Lucan 9.807 *magnanimo iuveni miratorique Catonis.*

519. **suo...nomine:** supply *dabit,* "will give in his own name," "on his own account."

520-53. While Aeneas and Achates gloomily ponder Evander's words, there is sudden thunder and lightning and a vision of clashing arms in the sky. Aeneas tells Evander not to fear that this portends disaster, because Venus had promised to send such a sign and bring him arms made by Vulcan. Aeneas speaks with confidence about the war, saying that his enemies will pay for breaking treaties with him. He and the others sacrifice, and Aeneas chooses men for the trip to the Etruscans.

     In Vergil's imitation of Telemachus' travels, the omens recall a bird omen from the end of his visit to Sparta (*Od.* 15.160-81), interpreted (cheeringly) by Helen, but they also recall omens in Roman contexts, especially before or after Caesar's death in 44 BCE (Verg. *Geo.* 1.463-514 with the note of Mynors (1990) on 469ff. on the tradition, and cf. below 523 n., 529 n., 533 n.). Aeneas' wholly positive interpretation of the omens that frighten the others is not the only way to read them (533 n.), as Vergil presents one of a number of ambiguous omens in the poem. In 9.110-22, when Turnus misinterprets the celestial light and noise that accompany the voice of the Great Mother when the Trojan ships turn into nymphs, verbal echoes link the scene to this one (530 n.).

520. **defixi...ora tenebant:** *ora* is dependent on both *defixi* and *tenebant;* cf. 2.1 *intentique ora tenebant* and 7.249-50, quoted below. They set their faces and kept them set. **defixi:** can

Aeneas Anchisiades et fidus Achates,
multaque dura suo tristi cum corde putabant,
ni signum caelo Cytherea dedisset aperto.
namque improviso vibratus ab aethere fulgor
cum sonitu venit et ruere omnia visa repente,   525
Tyrrhenusque tubae mugire per aethera clangor.

---

suggest a downcast gaze (Aeneas *maesto defixus lumina vultu* 6.156), or merely a fixed one
(*dum stupet obtutuque haeret defixus in uno* 1.495, *talibus Ilionei dictis defixa Latinus | obtutu
tenet ora soloque immobilis haeret* 7.249-50).

521. **Anchisiades:** the patronymic calls attention to the father-son relationship of Evander and
Pallas, and to Aeneas' role as mentor to Pallas; cf. 10.822, where it is used of Aeneas after he
kills Lausus who died saving his father. For the four-word hexameter (ignoring *et*), cf. 103 n.

522. **suo tristi cum corde:** elsewhere Vergil uses *corde* by itself (e.g., 1.209); using both the
preposition and the possessive suggests archaic* Latin and Ennius in particular, as it does at
6.185 *suo tristi cum corde volutat.* Cf. *Ann.* 507 Sk. = 537 W *tristi cum corde*, and *Ann.* 50 Sk. =
48 W *aegro cum (tum?) corde meo.* Why are Aeneas and Achates grim? Because the offer of
help is so modest, as Servius suggests? Or because an old man with romantic ideas about war
and heroism (cf. Petrini (1997: 48-86)) has entrusted to them his only son? Fowler (1917: 86-9)
suggests than Aeneas "has an intuition of [Pallas'] death."

523. **ni signum...dedisset:** we expect *vix ea fatus erat* (520) to be followed by an inverted *cum*-
clause or a sentence in parataxis* as in the other seven times it occurs in the poem (three others
before omens or miracles). But after describing the despondency of Aeneas and Achates with
what look like ordinary imperfects *tenebant* and *putabant,* the plup. subjunctive *dedisset* makes
the sentence a contrary-to fact condition with an elliptical apodosis: "were thinking (and would
have kept thinking), if Venus had not...." Cf. the similar 6.358-61 *iam tuta tenebam, | ni gens
crudelis...invasisset,* and see AG §517b. **Cytherea:** Venus, after the island off the southern
Peloponnese sacred to her because she was born from the sea near it. **aperto:** thunder and lightning in a "clear" sky was an omen; cf. 528 *serena,* 529 *per sudum, Geo.* 1.487 *caelo...sereno* of
the omens after Caesar's death, Hor. *Carm.* 1.34.5-8 *Diespiter | ...per purum tonantis | egit
equos,* Ovid *Fasti* 3.369 *tonuit sine nube deus.*

524. **improviso:** adverb, not connected with *aethere.* **vibratus:** "hurled," but by whom? Venus?
Jupiter?

525-6. **ruere:** the heavens seem suddenly about to crash down, in this heavily dactylic line; cf.
caelique ruina 1.129. **visa:** supply *sunt; visa (sunt)* then governs *mugire* in 526 as well. **Tyrrhenus:**
the trumpet is "Tyrrhenian" already in fifth-century tragedy (Aesch. *Eum.* 567-8; Soph. *Ajax*
16-7; Eur. *Phoen.* 1377-8, *Rhes.* 988-9), but here the context of Aeneas' seeking Etruscan
help adds resonance. For the transference of epithet (enallage*), cf. Lucr. 5.24-5 *Nemeaeus...
hiatus | ...leonis,* and see Conte (2007: 98-100), who says on another passage (91) that such a
Vergilian syntactical inversion as enallage may "charge [a] phrase with expressive force" and
also "compresses a complex thought by leaping over the intermediate articulations through
a daring condensation."

suspiciunt, iterum atque iterum fragor increpat ingens.
arma inter nubem caeli in regione serena
per sudum rutilare vident et pulsa tonare.
obstipuere animis alii, sed Troius heros   530
agnovit sonitum et divae promissa parentis.
tum memorat: "ne vero, hospes, ne quaere profecto
quem casum portenta ferant: ego poscor Olympo.

---

527. **iterum atque iterum:** the triple repetition confirms the omen, cf. 7.141.

528. **inter nubem:** "amid a cloud." Apparently the rest of the sky is clear except for this cloud, on which the arms seem to be supported. Clouds are commonly introduced when the gods are referred to as taking up a position in the sky or moving through it; cf. 608; 9.111, 640; 10.38, 634; 12.792.

529. **sudum:** neuter used as a substantive. **pulsa tonare:** struck together, the weapons make a noise like thunder. This was often a sign of war and trouble; cf. 533 n., and *Geo.* 1.474-5 *armorum sonitum toto Germania caelo | audiit*, of the portents after the murder of Caesar.

530. **obstipuere animis alii, sed...:** the verb is often used of Aeneas (six times, e.g., 5.90 of his reaction to an ominous snake), but here the others are alarmed when an omen of war follows a speech ending in Pallas' name, and Aeneas is calm. The same contrast marks Turnus' response to an omen at 9.123-6 *obstipuere animis Rutuli...at non audaci Turno fiducia cessit*; cf. O'Hara (1990: 74-8; 1993).

532. **ne quaere:** for *ne* + imperative, cf. 39 n. In the underworld Anchises, answering Aeneas' question about the doomed Marcellus, says *o gnate, ingentem luctum ne quaere tuorum* (6.868). Pallas, Marcellus, and Lausus are connected as young men who die too early; cf. 589-91 n., Petrini (1997), Reed (2007: 40). For emphatic *ne...ne*, cf. 11.278, 12.72. **profecto:** repeats and intensifies *vero*; occurs only here in Vergil, and is a strange type of word to have at line-end. Williams: "Aeneas' anxiety to convince Evander that all is well leads him to an over-reliance on emphatic particles which is very common in such a situation."

533. **casum:** the word can mean "disaster" or the more neutral "outcome," which is what Aeneas must mean here, but the ambiguity is picked up by Evander at 578, who is not fully convinced by Aeneas' determined optimism here: see 578 n. **ego...:** emphatic: "*I* am the one summoned by heaven"—not Pallas. Aeneas picks up on Evander's *fatis...poscentibus* (477). But Aeneas is only partially correct, for the omens can be read in more than one way. The thunder and lightning can be see as an *augurium*, an assurance that the gods favor Aeneas' course of action. But the thunder and lightning and especially the clashing of weapons in the sky, reminiscent of omens associated with the civil wars after Caesar's death, can also be seen as a *prodigium* foreshadowing a disastrous war (cf. 529 n.) and the horrors that it will bring, including the death of Pallas. See O'Hara (1990: 49-50, with references), and cf. Carmenta's prophecy about the Aeneadae and Pallanteum (340-1 and 341 n.), Anchises' reading of horses as an omen both of war and of peace (3.539-43), and Lavinia's burning hair as an omen of fame for her but a great war for her people (7.79-80).

hoc signum cecinit missuram diva creatrix,
si bellum ingrueret, Volcaniaque arma per auras   535
laturam auxilio.
heu quantae miseris caedes Laurentibus instant!
quas poenas mihi, Turne, dabis! quam multa sub undas
scuta virum galeasque et fortia corpora volves,
Thybri pater! poscant acies et foedera rumpant."   540
    Haec ubi dicta dedit, solio se tollit ab alto
et primum Herculeis sopitas ignibus aras
excitat, hesternumque larem parvosque penatis

---

534. cecinit missuram: supply *se...esse* both here and with *laturam* (536). For reference in epic like this to scenes not mentioned earlier, cf. O'Hara (2011) on *Aen.* 4.351 (Aeneas talking about dreams of Anchises), and Nünlist (2009: 157-73) on comments in Homeric scholia. At 612-13 Venus refers to *promissa...munera*.

535. ingrueret: subjunctive in a protasis in indirect discourse (AG §589).

536. auxilio: dat. of purpose. For the half-line, cf. 41 n.

538-9. quas poenas mihi, Turne, dabis!: cf. 4.386 *dabis, improbe, poenas* (Dido to Aeneas), with the note there in O'Hara (2011) on models in Enn. *Ann.* fr. 95 Sk. = 103 W and Cat. 116.8, and Latinus at *Aen.* 7.595 *ipsi has sacrilego pendetis sanguine poenas*. **quam multa...volves:** the similarity of these words to those used by Aeneas of the Trojan river Simois in 1.100-1 stresses how the war in Italy will reenact the Trojan War, as the Sibyl has predicted (6.83-97), with particular reference to the Simois (88). At *Il.* 21.214-21, the other Trojan river, the Xanthus or Scamander, complains that Achilles has filled his waters with corpses.

540. foedera rumpant: Aeneas' claim that the Latins have broken treaties is one way to look at what has happened (cf. 118 n.). Latinus offered an alliance and his daughter to Aeneas, using the word *pax* (7.266) for the agreement, which is never formally established; after being enraged by Allecto Turnus calls for war *polluta pace* (467), which can mean either "breaking the agreement" or more likely "because (his) agreements (with Latinus) have been broken" (cf. 7.467, Horsfall (2000) ad loc., Syson (2013: 26-7)); soon Allecto says to Juno *foedera iungant* (7.546), "let them (try to) make treaties (now)." On Aeneas' shield Mettus will be cruelly punished for violating a treaty (642 and note), and in 12 the Latins will violate the truce arranged for Aeneas and Turnus' single combat (12.257-69), as Aeneas complains when he attacks Latinus' city: *multa Iovem et laesi testatus foederis aras* (496). Brief discussions of treaty-breaking in Galinsky (1988: 223-4) (very anti-Turnus), Gaskin (1992: 297) ("Turnus is not himself directly responsible for the breaking of either of the two treaties"), Johnson (2004: 237 n. 14 with references), Fratantuono (2007: 248-9), Lowrie (2010: 394-5).

542. Herculeis...ignibus: "with Herculean flames"; the epithet is transferred from "altars" to "fires" (enallage*).

543. hesternumque larem: the Lar to whom he had offered sacrifice yesterday. **parvos:** more stress on the simplicity of Evander's household; cf. Hor. *Carm.* 3.23.15-16 *parvos...deos*, of the humble *Penates* of "rustic Phidyle."

laetus adit; mactat lectas de more bidentis
Evandrus pariter, pariter Troiana iuventus.   545
post hinc ad navis graditur sociosque revisit,
quorum de numero qui sese in bella sequantur
praestantis virtute legit; pars cetera prona
fertur aqua segnisque secundo defluit amni,
nuntia ventura Ascanio rerumque patrisque.   550
dantur equi Teucris Tyrrhena petentibus arva;
ducunt exsortem Aeneae, quem fulva leonis
pellis obit totum praefulgens unguibus aureis.
       Fama volat parvam subito vulgata per urbem

---

544. **laetus:** often used of one who has become hopeful about the future; Wiltshire (2012). **adit:** "approach (in worship)" as in Lucr. 5.1229 *divum pacem votis adit*, Prop. 3.21.18 *prece adire deos*, Cic. *ND* 1.77 *deos ipsos...adire*. **mactat lectas de more bidentis:** repeated from 4.57; cf. Latinus' sacrifice, 7.93 *mactabat rite bidentis*. **de more:** "in accordance with custom," i.e., without blemish or fault, and perhaps of a certain age and appearance. **bidentis:** "sheep" that are one to two years old; at this age sheep have two prominent teeth, which appear to be their only ones.

546. **graditur:** sc. Aeneas, with abrupt change of subject.

547. **qui...sequantur:** relative clause of purpose.

549. **segnis:** without exertion, because they can flow with the current. **secundo defluit amni:** repeated from *Geo.* 3.447. The meter (with third-foot coincidence of ictus and accent; see Appendix A on meter) and sounds flow smoothly like the current (onomatopeia*). Their arrival at the Trojan camp is never mentioned.

552. **exsortem:** the Arcadians bring forth a "special" mount for Aeneas; cf. Latinus' gift of horses at 7.276-85.

553. **aureis:** a spondee by synizesis (see Appendix A on meter). For gilded claws on a lionskin, cf. the prize awarded at 5.352. Evander is not a complete pauper.

554-84. *The rumor of the embassy to the Etruscans fills Pallanteum with fear of the approaching war. Evander says goodbye to Pallas, lamenting that he no longer has the strength he displayed when once he killed the monster Erulus, and praying for life if he is to see his son again, or else for instant death.*

The pathos, structure, and rhetoric of Evander's speech are noteworthy. His sentences are unusually long (560-71, 572-7, 578-83), each featuring a tricolon* with anaphora* (564-6, 574-6, 580-1), and his words are awash in emotion: nostalgia for his own youthful strength, anger at Mezentius, desperate bargaining with the gods, love for his son, and fear for Pallas' safety. Vergil combines and compresses two long speeches by Nestor in which he wishes he were still young, at *Il.* 7.124-60 (esp. 132ff.) and 11.655-761 (esp. 669ff.); the speech in *Iliad* 11 ultimately inspires the ill-fated plan to imitate Achilles that leads to the death of Patroclus— the model for the role to be played in the *Aeneid* by Pallas. That speech also deals with

ocius ire equites Tyrrheni ad limina regis.   555
vota metu duplicant matres, propiusque periclo
it timor et maior Martis iam apparet imago.
tum pater Evandrus dextram complexus euntis
haeret inexpletus lacrimans ac talia fatur:
"o mihi praeteritos referat si Iuppiter annos,   560
qualis eram cum primam aciem Praeneste sub ipsa
stravi scutorumque incendi victor acervos

---

cattle-raiding, the subject of Evander's tale of Hercules and Cacus (*Aen.* 8.185-275). This emotionally wrenching farewell by a parent to a child is like that of Jason's parents in Apoll. Rhod. *Arg.* 1.260-305 and Aegeus to Theseus in Cat. 64.215-37 (cf. 514 n., 574-6 n.). The Homeric Nestor is also a father who loses a son, Antilochus who dies at Troy (*Od.* 3.111-17). There are also echoes and reminders of Aeneas' encounter with Dido (572 n., 584 n.), and later in the poem Evander's bitter enemy Mezentius will lament the loss of a son (10.843-66). Cf. Eden on 561ff., Thomas (1982: 107 n. 41) on Catullus 64, Nelis (2001: 364) on Apollonius, and Clausen (2002: 170-3).

555-7. **ocius:** the comparative is common as a variant for *ociter.* **equites:** acc. subject of *ire*, in indirect statements implied by *Fama volat.* **regis:** Tarchon. **propiusque periclo…:** fear moves through the Arcadians, "more imminent because of the danger," with *periclo* as abl., and "the image of Mars looms larger." When the orders to march are given, mothers begin to feel more anxious and to realize what war means. Some take *periclo* as dat., so that "fear treads more closely on the heel of danger" (Conington) or "fear goes closer to the danger (than they really are)" (Williams). See Fordyce for Vergil's fondness for initial *it* and for his varied use of *imago*.

558. **euntis:** i.e., Pallantis, since Evander is referred to as *pater*, as Servius notes.

559. **inexpletus lacrimans:** "weeping (still) unsatisfied," "unable to get his fill of weeping." For adjective with present participle, cf. 3.70 *lenis crepitans* "softly whispering"; *Geo.* 2.377 *gravis incumbens*.

560. **o…referat si:** in poetry *si* + subjunctive may express a wish, like English "if only," as at 6.187-8 *si nunc se nobis ille aureus arbore ramus | ostendat* (AG §442a). But this wish will turn out to be also the protasis of a condition, with the apodosis in 568-71, "(in that case) I would not be…."

561. **qualis:** in loose apposition to 560, as though he had said "young, such as I was when…." **Praeneste:** modern Palestrina, twenty-three miles from Rome, an important city during the period of Etruscan domination in Latium. The form is usually neuter as at 7.682, but feminine here and at Juvenal 3.190.

562. **scutorumque…:** Servius says that this practice was introduced by Rome's sixth king Tarquinius Priscus, who burned the shields of conquered Sabines in honor of Vulcan; cf. Livy 1.37, 8.30, 23.46.

et regem hac Erulum dextra sub Tartara misi,
nascenti cui tris animas Feronia mater
(horrendum dictu) dederat: terna arma movenda,   565
ter leto sternendus erat; cui tunc tamen omnis
abstulit haec animas dextra et totidem exuit armis:
non ego nunc dulci amplexu divellerer usquam,
nate, tuo, neque finitimo Mezentius umquam
huic capiti insultans tot ferro saeva dedisset   570
funera, tam multis viduasset civibus urbem.
at vos, o superi, et divum tu maxime rector

563-6. **Erulum:** a myth mentioned only here; Vergil imitates how Nestor tells a story also not mentioned elsewhere (*Il.* 11.672). The three-souled Erulus is like the three-bodied Geryon (*tergemini…Geryonae* 202) killed and robbed by Hercules, who seems in Aesch. *Ag.* 869ff. to have a separate life for each body. Servius notes that Evander claims for himself a Herculean feat (*attendendum sane, hoc sibi Evandrum vindicare quod fuit in Hercule; nam ut ille Geryonem extinxit, ita hic Erylum occidit*); cf. Petrini (1997: 51), Secci (2013), O'Hara (n.d.). McPhee (n.d.) argues that Nestor's tale at *Il.* 11.711-61 of fighting the Moliones, who may have been thought of as conjoined twins, is an intertext for Evander's tale of three-souled Erulus. **tris… terna…ter:** the anaphora* with variation helps organize the passage (cf. 574-6 and 580-1), but the Latin is difficult and disputed, and can be punctuated in different ways. It is clear that his mother gave him three souls (*nascenti…dederat*) and that he had to be killed three times (*ter leto sternendus erat*). With a dash after *terna arma movenda* (as in the text of Mynors (1969); Hirtzel (1900) starts a parenthesis there) those words represent a second direct object, so that his mother gave him three sets of armor to take into battle. With our colon after *dederat* (as in Geymonat (2008); Conte (2009) has a dash), the words *terna arma movenda* are the first of two periphrastic constructions, "three times arms had to be moved (against him)…." Servius concisely says that *arma movenda* may refer to arms that are to be moved against him, or by him. Evander kills him three times and each time strips his arms. **Feronia:** a deity mentioned at 7.800. **leto:** dative, as in many expressions for killing in Latin like *dare morti*; cf. Weber (1969), O'Hara (2007: 52).

567. **armis:** abl. of separation, with slight enallage*.

568-70. **non…divellerer…neque…dedisset:** delayed contrary-to-fact apodosis to 560 (see note), with the imperf. subjunctive describing the present situation, the pluperfect what would have been different in the past. **usquam…umquam:** the repetition at successive line-ends suggests passionate emphasis. **finitimo:** could go with *capiti* (570) but it might be best to supply *mihi*.

571. **urbem:** Pallanteum, though we know nothing of any devastating attacks on it by Mezentius, and Evander had said that the Tiber protects them on the Etruscan side (473).

572. Evander turns from angry indignation to a prayer to the gods (cf. apostrophe*); Williams compares the change of mood in Dido's speech at 4.603-14. There are echoes of Dido in 574, 579, 584.

Iuppiter, Arcadii, quaeso, miserescite regis
et patrias audite preces. si numina vestra
incolumem Pallanta mihi, si fata reservant,   575
si visurus eum vivo et venturus in unum:
vitam oro, patior quemvis durare laborem.
sin aliquem infandum casum, Fortuna, minaris,
nunc, nunc o liceat crudelem abrumpere vitam,
dum curae ambiguae, dum spes incerta futuri,   580
dum te, care puer, mea sola et sera voluptas,
complexu teneo, gravior neu nuntius auris
vulneret." haec genitor digressu dicta supremo

---

573. **Arcadii...regis:** Fordyce calls this a "curious periphrasis" for a speaker to use of himself. Harrison (1984) suggests that Evander appeals to Jupiter as a fellow Arcadian, since some myths placed Jupiter's birth there.

574-6. **et patrias audite preces:** cf. 4.612 *et nostras audite preces* (Dido). **si...si...si...:** a second (of three; cf. 563-6 n.) tricolon* with anaphora* heightens the emotional tone. Thomas (1982: 107 n. 41) suggests that Aegeus' farewell to his son Theseus at Cat. 64.215-37 "may well have been in Virgil's mind at *Aen.* 8.574-584."

576. **in unum:** "to one and the same place."

577. **quemvis durare laborem:** cf. Lucr. 1.141 *quemvis efferre laborem* and Vergil's *perferre laborem* at *Geo.* 2.343, *Aen.* 5.617, 769; *duros perferre labores* at 6.437; *perferre labores* at 12.177.

578. **sin aliquem:** after *sin*, we expect *quem*, so *aliquem* is emphatic, "any at all." **infandum:** the father cannot mention the death of his son (Servius). **casum:** Wiesen (1973: 758): "Aeneas' ambiguous word *casum* [8.533] is taken up by Evander...when he is pondering Pallas' future." Cf. 533 n.; Evander is not convinced by Aeneas' confidence.

579. **crudelem abrumpere vitam:** "to break off" a life that has become cruelly painful. The phrase recurs at 9.497 (Euryalus' mother), and cf. 4.631 *invisam...abrumpere lucem* (Dido).

580-1. **dum...dum...dum:** a third tricolon* with anaphora* (563-6 n.), giving an intensely felt climax. **curae:** is both "affection" for Pallas and "anxiety, worry," while *spes* can be either "hope" for good or "expectation" of evil. **mea sola et sera voluptas:** at 3.660 the blind Polyphemus' sheep are his *sola voluptas*. Cf. also 514 *spes et solacia nostri*, and Amata's words to Turnus at 12.57-8 *spes tu nunc una, senectae | tu requies miserae*.

582. **neu:** "and let no..."; negative jussive, as with *neve* at 7.265. It could also be read as a neg. purpose cl., but that may make for weaker rhetoric. Evander's reaction to Pallas' death is described at 11.139-81.

fundebat; famuli conlapsum in tecta ferebant.
    Iamque adeo exierat portis equitatus apertis   585
Aeneas inter primos et fidus Achates,
inde alii Troiae proceres, ipse agmine Pallas
in medio chlamyde et pictis conspectus in armis,
qualis ubi Oceani perfusus Lucifer unda,
quem Venus ante alios astrorum diligit ignis,   590
extulit os sacrum caelo tenebrasque resolvit.

---

584. **fundebat...**: imperf.: he was still speaking when he collapsed. **famuli conlapsum...**: close echo of Dido's collapse at 4.391-2 *suscipiunt famulae conlapsaque membra | marmoreo referunt thalamo stratisque reponunt*; see O'Hara (2011) on those lines. For Dido, cf. 538-9 n., 572 n., 574-6 n., 579 n.; and for thematic connections between Evander, Dido, and in Book 9 Euryalus' mother, see Petrini (1997: 55-6), who stresses the clash between heroism and domestic concerns.

585-607. *As fearful mothers watch, the Trojans and Arcadians ride towards Etruscan Caere, with Pallas in their center, bright and beautiful as the morning star. They camp for the night in a sacred grove of Silvanus; from nearby hills they can see the forces of the Etruscan Tarchon.* Henry (1889: vol. 3, 755) compares 585-96 with the start of Dido and Aeneas' hunt at 4.129-50: "To the reader unacquainted with the sequel both pictures are as gay and exhilarating as they stand to him who reads the story for the second, or it may be for the hundredth time, in the saddest contrast to the grim catastrophes by which their sunny morning brightness is so soon, so very soon, to be overcast, and for ever extinguished. Each picture may be regarded as the last glimpse of a blue sky immediately to be enveloped in clouds and storm...."

585. **iamque adeo**: "and now indeed"; *adeo* as always emphasizes the word before it. **equitatus**: noun, "the cavalry," with the successive names in apposition.

587-8. **proceres, ipse agmine Pallas | in medio**: with this text and punctuation, the list of men on horseback continues with asyndeton*. Mynors (1969) has a semi-colon after *proceres* and to start 588 prints Markland's emendation of *in* to *it*. **conspectus**: used of one "on whom every eye is turned"; cf. *Geo.* 3.17 *Tyrio conspectus in ostro*; Hor. *A. P.* 228 *regali conspectus in auro... et ostro.*

589-91. **Oceani**: a detail not in Homer, borrowed from Apollonius' comparison of Jason's beauty, in Medea's longing eyes, to that of Sirius rising from Oceanus (*Arg.* 3.956-9); cf. Nelis (2001: 319-23) for several Apollonian models for the simile here. **Lucifer**: Conte (1986: 193) shows that the frequent association in sepulchral iconography between Lucifer the morning-star and those who die young makes this simile suggest "splendid but *ephemeral* beauty," and so foreshadow Pallas' death; more references in Nelis (2001: 321), Cucchiarelli (2001), Feldherr (2014: 315-16). The simile draws on *Il.* 5.4-7, where Diomedes' helmet blazes like the dog-star Sirius, as well as *Il.* 22.315-21, where Achilles' spear shines like the evening-star Hesperus "which is the brightest star in the heavens" (Lucifer and Hesperus are the same body, the planet Venus; cf. Cic. *ND* 2.53). Lucifer's rising also marks the end of the night Troy fell

stant pavidae in muris matres oculisque sequuntur
pulveream nubem et fulgentis aere catervas.
olli per dumos, qua proxima meta viarum,
armati tendunt; it clamor, et agmine facto   595
quadripedante putrem sonitu quatit ungula campum.
est ingens gelidum lucus prope Caeritis amnem,
religione patrum late sacer; undique colles
inclusere cavi et nigra nemus abiete cingunt.
Silvano fama est veteres sacrasse Pelasgos,   600
arvorum pecorisque deo, lucumque diemque,
qui primi finis aliquando habuere Latinos.
haud procul hinc Tarcho et Tyrrheni tuta tenebant

(2.801); Servius there quotes Varro as saying the star of Venus was visible to Aeneas from the time he left Troy until he reached Latium (cf. Gransden). **diligit ignis:** assonance*, with five straight syllables at line-end with the vowel *i*.

592. The women look out from the walls as they do when they watch Camilla at 11.877, and as the Trojan men do in *Il*. 3.121-244 (the *teichoscopia*, with Helen) and 22.462-6 (with Andromache), or the mother and daughter in Hor. *Carm*. 3.2.6-12, where Nisbet and Rudd (2004) list several parallels, including Enn. *Ann*. 418 Sk = 371 W *matronae moeros complent spectare faventes*.

594. **meta:** they take the quickest path to their "goal," cutting across the thornbushes; the word is used of the turning-post of a racetrack, as at *Geo*. 3.202.

596. This galloping line and the similar 11.614 are famous for their onomatopoeic* accommodation of sound to sense both through meter and the choice of consonants. Macrob. *Sat*. 6.1.22 says Vergil imitates lines in Ennius, especially *Ann*. 263 Sk. = 283 W *summo sonitu quatit ungula terram*. **quadripedante:** = "galloping," since horses lift all four feet to gallop; cf. Enn. trag. fr. 169 J = trag. frag. 189 W, Plaut. *Capt*. 814. **putrem:** "crumbling."

597. **est...lucus:** like the formulaic opening for description of a place; cf. 1.159 *est...locus*, 4.480-2, 7.563-7 with the note of Horsfall (2000), 11.522-5, G. Williams (1968: 637-57). The topography here is confusing and probably not meant to be realistic. **Caeritis:** irregular gen. of *Caere*; in 10.183 we have *Caerete* as the abl. Cf. 479 n.

599. **cavi:** not hollow but leaving a hollow in their midst, or "encircling." **abiete:** dactyl, with consonantal *i*; cf. 7.175 *ariete caeso*. Notice too the sing. used collectively.

600. **Silvano:** Silvanus was a Roman god of the woods; cf. *Ecl*. 10.24 with the note of Clausen (1994), *Geo*. 1.20, 2.494. **Pelasgos:** elsewhere in Vergil simply means "Greek" (1.624 Dido, 2.83 Sinon, 6.503 Aeneas), as in Enn. *Ann*. 14 Sk. = 15 W; Evander's use of it for predecessors of the Etruscans in Italy follows a tradition mentioned in Dion. Hal. *Ant. Rom*. 1.17.

601. **diemque:** "and a festival," a day set apart in his honor.

603. **Tarcho:** this spelling only here, the Greek *Tarchon* nine times; cf. as Servius does Apollo(n) in Greek and Latin. **tuta:** with *locis*, "in a well-defended spot," lit. "protected by its location," with abl. of instrument or cause, as at 6.238 *tuta lacu nigro nemorumque tenebris*.

castra locis, celsoque omnis de colle videri
iam poterat legio et latis tendebat in arvis.   605
huc pater Aeneas et bello lecta iuventus
succedunt, fessique et equos et corpora curant.
    At Venus aetherios inter dea candida nimbos
dona ferens aderat; natumque in valle reducta
ut procul egelido secretum flumine vidit,   610

---

604. **celso...de colle:** if this refers to Aeneas and the others, it would mean they can see the
    Etruscans from the top of one of the hills mentioned in 598, which they cross before
    descending to the grove. It could also mean that the Etruscan *legio* can be seen in its position
    on a hill.

605. **legio:** Roman technical term, used loosely of any armed force. **et latis...:** an explanatory
    clause; the Etruscans could be seen because of where they had "pitched their tents" (*tendebat*,
    as in 2.29 *hic saevus tendebat Achilles*).

606. **huc:** i.e., into the grove mentioned in 597; Aeneas reaches the camp of Tarchon at 10.148.
    Aeneas will be absent throughout Book 9.

608-731. Venus brings Vulcan's arms to Aeneas, and we see him looking at them (608-25). The poet
    describes the scenes from future Roman history on the shield (626-728; see note there for full
    introduction to the shield), which Aeneas delights in though he cannot understand (729-31).

*608-25. Venus brings the armor made by Vulcan to Aeneas, and embraces him; Aeneas cannot gaze
    on the marvelous armor enough.*

Vergil adapts *Iliad* 19.1-20, where Thetis brings Achilles the arms made by Hephaestus, after
    we have watched Hephaestus make the scenes upon the shield, while Vergil has Venus bring
    the shield, and then we and Aeneas see it together. There are influences too from Apollonius'
    description of Jason as he sees the Golden Fleece in *Arg.* 4.123-82. Cf. Johnson (1976: 111-14),
    Nelis (2001: 356-7), Clausen (2002: 173-5).

608. **inter...nimbos:** she comes "amid clouds," which are imagined as conveying her to the spot,
    cf. 528 n.

609. **dona ferens:** cf. *Il.* 19.3, of Thetis "carrying the gifts of the god." **in valle reducta:** the same
    phrase at 6.703 describes the Elysian fields, where Aeneas with his other parent, his father, sees
    the souls of his Roman descendants, whose exploits are here about to be described on Vulcan's
    shield; the repetition ties together two of the three major prophecies of Rome.

610. **egelido:** sometimes means "warm," with a privative prefix, but here must mean "very cold,"
    with an intensifying prefix, as Servius notes; cf. Fordyce. Several manuscripts have *e gelido*,
    but modern editors prefer the reading of M and of Servius. **secretum:** that Aeneas is "apart,"
    withdrawn from his comrades, unlike Achilles, who is with the Myrmidons when Thetis
    comes, tells us something about Aeneas' role in this poem. **flumine:** local abl., unless *secretum
    flumine* means "cut off by the river."

talibus adfata est dictis seque obtulit ultro:
"en perfecta mei promissa coniugis arte
munera. ne mox aut Laurentis, nate, superbos
aut acrem dubites in proelia poscere Turnum."
dixit, et amplexus nati Cytherea petivit,   615
arma sub adversa posuit radiantia quercu.
ille deae donis et tanto laetus honore
expleri nequit atque oculos per singula volvit,
miraturque interque manus et bracchia versat
terribilem cristis galeam flammasque vomentem,   620
fatiferumque ensem, loricam ex aere rigentem,

---

611. **se...obtulit:** also of Venus at 2.589-90. Because Vergil mentions her addressing Aeneas before he says that she appears, Servius calls this hysteron proteron* (cf. also 615). **ultro:** she appears "of her own accord," without prior arrangement.

612-14. **en perfecta... | munera:** *en*, "behold," may be followed by a nom. or acc. of exclamation; cf. *Ecl.* 5.65 *en quattuor aras, Aen.* 7.452 *en ego victa situ,* 545 *en, perfecta tibi bello discordia tristi.* **promissa:** cf. 534 *cecinit.* **ne...dubites:** with a full stop after *munera,* neg. jussive; with a comma, neg. purpose.

615. **amplexus:** Aeneas finally gets a hug. At 1.402-9, Venus slips away as he protests her appearing to him in disguise (*cur dextrae iungere dextram | non datur...?* 408-9), and at 2.790-4 and 6.697-702 he tries in vain to embrace the insubstantial shades of his wife and father. Oliensis (2009: 67) finds this scene "disturbingly reminiscent of Cupid's earlier attack on Dido" in 1.707-22, which is "likewise carried out by a combination of caresses and splendid gifts." Cf. too the embrace of Ascanius by Aeneas at 12.433-4.

616. Similar to a golden line*. **quercu:** at Apoll. Rhod. *Arg.* 4.123-5 the golden fleece is found on an oak. (Note that the term "golden line" is not ancient.)

617. **laetus:** cf. *gaudet* 731, *miratur* 619, 730, *Il.* 19.18 for Achilles' delight in Hephaestus' shield, *Arg.* 4.167-71 for Jason's in the golden fleece; cf. Nelis (2001: 356-7).

618. **expleri nequit:** cf. 265; contrast *Il.* 19.19, where Achilles does satisfy or at least please his heart (Gr. *tetarpeto*) by looking at his shield.

620. **flammasque vomentem:** at *Il.* 5.4 Athena makes Diomedes' helmet and shield glow with fire (cf. 589-91 n.). The image associates Aeneas with Augustus, but not exclusively: flame is poured forth from the Chimaera on the helmet of Turnus, *Aetnaeos efflantem faucibus ignis* (7.786), by Cacus, *Cacum in tenebris incendia vana vomentem* (8.259), from Augustus' head on Aeneas' shield, *tempora flammas | laeta vomunt* (680-1, see note), and from the shield and head of Aeneas, *ardet apex capiti cristisque a vertice flamma | funditur et vastos umbo vomit aureus ignis* (10.270-1).

621. **fatiferum:** "death-dealing," but with also a sense of "fateful" here and in Ascanius' *fatifer arcus* 9.631. Henderson (1998) translates *fatum* in Lucan as "deathstiny."

sanguineam, ingentem, qualis cum caerula nubes
solis inardescit radiis longeque refulget;
tum levis ocreas electro auroque recocto,
hastamque et clipei non enarrabile textum.   625

622-3. sanguineam, ingentem: "blood-red, huge." The asyndeton* adds weight to the sense of terror which the adjectives convey, heightened also by the use of *sanguineam* instead of an adj. like *rutilus*; Faber (2000) argues that the prominence of blood in the pseudo-Hesiodic *Scutum* stands behind the references to blood here and on Aeneas' shield. **qualis:** the simile* is adapted from Apoll. Rhod. *Arg.* 4.125-6, where the golden fleece is "like a cloud that grows red from the fiery beams of the rising sun" (Race 2008); cf. Faber (2000), Nelis (2001: 356-7), Clausen (2002: 174). Cf. above 22-5 and note for another simile on the effect of light adapted from Apollonius.

624. levis ocreas: "smooth" or polished (from *lēvis*, not *lĕvis*, "light") greaves or shin-guards, as at 7.634; the first syllable of *ocreas* scans as short before the mute and liquid. **recocto:** smelted again and again.

625. non enarrabile: [Hes.] *Scutum* 144, 161 has οὔ τι φατειός and οὔ τι φατειῶν, "unspeakable," with the negation but without a version of the prefix *e-*. But the prefix is important: the shield cannot be "fully described" (cf. 628 *omne*), so Vergil's lines will be selective; Zetzel (1997: 200), Kania (2016: 92). Cf. also Laird (1993: 27; 1996: 78-9 and 100-1), with good discussion of Servius here; Smolenaars (1994) on Stat. *Theb.* 7.652 *clipei penetrabile textum*; Eigler (1994); Putnam (1998: 187-8); Faber (2000); Casali (2006: 196); Ross (2007: 118), who paraphrases *non enarrabile textum* as "complexity beyond description"; and Lowrie (2009: 164). **textum:** literally suggests that the shield is a composition of plates or pieces of metal (cf. 449 *impediunt*), but also likens the shield to woven fabric, often used metapoetically of finely crafted Callimachean poetry; cf. 409 n., Bartsch (1998: 327-8), and Casali (2006), who notes that Jason's cloak (above 426-8 n.) is a model for the shield.

626-728. A description of what's on the shield: Romulus and Remus and the wolf (630-4); the rape of the Sabine women and the war that followed (635-41); the savage punishment for treachery of Mettus (642-5); Porsenna's failed attempt to restore the last Tarquin as king (646-51); the defense of the Capitol against the Gauls (652-62); various sacred rites of Rome (663-6); the underworld where Catiline is punished and Cato presides over the just (666-70); then the sea (671-4) and, in the center, the battle of Actium, where Augustus and Agrippa defeat Antony and his Egyptian wife and foreign troops, as Roman gods and especially Apollo fight the gods of Egypt, and Cleopatra flees to the Nile (675-713); Caesar returns to Rome and is honored in a triumph (714-19), and receives the gifts of conquered nations on the threshold of the temple of Palatine Apollo (720-28).

The shield has two main sections, with a brief transitional section between. First come scenes from early Roman history (626-66), all from the period that could have been covered in Ennius' *Annales*. Only four and a half lines (666-70) refer to events from later Republican history, then the rest of the shield (671-728) describes the Battle of Actium and its aftermath.

The shield evokes a rich series of literary intertexts, historical referents, and thematic connections within the *Aeneid*. The major intertext for the shield is Homer's shield of Achilles, which is described as Hephaestus (= Vulcan) makes it in *Il.* 18.468-607. Achilles actually needs new armor, since Hector has taken his from Patroclus, while Aeneas gets new armor in part to show the gods' support for him, in part simply to allow Vergil to rival Homer. Hephaestus makes first the cosmos of earth, sky, sun, moon, and stars (18.483-9), then two mortal cities, one at peace with marriages and a courtroom dispute and one at war featuring a council and an ambush (491-540). Five scenes depict agriculture (541-89); young men and women dance (590-606); and along the outermost rim flows the Oceanus River (607-8). On Aeneas' shield are scenes from the Roman future, from Aeneas' perspective, or Roman history, from that of the Augustan reader: first early stories that would have been in Ennius (630-66), then two figures from recent history (666-70), then the battle of Actium and Augustus' triumph (671-728). The shield is thus one of three major prophecies in the poem (cf. 627 n. on *vatum*), along with Jupiter's speech to Venus (1.257-96), and Anchises' review of the souls of future Romans (6.756-853, cf. too 4.229-31, 7.96-101, 12.834-40). The long tradition of "ecphrases" or poetic descriptions of works of art also includes the pseudo-Hesiodic *Scutum Heraclis*. Faber (2000) notes borrowings from the *Scutum* and argues that Vergil draws from that text a sense of war as bloody and frightening not present in Homer's shield; cf. 622-3 n., and also Heckenlively (2013).

The practice of Hellenistic ecphrasis in Callimachus, Theocritus, Moschus, and especially Apollonius will have influenced Vergil as well; cf. Clausen (2002: 177-84) in general, and Nelis (2001: 350-6) and Casali (2006) on the ecphrasis of Jason's cloak in *Arg.* 1.721-68. Other descriptions of works of art in the *Aeneid*: the scenes of the Trojan War on Juno's temple at Carthage (1.456-93), the Ganymede story on a cloak offered as a prize at games (5.250-7), the story of the Minotaur engraved by Daedalus on Apollo's temple doors at Cumae (6.20-30), the metamorphosis of Io on Turnus' shield (7.789-92), and the Danaids' murder of their bridegrooms on Pallas' baldric (10.497-9, 12.941-6).

Other influences on the shield include the golden shield the Senate awarded Augustus in 27 BCE, praising him for his *virtus, pietas, clementia, iustitia*, "valor, piety, clemency, and justice"; see *Res Gestae* 34, West (1990b: 296), who is skeptical of a connection, and Harrison (1997). The shield of the Athena Parthenos of Pheidias in the Parthenon at Athens has also been cited as a model; Cohon (1991), Hardie (1986: 99), McKay (1998). From (probably) later in the Augustan period, one may compare the decorated breastplate of the Augustus of Prima Porta statue. McKay (1998) argues that even before getting to Augustus' triumph in 714, the shield features scenes relevant to triumphal parades and to monuments and topographical features they would pass. Of literary influences that of Ennius' *Annales* must be foremost, especially on the scenes from early Roman history. Servius says the whole description of Romulus and the wolf (630-4) is "Ennian" (*sane totus hic locus Ennianus est*), and numerous borrowings, as well as resemblances to the version in Livy's recent *Ab Urbe Condita*, support this claim. Indeed only the four-and-a-half lines on the Underworld refer to events from the period between the end of what was covered in Ennius and the start of the Battle of Actium (666-70 n.). Livy's own early books, the first ten of which were probably available to Vergil, will also be an influence, but Ennius influenced Livy as well; cf. notes to various passages in 632-66, Woodman (1989), Feldherr (2014: 301). On the importance of Ennius, see Barchiesi (1997: 271-81) (the shield represents Ennian "poetics" and the "road not taken" in most of the *Aeneid*); Eden, who cautiously suggests that "the Shield is Virgil's most sustained tribute to Ennius in the *Aeneid*" (164-5); Hardie (1993: 105), Zetzel (1996: 314); Goldschmidt (2013: 167-79, and index s.v. *Aeneas, shield of*).

As an ecphrasis, the shield has a peculiar and fascinating status as a description of an imaginary work of art; on ecphrasis see Heffernan (1993), Becker (1995), Boyd (1995), Laird (1996), Putnam (1998), De Jong (2011), Feldherr (2014). We watch as Aeneas first sees it (cf. 630-1 n.), and the poet addresses us several times (650 *aspiceres*, 676 *videres*, 691 *credas*; cf. esp. Laird (1996: 80-7), Feldherr (2014)), indicates where scenes are located on the shield (642 *haud procul inde;* 652 *in summo,* 663 *hic,* 666 *hinc procul,* 671 *haec inter,* 675 *in medio*; cf. Clausen (2002: 178)), and comments on the metals used (655, 658-60, 671-2, 675, 701). The description is far from that of an impartial reporter: it is clear that it covers only a selection of what Vulcan's divine skill can depict (cf. 625 *non enarrabile* and note, 628 *genus omne* and note). The poet also uses words that represent value judgments (635, 643, 688, and perhaps 721; cf. Zetzel (1996)) and describes pictures that either move through Vulcan's divine skill or are so vivid that they seem to move (632-4 and note). Some details and some intratexts within the *Aeneid* suggest that the shield is presenting only one version of a story (cf. 629 n. on Ascanius, 630-1 n. on the Lupercal, 657 n. on the Gallic sack, and 702 n. on Discordia). In the description of Augustus' triple triumph that concludes the ecphrasis (714-28), the poet goes beyond sober history, both in having the triumph of 29 BCE culminate in the temple of Apollo dedicated in 28 and then in listing, among those who bring gifts to Augustus, peoples who had little or nothing to do with Actium and were pacified either later or never at all (see 720-8 n., as well as 688 n., 705-6 n.).

The shield lends itself to a variety of interpretive approaches; Feldherr (2014: 289) says its "multiplication of perspectives...complicates audience response by allowing for the adoption of divergent points of view on the same event." Whether, for example, the fantastic hyperbole with which the ecphrasis concludes works as dazzling and effective encomium of Augustus as world-conqueror (perhaps reflecting the exaggerations of Augustus' actual triumph, as Östenberg (1999) suggests), or serves to undercut the shield as a piece of false propaganda more simplistic than the rest of the poem, is a question different readers will answer in different ways (720-8 n.). The shield can be seen as complementing Evander's Hercules-Cacus story (184-279) in presenting the triumph of good over evil, in ways that look forward to Aeneas' victories over Mezentius in Book 10 and Turnus in 12. Most of the scenes on the shield depict or allude to threats to Rome—from the Sabines, Mettus, and Porsenna in Rome's infancy, from the Gauls in 390 BCE, from Catiline in 63, and finally from Antony and Cleopatra— threats that were avoided through Roman *virtus* and the help of the gods; Harrison (1997), Clausen (2002: 182-3). In the climactic battle of Actium, we see "the victory of order over disorder, of West over East, of male over female, of civilisation over barbarism," in short "a victory of cosmic order, reflecting the mythological victory of the gods over the giants"; Zetzel (1996: 198); see also 675 n. The theme of gigantomachy on the shield ties in with its use in the whole poem, including the Hercules-Cacus story (184-279 n.), as has been richly described by Hardie (1986) (see also O'Hara (2007: 96-101)); Hardie also shows that the allegorical aspects of Vergil's shield reflect centuries of speculation by commentators analyzing Homer's shield. Alternately, the shield's treatment of Actium, like the story of Hercules and Cacus, can be seen as depictions of the world that are *quoted* by the main narrator but are much simpler in their moral outlook than his own handling of the stories of Aeneas (cf. Petrini (1997) on Hercules quoted 299-300 n.). The exaggerations and fantasies of the depiction of Actium and the triumph can also be viewed in the context of the regular practice of deception in prophecies in the *Aeneid*; O'Hara (1990; 1997: 78-82). The initial scene focuses on the founder Romulus, and several other passages suggest Romulus and associate Augustus with him (or with both him and the savior of 390 BCE Camillus). Romulus too is an ambivalent

illic res Italas Romanorumque triumphos
haud vatum ignarus venturique inscius aevi
fecerat ignipotens, illic genus omne futurae
stirpis ab Ascanio pugnataque in ordine bella.

figure suggesting on the one hand power and majesty (some thought Octavian should take his name, Suet. *Aug.* 7.2), but also violence, fratricide, civil strife, and kingship on the other hand; cf. 632-4 n., 635 n., 642 n., Hor. *Epod.* 7.17-20, Dio Cassius 53.16.7-8 ("kingship"). Whether readers think the shield complements or stands apart from the rest of the poem will probably depend on how they read the rest of the poem.

From a vast bibliography, see West (1975-6), G. Williams (1983: 152-6), West (1990b), Hardie (1986: 97-110, 336-76; 1998: 75-6, 97), Clausen (1987: 76-82; 2002: 173-84), O'Hara (1990: 172-5), Quint (1993: 21-46), Boyd (1995), Gurval (1995: 209-47), Zetzel (1996; 1997), Toll (1997), Boyle (1999), Casali (2006), Farrell (1997), Harrison (1997), McKay (1998), Putnam (1998: 119-88), Nelis (2001: 345-59), Thomas (2001: 198-207), Ross (2007: 113-19), Miller (2009: 54-94), Rossi (2010), Heckenlively (2013), and Feldherr (2014).

626. **res Italas Romanorumque triumphos:** elegant chiasmus* linking Italy and Rome—a contested issue in Vergil's North Italian youth and the years before he was born, in which Rome and her allies fought the Social Wars of 91-88 BCE. The careful reader may note that the introduction to the shield suggests that we will see plural "triumphs of Romans," but only the triple triumph of Augustus is mentioned. The restriction matches the historical process in which triumphs became the sole prerogative of Augustus and the imperial family; cf. Beard (2007: 68-71).

627. **haud vatum ignarus:** litotes*. **-que:** disjunctive, "or." The term *vates* usually refers to humans who possess knowledge of the divine (cf. 4.65 *heu vatum ignarae mentes*) or to poets. Vulcan can be thought to have learned the future from gods with prophetic power like Apollo, but *vatum* can also suggest poets like Ennius, so that "the authority of the Vergilian text is no more or less than that of the other texts on which it draws, and which it completes"; Hardie (1998: 97), Casali (2006: 186). Cf. 730, of Aeneas: *miratur rerumque ignarus imagine gaudet.*

628. **genus omne:** implies that by Vulcan's divine skill the shield portayed *all* of the Roman or at least Julian race, and perhaps even all their wars in order (*in ordine*), whereas Vergil's description must involve a selection; cf. 625 *enarrabile* and note, 718 *omnibus arae* and 718-19 n. We are alerted that this description, like any piece of writing, will involve choice, emphasis, and a certain point of view; Zetzel (1997: 200-1; 1996: 313-14), Putnam (1998: 187-8).

629. **stirpis ab Ascanio:** with his usual (and challenging) fondness for using incompatible variants of myth Vergil has both Vulcan's shield and Jupiter's prophecy to Venus (1.267-74) present the Trojan Ascanius as the ancestor of the Julians, while Anchises in his underworld prophecy to Aeneas puts Aeneas' half-Italian son Silvius Postumus in that position (6.763-6). See O'Hara (2007: 88-9), Quint (2015: 20), Rogerson (2017), and for other inconsistencies or allusions to variant versions on the shield, cf. 630-1 n., 657 n., 663-6 n., 702 n.

fecerat et viridi fetam Mavortis in antro					630
procubuisse lupam, geminos huic ubera circum
ludere pendentis pueros et lambere matrem
impavidos, illam tereti cervice reflexa
mulcere alternos et corpora fingere lingua.

630-1. **fecerat…**: as Lessing famously noted in 1766, Homer describes Achilles' shield as it is made, while Vergil has Aeneas looking at the shield that Vulcan "had made." Lessing prefers Homer, but Servius on 625 praises Vergil's choice; see Lessing (1984), Laird (1996). Putnam (1998: 119-88) discusses this opening scene on the shield several times. **fetam:** can mean "pregnant," or "having recently given birth." **Mavortis in antro:** the Lupercal, recently restored by Augustus, associated with Mars because of his fathering Romulus and Remus; see map 1, and cf. 1.276-7 *Romulus…Mavortia condet | moenia*, 6.777-8 *Mavortius… | Romulus* born to Ilia, and the story in Livy 1.4, Dion. Hal. *Ant. Rom.* 1.79. This passage implies that the name Lupercal derives from this wolf, whereas in 342-4 Evander had shown Aeneas the Lupercal and linked the name to Pan Lykaeus (< Gk. "wolf"). Ovid *Fasti* 2.421-4 argues that both etymologies can be true and calls attention to Vergil's two derivations; O'Hara (2017: 266-7). **procubuisse:** as direct obj. for what Vulcan is portaying on the shield, Vergil will sometimes use an acc. noun, sometimes an acc. + infin., as here. The tenses of *fecerat…procubuisse* mean that Vulcan "had represented that the wolf had…," then the present infinitives of 632-4 describe later actions. Cf. Ovid *Met.* 6.108 *fecit et Asterien aquila luctante teneri*; Cic. *ND* 1.19 *Plato…construi…a deo…mundum facit*.

632-4. **matrem:** "as a mother"? On the "ambivalence of the wolf" as an image of "the Roman military spirit" that must be "safely channelled into conflict with the outsider, and prevented from turning against itself," see Hardie (1990: 230). **tereti cervice reflexa:** Hirtzel (1900) and Mynors (1969) print this text; Conte (2009), Geymonat (2008), and Gransden (1976) *reflexam*, also found in some manuscripts (Conte notes Vergil seldom has the same case for three words in a row). Vergil adapts the *tereti cervice reposta* of Lucr. 1.35 from the Mars-Venus passage he also imitated in his Venus-Vulcan scene (cf. notes to 370-453, 373, 394). Resemblances between Livy's and Vergil's treatment of the twins (Ogilvie (1970: 46-8), Woodman (1989)), as well as Cicero, *Aratea* frag. 9.5 *a tereti cervice reflexum*, suggest that all draw upon Ennius. Servius on 631 says *sane totus hic locus Ennianus est*; cf. 626-731 n., Goldschmidt (2013: 173). **mulcere alternos:** is the caressing them "by turns" only suggested by the artist's work, or can Vulcan's art make pictures that move, like photographs in Harry Potter's world? We know that the god can make devices that move like robots (tripods at *Il.* 18.372-7, bellows at 417-20, golden maidservants at 468-73; cf. Kalligeropoulos and Vasileiadou (2008)) and some have thought Hephaestus in the *Iliad* makes pictures that move on Achilles' shield. Others argue that such passages in both Homer and Vergil reflect merely the amazing verisimilitude of the artist. Cf. 437-8 n., and the discussion with references of de Jong (2011), who argues that the impression of movement in Homer is created by artistry and not magic. See Bartsch (1998) for *mulcere*'s associations with Vulcan Mulciber (724) as artist and with Donatus' comment (*Vita Donati* 22) that the poet claimed to lick his poem into shape as a she-bear does her cubs.

nec procul hinc Romam et raptas sine more Sabinas 635
consessu caveae, magnis Circensibus actis,
addiderat, subitoque novum consurgere bellum
Romulidis Tatioque seni Curibusque severis.
post idem inter se posito certamine reges
armati Iovis ante aram paterasque tenentes 640
stabant et caesa iungebant foedera porca.

---

635. **sine more:** "lawlessly," "in an uncivilized manner," which must be a comment by the poet. Cf. 316 *quis neque mos neque cultus erat* (before Saturn), Ovid, *Ars* 1.119 *sic illae (Sabinae) timuere viros sine more ruentes.* For the kidnapping and rape of the Sabine women after Romulus had invited the Sabines to a religious festival, cf. Livy 1.9-13, Ovid *Ars* 1.101-34, and (largely on Livy and Ovid) Joshel (1992), Miles (1995: 179-219), Brown (1995), Beard (1999), and Labate (2006). Thomas (2001: 199-200) notes attempts to amend Vergil here to mitigate the lawlessness. A stolen bride is of course crucial to the war fought in *Aen.* 7-12 (cf. 291 n. on Oechalia, 6.93 *causa mali tanti coniunx iterum*, 9.138 *coniuge praerepta*) as it was to the Trojan War; cf. also 637-8 n.

636. **consessu caveae:** from the seated crowd, in the sloping tiers of seats, cf. Lucr., 4.78 *consessum caveai*, *Aen.* 5.340 *caveae consessum*. **Circensibus:** suggests the games of the Circus or *ludi magni* (see map 1), though both Livy 1.9 and Servius put the rape at the different games called Consualia, so it perhaps just refers to that type of games. **actis:** "being held," with the perf. participle used as often with present sense, cf. 407 *noctis abactae* "departing night."

637-8. **novum consurgere bellum:** the inf. is like a noun, "the outbreak of...." **Romulidis:** the lawless kidnappers are boldly called "the people of Romulus," as at Lucr. 4.683; cf. *Aeneadae* at Lucr. 1.1, *Aen.* 1.157, 565, etc. Clausen (2002: 183) notes that Romulus "is kept before the reader" often in these early scenes. **Tatioque seni:** for the story of this Sabine king, see Livy 1.10-14. As Gurval (1995: 219) notes, Tatius is *senex* only here: this war over stolen brides is made to parallel that of *Aen.* 7-12, where Aeneas fights against *Latinus... | iam senior* (7.45-6), who will be his father-in-law (cf. also 291 n. on the Hymn to Hercules and the war of *Aen.* 7-12). After the Romans and Sabines make peace and become one people, the Romans took the name *Quirites* from Tatius' hometown of Cures, just as after Aeneas' victory the Trojans will adopt the Latin name (*Aen.* 12.824-35). **severis:** for the well-known strictness and severity of the Sabine character, cf. *severa* used of the Sabine mother of Hor. *Carm.* 3.6.39-40, and the depictions in *Geo.* 2.532, Hor. *Epod.* 2.39-48.

639-41. **idem:** plural. **posito:** "laid aside," as if *deposito*; cf. 329 *posuit*. **armati:** probably nom. with *reges*, but could it be genitive with *Iovis*? Woodman (1989: 137 and 141 n. 30) notes that *-que* in 140 would have to be coordinate with *et* in 141. **stabant:** the first finite verb used for events on the shield. **caesa iungebant foedera porca:** a pig slain while making a treaty invoked on those who slew it similar destruction if they broke the treaty; cf. Livy 1.24 *tum illo die, Juppiter, populum Romanum sic ferito ut ego hunc porcum hodie feriam*, and Servius here who says *foedus* is derived etymologically *a porca foede et crudeliter occisa*. Aeneas and Latinus will make a treaty (soon to be broken) at 12.161-215, with mention of a pig and other animals at 170-1.

haud procul inde citae Mettum in diversa quadrigae
distulerant (at tu dictis, Albane, maneres!),
raptabatque viri mendacis viscera Tullus
per silvam, et sparsi rorabant sanguine vepres.   645
nec non Tarquinium eiectum Porsenna iubebat
accipere ingentique urbem obsidione premebat:
Aeneadae in ferrum pro libertate ruebant.
illum indignanti similem similemque minanti
aspiceres, pontem auderet quia vellere Cocles   650
et fluvium vinclis innaret Cloelia ruptis.

---

642. **haud procul inde:** i.e., on the shield. The Alban king made peace with Tullus Hostilius
after what Livy 1.23.1 describes as like a civil war, since Rome was founded from Alba. But
Mettus treacherously held back in a battle to see which side would win, and was punished
by being torn to pieces by horses sent in opposite directions. Livy 1.27-8 tells the story, cf.
1.28.10 *diversum iter equi con<u>citati</u>,* and his comment that this barbaric punishment was
unique: *Primum ultimumque illud supplicium apud Romanos exempli parum memoris legum
humanarum fuit.* Again Ennius is likely a source: *Ann.* 124-6 Sk. = 140-2 W *tractatus per
aequora campi...volturus in † spineto † miserum mandebat homonem: | heu quam crudeli
condebat membra sepulcro;* cf. Goldschmidt (2013: 173).

643. **at tu...:** Vergil addresses Mettus in apostrophe* (Quintilian, *IO* 9.3.26 comments on this
parenthesis-plus-apostrophe; on apostrophe in Vergil, see Behr (2005)), and with a kind of
past jussive subjunctive or unfulfilled wish (for unfulfilled obligation, AG §439b; unfulfilled
wish, AG §441) says that he should have kept his word; cf. 4.678, 10.854, 11.118, 162. Cf. *Il.*
23.545-6, "he should have prayed to the gods."

646-7. **Tarquinium...Porsenna:** after the Romans drove out their last king, Tarquinius Superbus
(6.817 *Tarquinios reges,* and cf. above 493 n. on Mezentius), one tradition, seen in Livy 2.9-
13, said that the Etruscan Lars Porsenna tried to force them to take him back (understand
Romanos as subject of *accipere*), but was foiled by the heroism described in 648-51; another
tradition says that Porsenna in fact captured Rome (Tac. *Hist.* 3.72.1; Pliny, *N.H.* 34.139,
and cf. 657 n. on the Gauls' capture of Rome).

648. **libertate:** Romans who had recently driven out their king fight for their freedom. *Libertas*
was a "catchword" in the late Republic for "freedom from the rule of a tyrant or a faction";
Syme (1939: 155). Brutus the assassin of Caesar put *libertas* on his coins and was the descendant
of the Brutus who drove out the Tarquins and gave Rome *libertas* (cf. Livy 2.1). But Augustus
also says he "freed" (*liberavi, Res Gestae* 1) the state from the domination of a faction, and
coins of 28 BCE call him *libertatis vindex.* Later authors, e.g., Lucan *B.C.* 7.691-7 and Tacitus,
lamented that *libertas* died with the establishment of the Principate. Cf. Wirszubski (1950:
passim, 163-7) on Tacitus, Clausen (1994: 31) on *Ecl.* 1.27, Galinsky (1996: 54-7). **ruebant:**
cf. 9.182 *in bella ruebant* (Nisus and Euryalus), *Geo.* 2.503-4 *ruuntque | in ferrum.*

649-51. **similem...aspiceres:** the address to the reader uses an indefinite second person singular
with a potential subjunctive: if you were looking at the shield "you would see." This

in summo custos Tarpeiae Manlius arcis
stabat pro templo et Capitolia celsa tenebat,
Romuleoque recens horrebat regia culmo.

---

is the language of ecphrasis, and it comments on Vulcan's ability to portray realistically
Porsenna's anger and threats; cf. 676 *videres*, 691 *credas*, Laird (1996: 80-7), Putnam (1998:
127), Feldherr (2014: 289), who also notes more broadly that Vergil's inclusion of the reactions
of viewers like Porsenna (or Apollo or Cleopatra below) "complicates audience response by
allowing for the adoption of divergent points of view on the same event." **auderet quia:** the
subjunctive because it reports his reasoning second-hand, cf. 129 n. Livy 2.10 tells how Horatius
Cocles held the Tiber crossing of the Pons Sublicius while his countrymen cut it down behind
him; cf. Hardie (1994) on *Aen.* 9.815-19, where Turnus' leap into the Tiber recalls that of
Horatius; Livy 2.13 tells how Cloelia, given as a hostage to Porsenna after a peace treaty,
escaped, and swam across the Tiber.

652. **in summo:** top of the shield, or of the citadel of Rome? Or both? For words marking
position on the shield, cf. 642 *haud procul inde*, 663 *hic*, 666 *hinc procul*, 671 *haec inter*, 675
in medio; Vergil provides much more spatial orientation than there is on Achilles' shield.
Tarpeiae...arcis: cf. 347 n. for Tarpeia. Since Manlius both saved the citadel (next note)
and was later found guilty of treason and hurled from the Tarpeian rock, line 652 fits the type
of optimistic prophecy that hides the negative side of the future; O'Hara (1990; 2007: 89),
Feldherr (2014: 304). Livy 6.20.12 supports such a reading: *Tribuni de saxo Tarpeio deiecerunt
locusque idem in uno nomine et eximiae gloriae monumentum et poenae ultimae fuit.*

653. **Capitolia:** in 390 BCE the Gauls attacked Rome, and those who had not fled retreated to
the citadel on the Capitol; Livy 5.47 tells how though starving, the Romans refrained from
eating the sacred geese, which when the Gauls scaled the back of the hill, warned Manlius of
their approach and saved the day. Manlius acquired the cognomen *Capitolinus* (Livy 5.31):
Vergil often alludes to names or cognomina in this way, cf. 661 n., O'Hara (2017: 179-81).
For the alternate version in which the Gauls were successful, cf. 657 n.

654. **Romuleoque...:** alliteration* of *r* and nearly a golden line*, with enallage* or transferred
epithet as the straw or thatch rather than the structure is said to be "Romulean." At this
moment of danger, Vergil stops to provide continuity between Rome's founding, the danger
here in 390 BCE, and the Augustan present by noting that on the Capitol at this time, as in
his, the Romans kept in good repair a hut said to be the *regia* of Romulus (cf. Vitruvius 2.1.5,
Sen. *Cont.* 2.1.4, Mart. 8.80.6). Other sources refer to a hut on the Palatine not far from
Augustus' house (Dion. Hal. *Ant. Rom.* 1.79.11; Plut. *Rom.* 20.4). Kondratieff (2014: 200)
says the hut here on the shield is not the hut of Romulus but the Auguraculum from which
birds were observed, but that it's called a *regia* with Romulean thatch seems hard to square
with this claim. For references and for the symbolism and associations of both huts in various
writers, see Edwards (1996: 27-42). Clausen (2002: 182-3) notes that Vergil will have read
Camillus' reference to the hut at Livy 5.53.8: the poet "wishes to associate Augustus with
Romulus." Archaeologists have found on the Palatine and in the Forum what seem to be post
holes for iron-age huts: see McKay (1970: 133), Holloway (1994: 51-67), Forsythe (2005: 82-
93), Coarelli (2007: 133-4).

atque hic auratis volitans argenteus anser   655
porticibus Gallos in limine adesse canebat;
Galli per dumos aderant arcemque tenebant
defensi tenebris et dono noctis opacae.
aurea caesaries ollis atque aurea vestis,
virgatis lucent sagulis, tum lactea colla   660
auro innectuntur, duo quisque Alpina coruscant
gaesa manu, scutis protecti corpora longis.

---

655. **auratis...argenteus:** Vulcan skillfully uses various metals for contrasting colors (cf. 672-3 *aurea... | argento*), but by Vergil's days the temple of Jupiter on the Capitoline Hill had literally been gilded (348 and note), and (Servius tells us) a silver statue of the goose (cf. 653 n.) stood on the Capitol.

657. **arcemque tenebant:** the imperfect can be used of actions merely begun or attempted (inceptive or conative, AG §470c), but four lines after *tenebant* is used of Manlius in a different sense, that usage would be strange here. Vergil seems at least to allude to the alternative version of the story, in which the Gauls actually captured the Capitol, which was probably in Ennius fr. 227-8 Sk. = 251-2 W. Cf. Skutsch's note on Ennius, and Horsfall (1981: 306): "the literary evidence for the Gauls' capture of the Capitol stands firm."

658. **et dono...:** night favors the Gauls' attack as it did that of the Greeks in Book 2. But how was this depicted on a shield?

659-60. **aurea caesaries...aurea...auro** (661): gold is just right for the light-colored hair of the Gauls. Reed (2007: 56) notes the golden polyptoton* here as with Dido at 4.138-9, Latinus' horses at 7.278-9, and Chloreus at 11.774. **virgatis...sagulis:** the short cloaks (*sagulis* is a diminutive) are "striped," a meaning developed from the literal meaning of *virgatus*, "of wicker-work." Reed (2007: 56) calls attention to Servius' claim that Vergil alludes to *virga* = *purpura* in Gaulic; Ovid *Ars* 3.269 may allude to Vergilian wordplay with *purpureis...virgis*. **lactea:** Isidore 9.2.104 says that Vergil gives the Gauls "milky-white throats" because the name *Gallus* is derived from Greek *gāla*, "milk," because of the Gauls' skin coloring; cf. O'Hara (2017: 215). Hardie (1986: 121-2) notes that 660 and 10.137 (Ascanius) are the first uses of *lacteus* of flesh, and sees an allusion to an ivory relief on the doors of the Palatine temple of Apollo; this temple will be featured at 720-8.

661. **auro innectuntur:** "refers to the famous Gallic *torques,* the necklace from which Manlius' son got his cognomen Torquatus" (Williams); cf. 653 on Manlius Capitolinus. **quisque... coruscant:** the singular *quisque* with a plural verb is common when a plural subject is implied (AG §317e).

662. **gaesa:** Gaulic word for their weapons in, e.g., Caesar *B.G.* 3.4.1. **protecti:** middle, with *corpora* as direct object or retained accusative (286 n.).

hic exsultantis Salios nudosque Lupercos
lanigerosque apices et lapsa ancilia caelo
extuderat, castae ducebant sacra per urbem   665
pilentis matres in mollibus. hinc procul addit
Tartareas etiam sedes, alta ostia Ditis,
et scelerum poenas, et te, Catilina, minaci
pendentem scopulo Furiarumque ora trementem,
secretosque pios, his dantem iura Catonem.   670

663-6. Roman religious rituals, some with links to events of the early fourth century; Harrison
(1997). **exsultantis Salios:** the adj. glosses the name, as if from *salio*, "leap," or *sal(i)to*, "dance"
(Servius here, Varro *LL* 5.85, Ovid, *F.* 3.387), but also suggests the joyful emotions of religious
celebration. Evander's festival for Hercules included Salii who sing a hymn (285), but here they
appear "in more traditional Roman fashion"; Miller (2014: 451). **Lupercos:** they ran naked
through the city on February 15 in what seems to have been a fertility ritual (close to but not
actually connected to our Valentine's Day). Cf. Livy 1.5, Ovid *F.* 2.267-474, Shakespeare,
Julius Caesar Act 1, Scullard (1981: 76-8); Suet. *Aug.* 31 says that Augustus revived the rite.
lanigeros...: back to the Salii, who like the *flamines* wore conical headpieces topped by a tuft
of wool. Miller (2014: 452) notes that both the *apex* and *ancile* appear together on an Augustan
coin of 17 BCE. **lapsa ancilia caelo:** in Livy 1.20 Rome's second king Numa founds the priest-
hood of the Salii and puts them in charge of the twelve figure-eight-shaped shields called
ancilia; Ovid *F.* 3.351-88 tells how a shield descended from heaven to Numa as a pledge of
Jupiter's support for Rome, and he made multiple copies to foil any plot to steal the real one. In
7.187-9 Vergil depicts Latinus' grandfather Picus with an *ancile*. **castae...:** after the capture
of Veii (about 395 BCE), the Roman matrons contributed their jewelry to enable Camillus to
fulfil his vow of building a temple to Apollo, and in thanks the senate decreed *ut pilento ad
sacra...uterentur* (Livy 5.25; cf. Ovid *Fasti* 1.617-36). The *pilentum* was a covered two-wheeled
carriage. **mollibus:** i.e., cushioned, as in 11.64 *molle feretrum*.

666-70. Jumping centuries ahead to recent history, Vergil briefly sketches the underworld
punishments or reward of one villain and one hero from recent decades. Only these lines and
the description of Actium describe events that post-date Ennius's *Annales*. The shield, like
the Parade of Heroes in Vergil's underworld in Book 6, may stress events that were covered in
Ennius because of the decisive influence of that poet on Romans' conception of their history;
626-731 n., Goldschmidt (2013: 167-79). On the omission of most of Republican history,
see now Feldherr (2014: 301-4). **Catilina:** vocative, in apostrophe*, cf. 643 n. on *Albane*.
Catiline plotted revolution at Rome in 63 BCE, was thwarted by the speeches and actions of
the consul Cicero, and was killed in battle in 62; cf. esp. Sallust, *Catiline* and Cicero's speeches
In Catilinam. **minaci:** not "threatening to fall on him," which is inconsistent with *pendentem*,
but "towering high," cf. 1.162-3 *geminique minantur | in caelum scopuli*. His punishment seems
to be to "hang" chained on a rock like Prometheus, while the Furies torture him. **trementem:**
"trembling at." **his dantem iura:** like Minos in the underworld in *Od.* 11.568-71, Augustus
at *Geo.* 4.562 *per populos dat iura*, Romulus and Remus *Aen.* 1.291-2, Dido 1.507, Saturn
8.322. **Catonem:** the late Republican context and the role as lawgiver means that this is

haec inter tumidi late maris ibat imago
aurea, sed fluctu spumabant caerula cano,
et circum argento clari delphines in orbem
aequora verrebant caudis aestumque secabant.
in medio classis aeratas, Actia bella,   675

---

almost certainly Cato Uticensis, who committed suicide after losing to Caesarian forces in battle in 46 BCE. After death he was a symbol of Republican liberty and resistance to Caesar. Cicero wrote *Cato* praising him, and Sallust's *Catiline* praises both him and Caesar, but Caesar wrote *Anticato*, and later Augustus wrote *Rescripta Bruto de Catoni* (Suet. *Aug.* 85.1). Cf. Hor. *Carm.* 1.12.35-6 *Catonis | nobile letum*, 2.1.23-4 *et cuncta terrarum subacta | praeter atrocem animum Catonis*. Servius' view of the *Aeneid* as simple propaganda makes him claim that Vergil must be referring to Cato the Censor (234-149 BCE) rather than putting in charge of those who are *pius* the man who took up arms against Caesar. Thomas (2001: 202-7) discusses various attempts to delete or distort this passage. For interpretation of this whole underworld scene, see also Zetzel (1996: 310-12). It shares no features with the underworld of *Aeneid* 6.

671-4. **haec inter…**: we now learn that all the scenes described so far have been on the outer portion of the shield, and that within them is a depiction of the sea in gold, white, and sea-blue (for *caerula*, supply *maria*, "the dark blue waters") with dolphins (from [Hes.] *Scut.* 207-15) made to stand out in silver (*argento clari*) swimming around its edge (*et circum...in orbem*). In Hom. *Il.* 18.607-8 "Oceanos" forms the outmost rim of the shield, as it circles the world in ancient thought.

675. **in medio:** the center of the shield; Thomas (1999: 312-20) notes Vergil's Hellenistic practice of calling attention to the middle of ecphrases*, cf. *in medio* at *Ecl.* 3.40 and 46, *Geo.* 3.16 *in medio mihi Caesar erit*, Clausen (2002: 183), Lowrie (2009: 164). **Actia bella:** in loose apposition to *classis*. The naval battle of Actium off the coast of Western Greece in 31 BCE (see map 2), in which Octavian (later Augustus) and Agrippa seemed decisively to defeat the forces of Antony and Cleopatra, established Octavian as sole ruler of the Roman world. In reality the actual battle was a meager affair after a series of smaller victories by Agrippa leading up to it, but afterwards Octavian had the upper hand and never relinquished it; Carter (1970), Gurval (1995: 2), Pelling (1996: 54-9). For descriptions of the battle, cf. Hor. *Carm.* 1.37, *Epod.* 1 and 9; Prop. 3.11, 4.6, and 2.34.59-66 where the vocabulary suggests familiarity with an early version of parts of the *Aeneid*. Vergil's depiction stresses the conflict of the Italian West versus the decadent East as a clear battle of good versus evil, though with some more complex undertones. It praises both Augustus and Agrippa by name while asserting that Antony had mainly foreign, "barbaric" support, and it has the Roman gods enter the fray against the horrible Egyptian gods, all against a backdrop suggestive of gigantomachy and stressing the cosmic consequences of the victory. Specific echoes also link Augustus and Aeneas (666-70 n., 680 n.). On the depiction of Actium, see Hardie (1986: index s.v. *Actium*), Quint (1993: 21-49), Gurval (1995), Toll (1997), Zetzel (1997: 199), Putnam (1998: 138-49), Miller (2009: 54-94), Feldherr (2014).

cernere erat, totumque instructo Marte videres
fervere Leucaten auroque effulgere fluctus.
hinc Augustus agens Italos in proelia Caesar
cum patribus populoque, penatibus et magnis dis,
stans celsa in puppi, geminas cui tempora flammas   680

676-7. **erat:** "it was possible," a poetic usage developed from Greek (Smyth (1920: §1985)) and found at 6.596 *cernere erat*; *Geo.* 4.447 *neque est te fallere quicquam*. **videres:** cf. 649-51 n. **fervere:** archaic* third conjugation form (*VE* p. 846). **Leucaten:** promontory on the island of Leucas (3.274), some thirty miles north of which the battle took place.

678. **hinc Augustus...Caesar:** the name Augustus (in the *Aeneid* only here and at 6.792, both times at the climax of a prophecy) was not used until 27 BCE, but much of the shield's treatment of Actium and of Augustus' triple triumph conflates chronologically separate events (cf. 720-8 n.). **agens:** there is no finite verb for the pictures of Augustus and Agrippa. **Italos:** Augustus leads Italians, in contrast to Antony, said to command foreigners (*ope barbarica variisque armis* 685), though in fact Antony had many senators with him (679 n). But much of Augustus' success lay in appealing both to Romans and Italians; cf. Toll (1997), Ando (2002), Fletcher (2014), Wimperis (2017) and Aug. *Res Gestae* 25 *iuravit in mea verba tota Italia sponte sua, et me belli quo vici ad Actium ducem depoposcit*. In the *Aeneid*, cf. 8.4-5 *omne...coniurat... Latium* (and 4-6 n.) and Juno's words at 12.827 *sit Romana potens Itala virtute propago*. Aeneas fights against Italians, but in the future Augustus leads them into battle.

679. **cum patribus populoque:** cf. SPQR, *senatus populusque Romanus*; in fact Antony probably had more than three hundred senators (and many Roman soldiers) with him, Octavian seven hundred; cf. Aug. *Res Gestae* 25 for Octavian, Syme (1939: 278) and Reinhold (1988: 89-90) for Antony. **penatibus et magnis dis:** repeated from 3.12 where it is used of Aeneas, thus linking Augustus to him. Both passages look to Enn. *Ann.* 190 Sk. = 193 W, *volentibus cum magnis dis*; the archaic*-sounding rhythm produced by the final monosyllable (see Appendix A on meter) helps the recall. Some sources say that *magni di* is another name for the *penates* or for Samothracian gods associated with them, but on the shield we will see the major Roman gods on Augustus' side (699, 704). Cf. Horsfall (2006) on 3.12, Rebeggiani (2013); Miller (2009: 66) argues for deliberate ambiguity.

680. **stans celsa in puppi:** used of Aeneas as he enters the battle at 10.261, further linking Augustus and Aeneas; cf. also 3.527, of Anchises. At 4.554 Aeneas sleeps *celsa in puppi*, before the second visit of Mercury. **geminas...tempora flammas...vomunt** (681): literal flames or a kind of divine radiance? The image links the passage to several others: the harmless flames on the head that mark Ascanius (2.683-4) and Lavinia (7.71-80), and again Aeneas arriving at the battle carrying this very shield (*ardet apex capiti cristisque a vertice flamma | funditur et vastos umbo vomit aureus ignis* 10.269-70, right after which he is compared to the baleful dog-star). But cf. too passages in which fire is "poured forth" by Turnus' helmet and by Cacus (620 n.); and for another odd connection between Augustus and Cacus, cf. 721-2 n. on *superbis*. Rebeggiani (2013) argues that the flame suggests what we call now St. Elmo's fire: the presence of the Dioscuri Castor and Pollux. On *geminas*, cf. 697 n., with references.

laeta vomunt patriumque aperitur vertice sidus.
parte alia ventis et dis Agrippa secundis
arduus agmen agens, cui, belli insigne superbum,
tempora navali fulgent rostrata corona.
hinc ope barbarica variisque Antonius armis,   685
victor ab Aurorae populis et litore rubro,
Aegyptum virisque Orientis et ultima secum
Bactra vehit, sequiturque (nefas) Aegyptia coniunx.

---

681. **patrium...sidus:** i.e., the "star" of his adopted father Julius Caesar, a comet that appeared during games Octavian held in honor of Caesar a couple of months after his death and was supposed to mark his reception into heaven; cf. *Ecl.* 9.47 *Dionaei...Caesaris astrum, Aen.* 2.692-8, Hor. *Carm.* 1.12.47 *Iulium sidus,* Suet. *Jul.* 88, Plut. *Caes.* 69.3, Pliny *N.H.* 2.93, Prop. 4.6.59, Ramsey and Licht (1997), Pandey (2013).

682. **Agrippa:** M. Vipsanius Agrippa, who ran Augustus' military operations. He commanded the fleet at Actium, was consul in 37 BCE and with Octavian in 28 and 27, controlled Rome in his absence in the mid-20s and when Augustus was ill in 23, and in 21 married Augustus' daughter.

683-4. **arduus:** similar to *stans celsa in puppi* (680), so that Augustus and Agrippa are described in similar ways. **cui...:** the *corona navalis,* a crown adorned with figures of ships' beaks (cf. *rostrata*), was a special distinction, and Sen. *de Ben.* 3.32 and Vell. 2.81 say that Agrippa alone won it for defeating Sextus in 36; but Pliny *N.H.* 16.3 says that Varro was given it by Pompey. **insigne superbum:** used in loose apposition to the whole sense of 684; cf. *tormenti genus* in 487 and see Fordyce's note here for other examples. Line 684 is similar to a golden line*.

685. **ope barbarica:** "with barbarian wealth," i.e., with all the riches of the East, in a phrase borrowed from a description of Priam's palace in Enn. *Androm.* fr. 89 J = trag. fr. 103 W (quoted in Cic. *Tusc.* 1.35). Aeneas, though himself a Trojan, refers to Priam's palace in this way at 2.504 *barbarico postes auro spoliisque superbi;* see Quint (1993: 23-5), Reed (2007: 105-6), and below 721-2 n. on *superbis postibus.* **variis:** cf. 723 *quam variae linguis, habitu tam vestis et armis.* The suggestion here and in 686-8 is that Antony's forces are all in foreign garb with foreign weapons, and develops the theme of West vs. East, though in fact he had 20,000 legionary troops, Roman commanders, and a large following of Roman senators (cf. 679 n.).

686. **victor...:** Antony was partially defeated by the Parthians in 36 BCE, but made a successful attack on Armenia in 34; cf. Carter (1970: 58-61), Pelling (1996: 27-40). Servius suggests that calling him *victor* amplifies Augustus' feat of defeating him. **litore rubro:** i.e., the shore of the *mare Erythraeum,* which is not our Red Sea but the Arabian Sea and Indian Ocean (cf. Hor. *Carm.* 1.35.32 *Oceanoque rubro* and see map 2). Antony had nothing to do with it.

688. **Bactra:** capital of Bactria, a kingdom further east than the Parthians (part of it is now northern Afghanistan; see map 2), mentioned as a land of riches in Augustan poetry (*Geo.* 2.138; Hor. *Carm.* 3.29.28; Prop. 3.1.16, 4.3.63), but Antony and Cleopatra had no connection with

una omnes ruere ac totum spumare reductis
convulsum remis rostrisque tridentibus aequor.   690
alta petunt; pelago credas innare revulsas
Cycladas aut montis concurrere montibus altos,
tanta mole viri turritis puppibus instant.
stuppea flamma manu telisque volatile ferrum
spargitur, arva nova Neptunia caede rubescunt.   695

---

it. Much in the description of Actium and the aftermath is poetic fantasy (cf. 705-6 n., 720-
8 n.). **Aegyptia coniunx:** Roman poets never name Cleopatra: *regina* (696), *mulier, femina*,
or *monstrum* at Prop. 4.6.57, 65; Hor. *Epod*. 9.12, *Carm*. 1.37.21 (though Horace's ode pivots
to show respect for her in its second half). Roman citizens could not legally marry foreigners,
and Antony was married to Octavian's sister when he took up with Cleopatra. On Cleopatra
in Augustan poetry, cf. Keith (2000: 118-22 and index, with further references), Wyke (2007);
on the *Aeneid*, see Hardie (2006).

689. **ruere...spumare:** historic infinitives.

690. Repeated from the boat race at 5.143. **rostrisque tridentibus:** three-pronged beaks on the
prows.

691-2. **credas:** for the second person, cf. 649-51 n. Many sources suggest that Agrippa had
smaller, nimbler ships than Antony (Hor. *Epod*. 1.1-2 *ibis Liburnis inter alta navium,* | *amice,*
propugnacula), but there is no trace of this in Vergil, and the idea may have been a canard
that Augustus promoted to emphasize his victory; cf. Watson (2003: 57-8) on Horace,
with references. Dio 50.33.8 compares attacking the large ships at Actium to assaults on
walled towns, or islands besieged from the sea. Vergil's image of islands ripped from the sea or
mountains crashing into mountains suggests too the warfare of giants, interacting in particular
with Hercules' ripping the top off the Aventine in fighting Cacus (236-40) and more generally
with the theme of gigantomachy in the poem, in which forces of order fight against gigantic
forces of disorder; see 184-279 n., 698 n., Hardie (1986: 100-10), Miller (2009: 68). The
Cyclades torn loose may also suggest the myth of Delos, a floating island until fixed by Apollo
after his birth there (3.73-7).

693. **tanta mole...:** lit. "the men stand on towered decks of such huge bulk," or "so huge are the
towered decks on which the men stand." The line explains the idea in 691-2.

694. **stuppea:** adj., "made of twisted flax or hemp," which would be smeared with pitch and lit
on fire, 7.462-3 *flamma...* | *virgea*. The words *flamma* and *ferrum* form a kind of hendiadys*
for a weapon, the malleolus, consisting of flamable material attached to a weapon that could
be launched by hand, by bow, or by some kind of catapult. "Dio 50.34-5 gives a long and vivid
account of the havoc wrought by Octavian on Antony's ships with fire-bolts and fire-pots"
(Fordyce; cf. also Eden).

695. **arva...Neptunia:** a metaphor perhaps borrowed from Ennius; cf. Cic. *Arat*. 129 *Neptunia*
prata, Enn. *Ann*. 127 Sk. = 149 W (*pont*)*i caerula prata*. **nova:** "new," both "fresh" (cf. the
inceptive *rubescunt*) and "strange"; cf. *recenti* | *caede* 195-6, of Cacus' lair, and for the bloodiness
of the shield, cf. *sanguineam* 622, the slaughter of Mettus at 642-5, and Faber (2000), who
cites the influence of [Hes.] *Scutum*.

regina in mediis patrio vocat agmina sistro,
necdum etiam geminos a tergo respicit anguis.
omnigenumque deum monstra et latrator Anubis
contra Neptunum et Venerem contraque Minervam
tela tenent. saevit medio in certamine Mavors   700
caelatus ferro, tristesque ex aethere Dirae,

---

696. **regina in mediis:** Cleopatra did not in fact take a leading role in the battle but hung back in the rear or just behind the middle; cf. Carter (1970: 217-25), Pelling (1996: 58-9). **patrio vocat:** she is never named, but these two words may provide an etymological gloss of both parts of her name, with the first element linked to Greek *kaleo*, "call," or *kleos*, "fame"; cf. Chaudhuri (2012) who notes that Vergil glosses a name he has called "unspeakable" (*nefas*, 688). **sistro:** a rattle used in the worship of Isis; cf. Prop. 3.11.43 *Romanamque tubam crepitanti pellere sistro*, Lucan 10.63 *terruit illa suo, si fas, Capitolia sistro* (both of Cleopatra).

697. **geminos...anguis:** the historians (and Shakespeare's *Antony and Cleopatra*) speak of one asp or of a self-administered poison; Vergil's twin snakes resonate with the *gemini...* | *...angues* that attack Laocoon (2.203-4), the *geminos...anguis* in Allecto's hair (7.450), and the two snakes sent after baby Hercules (8.289 and note). Horace, *Carm.* 1.37.27 has plural *serpentes* before Vergil; he may have known an early version of *Aeneid* Book 8. Tronson (1998) surveys the evidence; Putnam (1998: 122) discusses "twins" in the poem and on the shield.

698. **omnigenum:** gen. pl., probably from an adj. *omnigenus.* **monstra:** cf. 6.285 *variarum monstra ferarum* and the insults at Plaut. *Poen.* 273 *monstrum mulieris*, Ter. *Eun.* 696 *monstrum homini(s).* Vergil adapts the Homeric theomachy of *Il.* 20.54-75 and the myth of gigantomachy, applied recently to Augustus' imposition of order by Hor. *Carm.* 3.4.42-64; cf. 184-279 n., 691-2 n., Hardie (1986: 87-8, 98-100), Miller (2009: 67-70). **latrator Anubis:** so Prop. 3.11.41 *ausa Iovi nostro latrantem opponere Anubim*; he had the head of a dog. For the monstrous Egyptian gods, cf. Juv. 15.1-8; Miller (2009: 68) cites slurs against Egypt's animal-shaped gods by Octavian (Dio Cassius 50.24.6, 51.16.5, Suet. *Aug.* 93).

699. **Neptunum:** opposed to Troy in the *Iliad* but helpful to Aeneas in *Aen.* 1.124-56 and 5.779-832. Sextus Pompey claimed Neptune's support until he was defeated in 37 and 36 BCE, but Neptune's support for Octavian became part of the iconography of Actium; cf., e.g., Zanker (1988: 97), Miller (2009: 70). With the list of gods, cf. the two amazing hexameters in Ennius, *Ann.* fr. 240-1 Sk. = 60-1 W: *Iuno Vesta Minerva Ceres Diana Venus Mars | Mercurius Iovis Neptunus Volcanus Apollo.*

700. **saevit medio in certamine Mavors:** cf. *Geo.* 1.511 *saevit toto Mars impius orbe*, of the civil (*impius*) war between Octavian and Antony. Mars is not presented on the shield as the father of Romulus who supports the Romans (630-1 and note) but as the god of battle whose nature places him with the Furies, Discord, and Bellona "amid the combat," inspiring both armies. Gurval (1995: 238-9) argues that "the gods that [in 700-3] represent the senselessness, violence, and destruction of war are not allied with Antony and his Eastern throng" and so "the madness of war is not partisan." Miller (2009: 70) tries nevertheless to read Mars and the Dirae as Roman, Discordia and Bellona as Eastern.

701. **Dirae:** identified with the Greek Eumenides, they appear, also with Discordia, at the entrace to the underworld, *ferreique Eumenidum thalami et Discordia demens* (6.280). Juno sends

et scissa gaudens vadit Discordia palla,
quam cum sanguineo sequitur Bellona flagello.
Actius haec cernens arcum intendebat Apollo
desuper: omnis eo terrore Aegyptus et Indi,   705
omnis Arabs, omnes vertebant terga Sabaei.
ipsa videbatur ventis regina vocatis
vela dare et laxos iam iamque immittere funis.

Allecto *dirarum ab sede dearum* to drive Amata and Turnus into the madness of war (7.324),
and at the close of the poem Jupiter sends a Dira to show Turnus and his sister that he is doomed
(12.843-69, 913-14). Syson (2013: 95): "it is never entirely clear whether or to what extent
specific members of the group *Dirae, Erinyes, Eumenides, Furiae, Harpyiae* share an identity
in the poem."

702. **scissa...Discordia palla:** though most of the portrayal of Actium makes it seem as though
Augustus and the Romans are fighting against Antony and foreigners, the mention of the personification* Discordia acknowledges that this is a civil war. Her "torn robe" represents the
division that she causes. Ennius' Discordia at *Ann.* fr. 225 Sk. = 258 W *postquam Discordia
taetra | belli ferratos postes portasque refregit* (quoted in Hor. *Serm.* 1.4.60-1) influenced both
Vergil's portrayal of Allecto (cf. 7.286-640) and the scene in which Juno opens the gates of
War (7.601-22). The Homeric *Eris*, "Strife," *Il.* 4.440-5, is a companion of Ares (Mars) and
also contributes to the picture here.

703. **Bellona:** another personification* of war (*bellum*); cf. 7.319. Her whip suggests the self-
wounding rites practiced by the fanatical devotees of the Eastern goddess with whom Bellona
had become identified; Fordyce; cf. Tib. 1.6.45, with the note of Maltby (2002), *gaudens Bellona
cruentis* at Hor. *Serm.* 2.3.223.

704. **Actius...Apollo:** Apollo long had a temple at Actium (Thuc. 1.29.3), which Augustus
restored and enlarged after his victory (Suet. *Aug.* 19), and he always regarded the deity as his
special patron. On how Augustus and the poets enhanced the position of Apollo in contemporary thought, see Miller (2009: esp. 71-5 on this scene). Aeneas visits Actium at 3.274-89.
Nelis (2001: 354) notes that Apollo shoots an arrow at the giant Tityos in the ecphrasis of
Jason's cloak at Apoll. Rhod. *Arg.* 1.759-62.

705-6. **omnis...omnis...omnes:** tricolon* with anaphora*. **eo terrore:** "at that terror"; i.e., at the
sight of Apollo's death-dealing bow. **Indi... | Sabaei:** Fordyce: "Antony had not drawn troops
either from the Far East or from the region in South Arabia where the Sabaeans inhabited the
country of Sheba, the modern Yemen" (for India and Sheba, see map 2). As with Bactria (688
n.), here and later (720-8 n.) Vergil mentions peoples not involved in Actium. Cf. Mayer
(2012) on Hor. *Carm.* 1.29.3 on "a bungled campaign against the Sabaeans" in 26-25 (or 27)
BCE by the Roman prefect of Egypt, and the false impression given by Augustus in *Res Gestae*
26.5 (cf. Cooley (2009)) that the campaign was successful.

708. **iam iamque:** expresses eager haste; she can hardly wait until the ropes can be set free.

illam inter caedes pallentem morte futura
fecerat ignipotens undis et Iapyge ferri,　　　　　　710
contra autem magno maerentem corpore Nilum
pandentemque sinus et tota veste vocantem
caeruleum in gremium latebrosaque flumina victos.
at Caesar, triplici invectus Romana triumpho
moenia, dis Italis votum immortale sacrabat,　　　　715
maxima ter centum totam delubra per urbem.
laetitia ludisque viae plausuque fremebant;
omnibus in templis matrum chorus, omnibus arae;
ante aras terram caesi stravere iuvenci.

709-13. **pallentem morte futura:** note the alliteration* of *m* in 709-13, the three participles of 711-12, the many mournful spondees in 709 and 711. Cleopatra committed suicide in Alexandria in August of 30 BCE. In 4.644 Dido is *pallida morte futura*, and the echo links the two African queens. **fecerat ignipotens:** our first reference to Vulcan since 665, using the same verb form as in 628 and 630, perhaps hinting through ring-composition that the ecphrasis is nearing its end. **Iapyge:** a west-northwest wind that would assist her flight east towards Egypt, as Horace, *Carm.* 1.3.4 imagines it will bring Vergil to Greece. **contra:** opposite the depiction of the fleeing queen. **sinus:** in one sense the "folds" of his robe (cf. Tiberinus in 33), which the Nile-god spreads wide open to welcome them in their defeat (*victos*), but of course a river will also have bends and bays (*OLD* s.v. *sinus* 10, 11). **latebrosa:** (1) as a place to hide, (2) with reference, as Servius notes, to the mystery of its source, cf. Hor. *Carm.* 4.14.45-6 *fontium qui celat origines | Nilusque.*

714. **triplici...triumpho:** the rest of the shield (714-28) seems to tell how Augustus celebrated on August 13, 14, and 15 of 29 BCE (recall that Aeneas arrived in Pallanteum on Aug. 12; cf. 102 n.) a triumph or victory parade for his victories at Actium, in Dalmatia, and in Alexandria (see names in boxes on map 2, and cf. Suet. *Aug.* 22), although from 720 on the setting will be the Temple of Apollo dedicated a year later (720 n.). On the Roman triumph, cf. Versnel (1970), Beard (2007), Östenberg (2009). Eden (165) thinks Vergil ends with Augustus' triumph because Ennius' *Annales* 15 ended with the triumph of his patron Fulvius Nobilior; cf. Zeztel (1996: 314). **invectus:** "riding into," i.e., in his triumphal carriage.

715-16. **votum...sacrabat:** "made a sacred oath," i.e., made an oath subject to religious sanction; sometimes wrongly thought to mean that he made offerings in keeping with a prior vow. Then 716 *maxima...*is in apposition to *votum.* Cf. Aug. *Res Gestae* 4.20 *duo et octoginta templa deum...consul sextum* (28 BCE)*...refeci,* Suet. *Aug.* 30, Hor. *Carm.* 3.6.1-4, Livy 4.20 *Augustum Caesarem templorum omnium conditorem ac restitutorem,* Ov. *F.* 2.63 *templorum positor, templorum sancte repostor.*

718-19. The depiction is of a *supplicatio,* when temples were opened and visited in thanksgiving; cf. Versnel (1970: 171-3) and *OCD* s.v. *supplicatio. Res Gestae* 4 says that during Augustus' reign they were held fifty-five times for a total of 890 days. **omnibus arae...:** stresses not that there were (of course) altars in every temple, but that by divine skill Vulcan depicted them all. **terram caesi stravere iuvenci:** the thing strewn is usually the object of *sterno,* but here is the

ipse sedens niveo candentis limine Phoebi   720

---

subject, as at Prop. 4.8.76 *sternet harena Forum*. A version of the phrase *caesi iuvenci* occurs three times in the *Georgics*: at 2.537 as a marker of the end of the Golden Age, at 3.23 in the imagined temple to Augustus, and at 4.284 of the animals slaughtered so that bees might miraculously grow from their carcass; cf. Dyson (1996), Putnam (1998: 159).

720-8. Vergil seems to continue the description of the triumph of 29 BCE, but a Roman triumph would and in that case did end at the temple of Jupiter on the Capitol (see map 1). In this "hyperbolic, anachronistic fantasy" (Miller (2009: 208)) Augustus is now in front of the temple dedicated to Apollo on the Palatine (see map 1) over a year later, in October of 28, the temple whose building discharges, after a millennium, the vow made by his ancestor Aeneas to the Apollo of Cumae: *Aen.* 6.69-70 *tum Phoebo et Triviae solido de marmore templum | instituam*; see Miller (2009: 138-41), Hor. *Carm.* 1.31; *Ep.* 1.3.17; Prop. 3.29. That bit of anachrony is topped by the list of *victae gentes*, who do not correspond to the peoples conquered in the three places for which Augustus was awarded a triumph (Actium, Illyria, and Alexandria; see names in boxes on map 2), but instead are presented as proof of Augustan control over most of the known world, naming distant lands and rivers from every corner of the map (see names in bold on map 2, and see 688 n. and 705-6 n. for more exaggerations in naming peoples at Actium). Östenberg (1999) argues that many of the peoples and rivers named here may have appeared in Octavian's triumphal processions even if he had not actually defeated them in battle, which would make the exaggerations his (in rivalry with the triumphs of Pompey and Caesar) and not simply Vergil's or Vulcan's. Some Roman readers may have considered the hyperbole appropriate for Augustus' extensive accomplishments, but others may have wondered why the encomium had to include so many false claims. Quint. *Inst.* 8.6.66-76 describes the thin line that separates effective from excessive hyperbole; the latter, he says, can look ridiculous, and one must consider carefully how far it is appropriate to exaggerate (he cites with approval 691-2 on the Cyclades). In a later age Tacitus would sneer at Domitian's exaggerations of his military successes over peoples he describes as *triumphati magis quam victi* (*Germania* 37). For a positive view of hyperbole in encomium, see Hardie (1986: 241-92) (mainly on hyperbolic expressions describing giants, heroes, and natural phenomena). Another approach would be to link these false claims to the tendency of prophecies in the poem to deceive; cf. 40-1 n., Zetzel (1996; 1997) as well as O'Hara (1990: 172-5; 1997: 78-82)—though neither of my books has much on the shield—and O'Hara (n.d.). On Vergil here, cf. Fordyce on 720ff. ("a crowded catalogue of romantic names...reflecting the vague dreams of distant conquest in which the politic flattery of Augustus' poets indulged"); Eden on 724ff.; Gransden on 722-5, who compares Trajan's column (which however contains no hyperbole); Gurval (1995: 34-6, 242-3); Toll (1997: 45) ("While it is conceivable that many" of Vergil's readers "were ignorant about precisely what forces were present at Actium, multitudes of them had actually witnessed the triumph, and could not have read Vergil's claim that there were Leleges and Geloni in the triumphal procession without sitting up straight in surprise and puzzlement"); Miller (2009: 206-10); Feldherr (2014: 305) (Vergil "makes what Livy defines as poetic subject matter look like history, and historical events look like myth").

720. **niveo:** the temple was made, according to Servius, of white marble. **candentis:** as the sun-god, identified with his white temple, and also glossing the Greek name Phoibos, "bright, radiant"; cf. Hor. *Carm.* 1.2.31 *nube candentes umeros amictus | augur Apollo*. Miller (2009:

dona recognoscit populorum aptatque superbis
postibus; incedunt victae longo ordine gentes,
quam variae linguis, habitu tam vestis et armis.
hic Nomadum genus et discinctos Mulciber Afros,
hic Lelegas Carasque sagittiferosque Gelonos   725

---

209), citing Hardie (1986: 355-6), notes that a "chariot of the sun-god...ornamented the
temple's roof just above where Octavian is sitting."

721-2. recognoscit: Weber (2014) notes that this is a "bureaucratic" word occuring more often in
prose, to describe the actions of magistrates. **aptatque superbis | postibus:** cf. 2.504 *barbarico
postes auro spoliisque superbi*, of Priam's palace as Aeneas looks back on the fall of Troy, and
8.196 *foribusque adfixa superbis*, of the gory skulls outside Cacus' cave. On the curious
intratextuality linking Augustus to Priam and Cacus and *superbia*, cf. Fowler (2000: 54),
Reed (2007: 123-4), Thomas (2001: 206). The adjective is in a sense focalized through the
perspective of the *victae gentes*; recall too that Vulcan who created this shield is the father of
Cacus (198). Cf. also 3.287, where Aeneas dedicates a shield at Actium, *postibus adversis figo*,
before celebrating "Actian games" (cf. 3.278-93).

723. quam variae: cf. 685 *variis* and note. For the sound of foreign languages as a part of triumphs,
cf. Östenberg (2009: 156).

724. Nomadum genus: the wandering tribes (*Geo.* 3.339, *Aen.* 4.320) of northwest Africa, an
area that sided with Antony (Plut. *Ant.* 61, Dio Cassius 50.6.4) but was not involved in the
three victories for which Augustus held his triumph (see map 2). **discinctos:** the *Afri* wore
"unbelted" flowing robes (cf. Livy 35.11.7), but the word also suggests that they are "undisci-
plined" (*OLD* 2) or lacking sword-belts and so "unarmed" of even "effeminate" (Gurval (1995:
242)); cf. a similar ambiguity at 4.41 *Numidae infreni cingunt*. **Mulciber:** Vulcan is called
Mulciber, a name found in Accius, as he shapes the shield. Servius and Macrobius note the
connection with *mulceo*, "stroke, soften"; cf. Clausen (1987: 121) = (2002: 219-20), Putnam
(1998: 155-6). Cf. also (as Putnam does) *mulcere* of the wolf in 634 and note.

725. Lelegas Carasque: this line full of names is metrically odd, with no main caesura, and also
makes suprising claims. The Leleges are a prehistoric people of Asia Minor often associated
with the Carians (*Il.* 10.428-9, Herod. 1.171; cf. map 2), but they had no part in the world of
Augustus or Vergil; cf. the survey by Vergil's contemporary Strabo 7.7.2 ("this tribe disappeared")
and Toll quoted at 720-8 n. Caria had been part of the province of Asia since 129 BCE.
Östenberg (1999; 2009: 148-9) notes that women labeled as legendary Amazons appeared
in Pompey's triumph of 61 BCE. **sagittiferosque Gelonos:** Scythian race on the north of the
Black Sea (see map 2), quiver-bearing in Horace, *Carm.* 3.4.35 *pharetratos Gelonos*, tattooed
in *Geo.* 2.115 *pictosque Gelones*. Horace also associates them with the Euphrates (726, cf. next
note) in a proposal to a friend to sing of Augustus' victories, *Carm.* 2.9.21-4 *Medumque flumen
gentibus additum | victis minores volvere vertices, | intraque praescriptum Gelonos | exiguis equitare
campis.* They had nothing to do with the triumph of 29 BCE, but Vergil's words, like Horace's
published in 23 BCE, may reflect negotiations with the Parthians later in the 20s; cf. Nisbet
and Hubbard (1978: 137-8). Östenberg (1999) suggests instead that the words of Horace and
Vergil mean that Octavian depicted the Geloni and Euphrates in his triumph regardless of
whether he had had actual victories there.

finxerat; Euphrates ibat iam mollior undis,
extremique hominum Morini, Rhenusque bicornis,
indomitique Dahae, et pontem indignatus Araxes.

---

726. **Euphrates ibat:** images of rivers were carried in a triumph (Östenberg (2009: 230-2));
the verb refers ambiguously to the depiction in the triumph and the movement of the river
itself. But if the Euphrates (see map 2) was pacified at all, it was years later; see also previous
note. Scodel and Thomas (1984) note that Vergil mentions the Euphrates six lines from the
end of both *Geo.* 4 (also in a discussion of Augustus) and *Aen.* 8, alluding to Callimachus'
programmatic reference to the Euphrates as a big river symbolic of the epic he disdains to
write, six lines from the end of his *Hymn* 2. Cf. Reed (2007: 123), as well as Feldherr (2014:
290): "The book takes us from a representation of a man looking at a river (Aeneas at the
Tiber), to a representation of a man (Aeneas) looking at a representation of a man (Augustus)
looking at rivers."

727. **extremique...Morini:** Gaulic tribe on coast of modern Belgium and France; see map 2,
and cf. Catullus 11.11-12 *ultimosque Britannos*. **Rhenusque:** 727-8 are marked by the
polysyndeton* of *-que...-que...-que...et*. The Rhine (which separates Germany from Gaul;
see map 2) and the Morini to some extent "simply mark the northern limits of Roman power"
(Eden), but they are the only names of 725-8 attested as part of the triumph of 29 BCE (Dio
Cassius 51.21.6), although a subordinate of Octavian's, Carrinas, also triumphed in 28 BCE
for his victories in this area. Cf. Östenberg (2009: 145-7), O'Hara (n.d.). **bicornis:** having two
mouths. The geographical swerves in 726-8 from east to north and then back to east led Eden
to suggest switching 727 and 728, but Worthington (1986) and Fowler (2000: 282-3) argue
against such a move.

728. **indomitique Dahae:** the adjective is used of Italian *agricolae* at 7.521, and could mean
"til now unconquered," but for that we would expect an expression such as at Horace, *Carm.*
1.29.3-4 *non ante devictis Sabaeae* | *regibus* and 4.14.4 *Cantaber non ante domabilis*, and this
Scythian tribe from east of the Caspian Sea (see map 2) was in fact not conquered by Augustus.
pontem indignatus Araxes: *indignatus* is used at 11.831 and 12.952 (the last line of the poem)
for the deaths of Camilla and Turnus, at 8.649 for the anger of Porsenna, and at *Geo.* 2.162 of
a lake's resentment of Agrippa's alterations of it (cf. Thomas' note). Servius and Servius *auctus*
report unreliable stories that Xerxes and Alexander bridged this violent Armenian River (see
map 2; its name was thought connected to ἀράσσω, "smash"), and that Augustus literally
rebuilt a bridge that the river had destroyed. The bridge is better seen as a Vergilian metaphor
for control of Armenia; cf. Manning (1988), Hardie (1986: 208-9), Feldherr (2014: 299). Quint
(1993: 30) argues that *indignatus* suggests that the control may be impermanent. Augustus did
nothing about Armenia soon after Actium but by 20 BCE a negotiated settlement allowed coins
to be issued with *Armenia capta* on them.

Talia per clipeum Volcani, dona parentis,
miratur rerumque ignarus imagine gaudet   730
attollens umero famamque et fata nepotum.

729-31. *Aeneas delights in the shield, though he does not understand it, and lifts it onto his shoulder.*

729-30. **parentis:** i.e., of Venus. **rerumque:** cf. *res Italas* (626); the genitive may be taken with both *ignarus* and *imagine*. Aeneas marvels at the beauty of the work, though he does not understand the subjects represented by the images, and lifts it onto his shoulders. On Aeneas' ignorance and his response, cf. Johnson (1976: 109-14), Lyne (1987: 209-10), Putnam (1998: 153-4), Lowrie (2009: 161-6), Feldherr (2014: 281-2).

731. **umero:** in Book 2 Aeneas had lifted his father Anchises to his shoulder (*umeros* 721, *sublato...genitore* 804, the last line); here he literally lifts the shield but also metaphorically the destiny of his ancestors. Cf. Hardie (1986: 372-5) on the connection to Atlas, whom Aeneas cites as an ancestor at 137 *aetherios umero qui sustinet orbis*. **famamque et fata:** *-que et* is grand and archaic* (cf. Eden here, Enn. *Ann.* 274 Sk., 216 W *malaque et bona dictu*). The nouns can be read as a hendiadys* for "glorious destiny," or problematized as questioning the link between "reputation" or "report" and "destiny." On *fama*, cf. Hardie (2012) and Syson (2013). Servius reports criticism of the line as superfluous and modern (*neotericus*) and lacking in gravity; modern critics admire "its dignified cadence and diction" (Williams). Clausen (2002: 184) says Servius' comment rightly marks the line as characteristic of post-Homeric poetry, but in a good way: "the line is un-Homeric, profoundly so."

Appendix A: Vergil's Meter[1]

Dactylic hexameter was the meter of Greek epic, and beginning with Ennius' *Annales* (early second century BCE),[2] it became the meter of Roman epic as well. Its basic rhythm can be felt in the following line from the opening of Longfellow's *Evangeline*:

Thís is the fórest priméval. The múrmuring pínes and the hémlocks

Here five dactyls (búm-ba-ba) are followed by a final disyllabic foot. These metrical units (as with English verse more generally) are created through the use of natural word stress to create patterns of stressed and unstressed syllables. Thus a dactyl in English poetry is a stressed syllable followed by two unstressed syllables (e.g., "Thís is the" and "múrmuring"). Classical Latin meter, however, differs in an important way. Metrical feet are based not on word stress but on the quantity of individual syllables (i.e. whether they are long or short). Thus, in Latin a dactyl contains one long syllable followed by two short ones (– ⏑⏑).

As the name indicates, "dactylic hexameter" literally describes a line that contains six (Gr. *hex*) measures or feet (Gr. *metra*) that are dactylic (– ⏑⏑).[3] In actual practice, however, spondees (– –) could substitute for dactyls within the first four feet,[4] and the line's ending was largely regularized as – ⏑⏑/ –x. The Latin dactylic hexameter can thus be notated as follows:

---

1   For more on Vergil's meter, see Jackson Knight (1944: 232-42), Duckworth (1969: 46-62), Nussbaum (1986), Ross (2007: 143-52), and Dainotti (2015).

2   The earliest Latin epics by Livius Andronicus and Naevius were composed in Saturnian verse, a meter that is not fully understood.

3   The word "dactyl" comes from the Greek word *dactylos*, "finger." A metrical dactyl with its long and two short syllables resembles the structure of a finger: the bone from the knuckle to the first joint is longer than the two bones leading to the fingertip.

4   More technically the two short syllables of a dactyl are "contracted" into one long, and a spondee is formed. The word "spondee" comes from a Greek word meaning

119

$$- \widemacron{\smile\smile} \ / \ - \widemacron{\smile\smile} \ / \ - \widemacron{\smile\smile} \ / - \widemacron{\smile\smile} \ / \ - \smile\smile \ / \ - \times$$

(Here, "/" separates metrical feet; "-" = a long syllable; "⌣" = a short syllable; and "x" = an *anceps* ("undecided") syllable, one that could be either long or short, but in an actual line will be one or the other.)

Very rarely (in Book 8 lines 54, 167, 341, 345, 402) a spondee is used in the fifth foot, in which case the line is called "spondaic."

To *scan* a line (i.e., to identify a line's rhythm and meter), long and short syllables must be identified. A syllable can be *long* in two ways: *by nature*, if it contains a vowel that is inherently long or is a diphthong;[5] or *by position*, if it contains a naturally short vowel followed either by a double consonant (*x* or *z*) or, in most cases, by two consonants—even if one or both consonants are in the next word.[6] In general, all other syllables are *short*, although at times a syllable is lengthened in the *arsis*, the first long of a foot that receives a special metrical emphasis known as the *ictus* (see discussion below, and 8.98-100 n., 363 n.). If, however, a word ending in a vowel, diph-thong, or vowel-plus-*m* is followed by a word that begins with a vowel, diphthong, or *h*, the first vowel or diphthong is *elided* (cf. *credo* in 4.12 below; elided syllables are enclosed in parentheses in the examples below). As a result the two syllables merge and are scanned as one—a phenomenon called *elision*. *Elision* occurs frequently in Vergil, though at times a final vowel is left unelided in what is called *hiatus* (there are no examples in Book 8, but see 4.235 *spe inimica*). When an extra syllable at the end of one line is elided before the next, it produces a *hypermetric* line (see 8.228, and the great ex-ample at 4.629). At times, two vowels usually pronounced separately will be

---

"libation," a liquid offering at one time accompanied by solemn verse featuring spondees.

5   We can determine if a vowel is long by nature by looking the word up in a dictionary or vocabulary to see if it has a macron over it or by checking inflected endings in a grammar; for example, some endings, like the first and second declension ablative singular (*-a*, *-o*), are always long; others, like the second declension nominative neuter plural (*-a*), are always short.

6   An exception to this general rule: if a short vowel is followed by a mute consonant (*b, c, d, g, p, t*) and a liquid (*l* or *r*), the resulting syllable can be either short or long. Cf. *Aen.* 2.663 where the first syllables of *patris* and *patrem* are short and long respectively: *natum ante ora pătris, pātrem qui obtruncat ad aras*. It should also be noted that *h* is a breathing, not a consonant; it therefore does not help make a vowel long by position.

pronounced together to make one syllable, in what is called *synizesis* (see 8.66, 292, 372, 553).

By applying these rules, we may scan hexameter lines as follows (8.18-21):

tālĭă / pēr Lătĭ/ūm. quāē / Lāŏmĕ/dōntĭŭs/ hērōs

cūnctă vĭ/dēns māg/nō cū/rārūm / flūctŭăt / āēstū,

ātqu(e) ănĭ/mūm nūnc / hūc cĕlĕ/rēm nūnc / dīvĭdĭt īllūc   20

īn pār/tīsquĕ ră/pīt vărĭ/ās pēr/qu(e) ōmnĭă / vērsăt,

A long syllable generally takes twice as long to pronounce as a short.

The flow of a line is affected not only by its rhythm but also by the placement of word breaks. A word break between metrical feet is called a *diaeresis*, while a word break within a metrical foot is called a *caesura*.[7]

ēxtēm/plō tūr/bāt(ī) ănĭ/mī, sĭmŭl / ōmnĕ tŭ/mūltū

(Aen. 8.4)

quīd strŭăt / hīs cōēp/tīs, quēm, / sī fōr/tūnă sĕ/quātŭr

(8.15)

In 8.4, diaeresis occurs after *simul*, while caesura occurs after each of the other words (except with the elision of *turbati*).[8] In 8.15, diaeresis occurs after *struat* and *quem*, caesura after the other words. In Latin word breaks are important mainly because they affect the interplay between the ictus and accent (see below), but scholars have also drawn attention to how they seem to divide most lines. The most important caesura in any given line often coincides with a sense break and is called the *main* or *principal caesura*.[9] It most frequently falls in the third foot, but also occurs not uncommonly in

---

7   When a *diaeresis* occurs just before the fifth foot, as in *Aen.* 8.4 quoted just below, it is often called a *bucolic diaeresis* because this type of diaeresis was used frequently in pastoral poetry: e.g., *nos patriam fugimus; tu, Tityre,* || *lentus in umbra* (Vergil, *Eclogues* 1.4).

8   In the combinations *qu, gu, su* (e.g., *-que, sanguis, suesco*), note that the *u* is consonantal but that the combinations themselves count as a single consonant for the purposes of scansion.

9   Readers may differ on where (or even if) there is a main caesura in a given line.

the second or fourth (or sometimes both); in 8.4 it occurs in the fourth foot, in 8.15 in the third. The slight pause implied in the main caesura helps shape the movement of each verse by breaking it into two (or more) parts. Here are the first seven lines of the *Aeneid*, scanned and with the principal caesurae marked ("||"):

ārmă vĭ/rūmquĕ că/nō, || Trō/iāē quī / prīmŭs ăb / ōrīs

Ītălĭ/ām fă/tō prŏfŭ/gūs || Lā/vīniăquĕ / vēnĭt

lītŏră, / mūlt(um) īll(e) / ēt tēr/rīs || iăc/tātŭs ĕt / āltō

vī sŭpĕ/rūm, || sāē/vāē mĕmŏ/rēm Iū/nōnĭs ŏb / īrăm,

mūltă quŏ/qu(e) ēt bēl/lō pās/sūs, || dūm / cōndĕrĕt / ūrbĕm

īnfēr/rētquĕ dĕ/ōs Lătĭ/ō, || gĕnŭs / ūndĕ Lă/tīnŭm

Ālbā/nīquĕ pă/trēs || āt/qu(e) āltāē / mŏēnĭă / Rōmāē. (*Aen.* 1.1-7)

(Note that in line 2, *Laviniaque* is pronounced as four (not five) syllables, with the second "i" treated as a consonant; cf. notes on 8.117
Troiugenas, 194 *semihominis*, 599 *abiete*.)

In addition to metrical length, words also have a natural stress accent.[10] This accent will either coincide with or clash with the metrical stress (*ictus*), which falls on the first long syllable of each foot. Coincidence of word accent and metrical stress produces fluidity in the verse; clashing of word accent and metrical stress creates tension. For example:

---

10   Two-syllable words have their accent on their initial syllable: *cáris, dábant, mólis*. For
words of three syllables or longer, the word accent falls on the penult (second to last
or "almost last" syllable), if it is long (*ruébant, iactátos*) but on the antepenult (the
syllable preceding the penult), if the penultima is short (*géntibus, mária, pópulum*).

```
  x      x      /      x      /      /
```
īnfān/dūm, rē/gīnă, iŭ/bēs rĕnŏ/vārĕ dŏ/lōrĕm   (*Aen.* 2.3)

```
/      x      x      x      /      /
```
īmpŭlĭt. / āgnōs/cō vĕtĕ/rīs vēs/tīgĭă / **flām**mae. (*Aen.* 4.23)

(Naturally accented syllables are in boldface; "/" = ictus that coincides
with word accent; "x" = ictus that clashes with word accent.)

In these two lines, there are clashes in three of the first four feet (wherein the
word accent generally does not coincide with the verse accent), followed by
coincidence in the final two feet.[11] In creating clashes, the placement of
"strong" caesurae is particularly important. When a caesura falls after the
first syllable of a foot, it is called "strong" (as after *cano* in 1.1 above); if it falls
after the second syllable in a dactylic foot, it is called "weak" (as after *arma*
in 1.1). In practice, "if a word of two or more syllables ends after the first long
of a foot (that is, producing a strong caesura), there will be a clash between
accent and ictus in that foot," because the final syllable of such words is not
accented.[12] The strong caesurae in 4.23 (above) and in four lines quoted below display this principle well.

One of Vergil's artistic feats was to manage the sequence of clash and
coincidence of ictus and word accent in such a way as to achieve a rhythmically varied and pleasing line. In general we find that Vergilian hexameters
are characterized by the clash of ictus and word accent in the first four feet
and by the coincidence of ictus and word accent in the last two feet, which
results in a pleasing resolution of stress at line end.[13]

```
    /      x      x      x      /      /
```
nec dulcis **natos Veneris** nec **prae**mia **noris?**   (4.33)

---

11   Classical Latin speakers would presumably have pronounced the word accents in
     reading lines, while still maintaining the basic rhythm of hexameter. Otherwise, the
     ictus would have transformed the basic sound of the word.

12   Ross (2007: 146). For word accentuation, see n. 10 (above).

13   Vergil can also make lines stand out and sound unusually smooth or harsh by using
     lines with much coincidence in the first four feet (cf. nn. on 8.393, 549), or by using
     final monosyllables or four-syllable words to produce clash in the fifth or sixth feet
     (cf. notes to 8.81-3, 679).

/   x   x   x   /   /

est(o): **aeg**ram **nul**li **quon**dam flexere mariti,   (4.35)

x   x   x   x   /   /

e**ven**tum **pug**nae **cu**piat, mani**fes**tius **ip**si   (8.16)

x   x   x   /   /   /

Ae**ne**as, **tris**ti tur**ba**tus **pec**tora **bel**lo,   (8.29)

Appendix B: Stylistic Terms

Vergil's skillful use of language is a defining element of his artistry. He often employs rhetorical figures and stylistic devices to reinforce the content of his poetry. Although the initial goals of the beginning student involve knowing how to translate Vergil into good English, careful attention should be paid both to what Vergil says *and* to exactly how he says it in Latin. The following list defines many of the stylistic terms and features that are encountered in studying Vergil. For discussion of the examples cited from Book 8, see the commentary notes. For more information on the terms, see Lanham (1991) and Brogan (1994). Fuller information on Vergilian style can be found in Jackson Knight (1944: 225-341), Camps (1969: 60-74), O'Hara (1997), Conte (2007: 58-122), and Dainotti (2015). Stylistic analyses of Vergilian passages are presented in Horsfall (1995: 237-48) and Hardie (1998: 102-14). This appendix is adapted from those of Ganiban (2008), Perkell (2010), and O'Hara (2011).

Alliteration: the repetition of the initial consonant sound in neighboring words. E.g., *magno misceri murmure* (4.160), *rauco strepuerunt cornua cantu* (8.2). *Alliteration* is often used to create **onomatopoeia**, and occurs frequently with **assonance** and **consonance**.

Anaphora (Gr. "bringing back"): the repetition of a word at the beginning of consecutive sentences or clauses. E.g., *nunc viribus usus, | nunc manibus rapidis, omni nunc arte magistra* (8.441-2).

Apostrophe (Gr. "turning away"): a sudden shift of address to a figure (or idea), absent or present. E.g., *at vos, o superi* (8.572), *distulerant (at tu dictis, Albane, maneres!)* (8.643).

Archaism (Gr. "old", "from the beginnings"): a word, expression, or construction used in a prior phase of Latin (or any language) but no longer current in spoken language or prose. In the *Aeneid*, the effect of archaism is of remoteness, solemnity, elevation, and the evocation of the epic tradition of, e.g., Homer or Ennius. E.g., **alliteration*** (8.3), monosyllabic line-endings (43, 679), the gen. plur. in -*um* (127), *polibant* for *poliebant* (436), and -*que et* (731).

Assonance (Lat. "answer with the same sound"): the repetition of vowel sounds in neighboring words or phrases. E.g., *Amphitryoniades armenta abitumque pararet* (8.214), *incipit et dictis divinum aspirat amorem* (8.373).

Asyndeton (Gr. "unconnected"): the omission of connectives between words, phrases, or sentences. E.g. *extemplo turbati animi, simul omne tumultu | coniurat* (8.4-5), *cognatique patres, tua terris didita fama* (132), *arduus arma tenens* (299).

Consonance (Lat. "sound together with"): the repetition of consonant sounds in neighboring words or phrases. See **alliteration, assonance**.

Dicolon Abundans: see **Theme and Variation.**

Ellipsis (Gr. "leaving out"): the omission of a syntactically necessary word or words, the meaning of which must be inferred. E.g., *turbati animi* (supply *sunt*) (8.4); *advectum* (supply *esse*) (8.11); *secuti* (supply *sunt*) (52); *huic* (supply *est*) (104); *disiectae...moles* (supply *sunt*) (191); *usus* (supply *est*) (441); *suo nomine* (supply *dabit*) (519); *visa* (supply *sunt*) (525); *cecinit missuram...| laturam* (supply *se...esse*) (534-6).

Enallage (Gr. "interchange," also called *hypallage*): a distortion in normal word order, whereby a word, instead of modifying the word to which it belongs in sense, modifies another grammatically. E.g., *et primum Herculeis sopitas ignibus aras* (542), where logically it is the altar and not the fires that should be called Herculean, and *Romuleoque recens horrebat regia culmo* (654), where it is actually the *regia* that is Romulean.

Enjambment (Fr. "crossing over," "straddling"): the continuation of the sense or syntactic unit from one line to the next. E.g., *et primum Herculeis sopitas ignibus aras | excitat* (8.542-3), *huc pater Aeneas et bello lecta iuventus | succedunt* (606-7), *Actius haec cernens arcum intendebat Apollo | desuper* (704-5).

Epanalepsis (Gr. "taking up again"): the repetition of a syntactically unnecessary word or phrase from a preceding line. E.g., *Atlas | idem Atlas* (8.140-1), *Atlantis duri caelum qui vertice fulcit, | Atlantis* (4.247-8).

Etymological wordplay: allusion to the etymological meaning of a word. E.g., *Romana potentia* and the etymology of *Roma* (8.98-100), *auxilium adventumque dei* and the etymology of the Aventine hill (8.201), *Latiumque... latuisset* and the etymology of Latium (8.322-3), *patrio vocat* and the etymology of Cleopatra (8.696). Cf. **Paronomasia**.

Golden Line: in dactylic hexameter, an artful arrangement of two substantive/ adjective pairs with a verb in between. It usually takes the form of ABCab, where Aa and Bb are both adjective-noun phrases, while C is a verb. E.g.,

    A   **B**   **C**   **a**   **b**

aurea purpuream subnectit fibula vestem. (4.139)

Examples in Book 8 involve prepositions or present the nouns and adjectives in a different order: *arma sub adversa posuit radiantia quercu* (616), *Romuleoque recens horrebat regia culmo* (654), *tempora navali fulgent rostrata corona* (684).

Hendiadys (Gr. "one through two"): the expression of one idea through two terms joined by a conjunction. E.g., *toro et villosi pelle leonis* (177) for a "cushion" consisting of a lion-skin, *squamis serpentum auroque*, "with serpent scales of gold" (436).

Hyperbaton (Gr. "transposed"): a distortion of normal word order. E.g., *frenaque bina meus quae nunc habet aurea Pallas* (168), *ipse...Tarchon* (505-6).

Hypotaxis: the frequent subordination of one clause to another, more common in prose than in Latin poetry, except in passages like 8.9-17 that reflect the style of prose used by historians. Contrast **Parataxis**.

Interpretatio: see **Theme and Variation**.

Irony (Gr. "dissembling"): saying one thing but with its opposite implied or understood. Possible examples in Book 8 include 394 where the poet has Venus call Vulcan, whose child she has never borne, *pater* as she asks him for help for her son Aeneas, and 461-2 where the phrase *limine ab alto* is used of Evander's humble home.

Litotes (Gr. "simplicity"): the description of something by negating its opposite. E.g., *haud incerta cano* (49), *haud vatum ignarus* (627).

Metaphor (Gr. "transference"): the application of a word or phrase from one field of meaning to another, thereby suggesting new meanings. E.g., in 224 Vergil is the first to use the metaphor "add wings to his feet" for running swiftly; and at 696 the sea is called *arva...Neptunia.*

Metonymy (Gr. "change of name"): the substitution of one word for another somehow closely related. E.g., *abies* is used for ship (91), *Ceres* and *Bacchus* for bread and wine (181).

Onomatopoeia (Gr. "making of a word" or "name"): the use or formation of words that imitate natural sounds. E.g., *rauco strepuerunt cornua cantu* (2), *secundo defluit amni* (549), *quadripedante putrem sonitu quatit ungula campum* (596).

Parataxis (Gr. "placing side by side"): the sequential ordering of independent clauses (as opposed to **hypotaxis**, the subordination of one clause to another). A famous example is Caesar's *veni, vidi, vici.* An example from *Aen.* 1: *et iam iussa facit, ponuntque ferocia Poeni / corda* (302-3). Though the two halves of the sentence are independent, in sense one is subordinated to the other: "after he has performed the commands, the Phoenicians set aside their fierce hearts." Much of Evander's narrative at 190-267 is set out in a paratactic style. Parataxis is particularly characteristic of Vergil and epic more generally.

Pathetic Fallacy: attributing human emotions (Gr. *pathos,* "feeling, emotion") to nature or to animals. Cf. the examples discussed under **Personification.**

Personification: (Lat. *persona,* "mask"): treating an inanimate object or abstract quality as though it were a living thing. Personification may be felt in the marveling of the woods and waves at 8.91-2, perhaps the reaction of the riverbanks at 240, and how the "walls" of cities sharpen weapons at 385-6.

Polyptoton (Gr. "in many cases"): the repetition of a word in its inflected cases. E.g., *non haec..., has..., hanc* (185-8), *aurea caesaries...aurea...auro* (659-60).

Polysyndeton (Gr. "much-connected"): the repetition or excessive use of conjunctions. E.g., *iramque minasque* (60), *extremique hominum Morini, Rhenusque bicornis, | indomitique Dahae, et pontem indignatus Araxes* (727-8).

Praeteritio (Lat. "passing by"): the figure in which a speaker pretends or claims to "pass over" a topic, but nevertheless discusses it in whole or in part. E.g., *quid memorem infandas caedes, quid facta tyranni | effera?* (483-4).

Simile (Lat. "similar"): a figurative comparison between two different things. It is an important component of epic style. E.g., Aeneas' angst is like flickering light reflected from water (18-25), Pallas is like the star Lucifer (589-91).

Synecdoche (Gr. "understanding one thing with another"): a type of **metonymy** that uses the part for the whole (or the reverse). E.g., the name of one Sicilian tribe, the Sicanae, is used for any inhabitant of Sicily (8.328), and in *fremunt...puppes* (497) the ships are referred to by a word for part of a ship, and are then said to do what men on them do.

Theme and Variation: the restatement of an initial phrase in different language, so that the same action or thing is seen from two slightly different perspectives. E.g., a description of dawn: *postera Phoebea lustrabat lampade terras | umentemque Aurora polo dimoverat umbram* (4.6-7); a possible example is *ut belli signum Laurenti Turnus ab arce | extulit et rauco strepuerunt cornua cantu* (8.1-2).

Transferred Epithet: see **Enallage.**

Tricolon (Gr. "having three limbs"): the grouping of three parallel clauses or phrases. When the third element is the longest, the resulting *tricolon* is called *abundans, crescens,* or *crescendo*. E.g., *non haec..., has..., hanc* (185-8), *quidquid...quod...quantum* (400-1), *nunc...nunc...nunc* (441-2).

Bibliography

Adams, J.N. (1982) *The Latin Sexual Vocabulary*. London.

Adkin, N. (2001) "A Virgilian Crux: *Aeneid* 8.342-43," *American Journal of Philology* 122.4: 527-31.

Adler, E. (2003) *Vergil's Empire: Political Thought in the* Aeneid. Lanham, MD.

Alföldi, A. (1965) *Early Rome and the Latins*. Ann Arbor.

Allen, G. (2000) *Intertextuality*. London.

Anderson, W.S. (2005) *The Art of the* Aeneid. 2nd ed. Wauconda, IL.

Anderson, W.S., and L.N. Quartarone. (eds.) (2002) *Approaches to Teaching Vergil's* Aeneid. New York.

Ando, C. (2002) "Vergil's Italy: Ethnography and Politics in First-Century Rome," pp. 123-42 in D.S. Levene and D.P. Nelis (eds.), *Clio and the Poets: Augustan Poetry and the Traditions of Ancient Historiography*. Mnem. Suppl. 224. Leiden.

Armstrong, D., J. Fish, P.A. Johnston, and M. Skinner. (eds.) (2004) *Vergil, Philodemus, and the Augustans*. Austin.

Austin, R.G. (ed.) (1955) *P. Vergili Maronis Aeneidos Liber Quartus*. Oxford.

———. (ed.) (1971) *P. Vergili Maronis Aeneidos Liber Primus*. Oxford.

Bacon, H.H. (2001) "Mortal Father, Divine Mother. *Aeneid* VI and VIII," pp. 76-85 in S. Spence (ed.), *Poets and Critics Read Vergil*. New Haven.

Barchiesi, A. (1984) *La traccia del modello: effetti omerici nella narrazione virgiliana*. Pisa. Revised edition transl. by I. Marchesi and M. Fox, *Homeric Effects in Vergil's Narrative*. Princeton, 2015.

———. (1997) "Virgilian Narrative: Ecphrasis," pp. 271-81 in Martindale, ed. (1997).

Barker, G., and T. Rasmussen. (1998) *The Etruscans*. Oxford.

Bartsch, S. (1998) "*Ars* and the Man: The Politics of Art in Virgil's *Aeneid*," *Classical Philology* 93.4: 322-42.

Batstone, W.W. (1994) "Cicero's Construction of Consular Ethos in the *First Catilinarian*," *Transactions of the American Philological Association* 124: 211-66.

Beard, M. (1999) "The Erotics of Rape: Livy, Ovid and the Sabine Women," pp. 1-10 in P. Setälä and L. Savunen (eds.), *Female Networks and the Public Sphere in Roman Society. Acta Instituti Romani Finlandiae* 22. Rome.

131

———. (2007) *The Roman Triumph*. Cambridge, MA.

Becker, A.S. (1995) *The Shield of Achilles and the Poetics of Ekphrasis*. Lanham, MD.

Behr, F. (2005) "The Narrator's Voice: A Narratological Reappraisal of Apostrophe in Virgil's *Aeneid*," *Arethusa* 38.2: 189-221.

Binder, G. (1971) *Aeneas und Augustus: Interpretationem zum 8. Buch der* Aeneis. Meisenheim.

Bonfante, G., and L. Bonfante. (2002) *The Etruscan Language: An Introduction*. 2nd ed. Manchester.

Boyd, B.W. (1995) "*Non enarrabile textum*: Ecphrastic Trespass and Narrative Ambiguity in the *Aeneid*," *Vergilius* 41: 71-90.

Boyle, A.J. (1999) "*Aeneid* 8: Images of Rome," pp. 148-61 in Perkell, ed. (1999).

———. (2003) "The Canonic Text: Virgil's *Aeneid*," pp. 79-107 in Boyle (ed.), *Roman Epic*. New York.

Briggs, W.W. (1980) *Narrative and Simile from the* Georgics *in the* Aeneid. Leiden.

———. (1981) "Virgil and the Hellenistic Epic," *Aufstieg und Niedergang der römischen Welt* 2.31.2: 948-84.

Brogan, T.V.F. (ed.) (1994) *The New Princeton Handbook of Poetic Terms*. Princeton.

Brown, R. (1987) *Lucretius on Love and Sex: A Commentary on* De rerum natura *IV, 1030-1287 with Prolegomena, Text, and Translation*. Leiden.

———. (1995) "Livy's Sabine Women and the Ideal of Concordia," *Transactions of the American Philological Association* 125: 291-319.

Buchheit, V. (1963) *Vergil über der Sendung Roms: Untersuchung zum Bellum Poenicum und zur* Aeneis. Gymn. Beiheft 3. Heidelberg.

Burke, E. (1958) *A Philosophical Enquiry into the Origin of Our Ideas of the Sublime and Beautiful*. Ed. J. T. Boulton. New York. Originally published 1757.

Burkert, W. (1983) Homo Necans: *The Anthropology of Ancient Greek Sacrificial Ritual and Myth*. Berkeley.

Cairns, F. (1989) *Virgil's Augustan Epic*. Cambridge.

———. (2006) "The Nomenclature of the Tiber in Virgil's *Aeneid*," pp. 65-82 in J. Booth and R. Maltby (eds.), *What's in a Name? The Significance of Proper Names in Classical Latin Literature*. Swansea.

Campbell, G. (2003) *Lucretius on Creation and Evolution: A Commentary on* De rerum natura *Book Five, Lines 772-1104*. Oxford.

Camps, W.A. (1960) *An Introduction to Virgil's* Aeneid. Oxford.

Carter, J.M. (1970) *The Battle of Actium: The Rise & Triumph of Augustus Caesar*. London.

Casali, S. (2006) "The Making of the Shield: Inspiration and Repression in the *Aeneid*," *Greece & Rome* 53.2: 185-204.

———. (2010) "The Development of the Aeneas Legend," pp. 37-51 in Farrell and Putnam, eds. (2010).

Chaudhuri, P. (2012) "Naming Nefas: Cleopatra on the Shield of Aeneas," *Classical Quarterly* 62.1: 223-6.

Claridge, A. (2010) *Rome: An Oxford Archaeological Guide*. 2nd ed. Oxford.

Clausen, W.V. (1987) *Virgil's* Aeneid *and the Tradition of Hellenistic Poetry*. Sather Classical Lectures 51. Berkeley.

———. (1994) *A Commentary on Virgil, Eclogues*. Oxford.

———. (2002) *Vergil's* Aeneid: *Decorum, Allusion and Ideology*. Munich. Revised and expanded version of Clausen (1987).

Clauss, J. (2017) "The Hercules and Cacus Episode in Augustan Literature: Engaging the *Homeric Hymn to Hermes* in Light of Callimachus' and Apollonius' Reception," pp. 55-78 in A. Faulkner, A. Vergados, and A. Schwab (eds.), *The Reception of the Homeric Hymns*. Oxford.

Coarelli, F. (2007) *Rome and Environs: An Archaeological Guide*. Berkeley.

Cohon, R. (1991) "Vergil and Pheidias: The Shield of Aeneas and of Athena Parthenos," *Vergilius* 37: 22-30.

Coleman, R. (1977) *Virgil:* Eclogues. Cambridge.

Commager, S. (ed.) (1966) *Virgil: A Collection of Critical Essays*. Englewood Cliffs, NJ.

Conington, J. (1963) *The Works of Virgil with a Commentary*. Rev. by H. Nettleship. Hildesheim. Repr. of 1883-4 London edition.

Conte, G.B. (1986) *The Rhetoric of Imitation: Genre and Poetic Memory in Virgil and Other Latin Poets*. Trans. C. Segal. Ithaca.

———. (1999) "The Virgilian Paradox: An Epic of Drama and Sentiment," *Proceedings of the Cambridge Philological Society* 45: 17-42.

———. (2007) *The Poetry of Pathos: Studies in Virgilian Epic*. Ed. S.J. Harrison. Oxford.

———. (ed.) (2009) *P. Vergilius Maro: Aeneis*. Berlin.

Cooley, A.E. (ed.) (2009) Res gestae divi Augusti: *Text, Translation and Commentary*. Cambridge.

Crook, J. (1996) "Political History: 30 B.C. to A.D. 14," pp. 70-112 in A. Bowman, E. Champlin, and A. Lintott (eds.), *The Augustan Empire: 43 B.C.–A.D. 69. The Cambridge Ancient History*. Vol. 10. 2nd ed. Cambridge.

Cucchiarelli, A. (2001) "Vergil on Killing Parthenius (*Aen.* 10.748)," *Classical Journal* 97.1: 51-4.

Dainotti, P. (2015) *Word Order and Expressiveness in the* Aeneid. Berlin.

de Grummond, N.T. (2006) *Etruscan Myth, Sacred History, and Legend*. Philadelphia.

de Jong, I.J.F. (2011) "The Shield of Achilles: From Metalepsis to Mise en Abyme," *Ramus* 4: 1-14.

Dekel, E. (2012) *Virgil's Homeric Lens*. Routledge Monographs in Classical Studies. New York.

Donlan, W. (1982) "Reciprocities in Homer," *Classical World* 75.3: 137-75.

Duckworth, G.E. (1957). "The *Aeneid* as a Trilogy," *Transactions of the American Philological Association* 88: 1-10.

Duncan, G. (2003) "The Hercules/Cacus Episode in *Aeneid* VIII: *monumentum rerum Augusti*," *AH* 33.1: 18-30.

Dyson, J.T. (1996) "*Caesi iuvenci* and *pietas impia* in Virgil," *Classical Journal* 91.3: 277-86.

———. (1997) "*Fluctus irarum, fluctus curarum*: Lucretian *religio* in the *Aeneid*," *American Journal of Philology* 118.3: 449-57.

Eden, P. T. (1975) *A Commentary on Virgil*: Aeneid *VIII*, Mnem. Suppl. 35. Leiden.

Edmunds, L. (2001) *Intertextuality and the Reading of Roman Poetry*. Baltimore.

Edward, C. (1993) *The Politics of Immorality in Ancient Rome*. Cambridge.

———. (1996) *Writing Rome: Textual Approaches to the City*. Cambridge.

Eigler, U. (1994) "*Non enarrabile textum* (Verg. *Aen*. 8, 625): Servius und die romische Geschichte bei Vergil," *Aevum* 68.1: 147-64.

Ellis, V.E. (1985) "The Poetic Map of Rome in Virgil *Aeneid* 8." M. Litt. thesis, University of Newcastle upon Tyne.

Faber, R. (2000) "Vergil's 'Shield of Aeneas' (*Aeneid* 8.617-731) and the *Shield of Heracles*," *Mnemosyne* 53: 49-57.

Fantuzzi, M. (2012) *Achilles in Love: Intertextual Studies*. Oxford.

Farrell, J. (1991) *Vergil's* Georgics *and the Traditions of Ancient Epic: The Art of Allusion in Literary History*. Oxford.

———. (1994) "The Structure of Lucretius' 'Anthropology' (*DRN* 5.771-1457)," *Materiali e discussioni per l'analisi dei testi classici* 33: 81-95.

———. (1997) "The Virgilian Intertext," pp. 222-38 in Martindale, ed. (1997).

———. (2005) "The Augustan Period: 40 BC-AD 14," pp. 44-57 in S.J. Harrison (ed.), *A Companion to Latin Literature*. Oxford.

Farrell, J., and M.C.J. Putnam (eds.). (2010) *A Companion to Vergil's* Aeneid *and Its Tradition*. Malden, MA.

Feeney, D.C. (1991) *The Gods in Epic: Poets and Critics of the Classical Tradition*. Oxford.

———. (1998) *Literature and Religion at Rome: Cultures, Contexts, and Beliefs*. Cambridge.

———. (2007) *Caesar's Calendar: Ancient Time and the Beginnings of History*. Sather Classical Lectures 65. Berkeley.

Feldherr, A. (2014) "Viewing Myth and History on the Shield of Aeneas," *Classical Antiquity* 33.2: 281-318.

Ferenczi, A. (1998-1999) "The Double-Faced Hercules in the Cacus-Episode of the *Aeneid*," *ACD* 34-35: 327-34.

Fletcher, K. (2006) "Vergil's Italian Diomedes," *American Journal of Philology* 127.2: 219-59.

———. (2014) *Finding Italy: Travel, Nation, and Colonization in Vergil's* Aeneid. Ann Arbor.

Fontenrose, J. (1959) *Python: A Study of Delphic Myth and Its Origins*. Berkeley.

Fordyce, C.J. (1977) *P. Vergili Maronis Aeneidos libri VII-VIII with a Commentary*. Ed. J.D. Christie. Oxford.

Forsythe, G. (2005) *A Critical History of Early Rome: From Prehistory to the First Punic War*. Berkeley.

Foster, F. (2013) "Virgilising Rome in Late Antiquity: Claudian and Servius," *New Voices in Classical Reception Studies* 8: 65-78.

Fowler, D.P. (1997) "On the Shoulders of Giants: Intertextuality and Classical Studies," *Materiali e discussioni per l'analisi dei testi classici* 39: 13-34.

———. (2000) *Roman Constructions: Readings in Postmodern Latin*. Oxford.

Fowler, W.W. (1917) *Aeneas at the Site of Rome: Observations on the Eighth Book of the* Aeneid. Oxford.

Fratantuono, L. (2007) *Madness Unchained: A Reading of Virgil's* Aeneid. Lanham, MD.

Gale, M. (2000) *Virgil on the Nature of Things: The* Georgics, *Lucretius and the Didactic Tradition*. Cambridge.

Galinsky, G.K. (1988) "The Anger of Aeneas," *American Journal of Philology* 109: 321-48.

———. (1990) "Hercules in the *Aeneid*," pp. 277-94 in Harrison, ed. (1990).

———. (1996) *Augustan Culture: An Interpretive Introduction*. Princeton.

———. (2003) "Greek and Roman Drama and the *Aeneid*," pp. 275-94 in D. Braund and C. Gill (eds.), *Myth, History, and Culture in Republican Rome: Studies in Honour of T. P. Wiseman*. Exeter.

———. (ed.) (2005) *The Cambridge Companion to the Age of Augustus*. Cambridge.

Ganiban, R. (2009) *Vergil:* Aeneid *Book 1*. Newburyport, MA.

Gantz, T. (1993) *Early Greek Myth*. Baltimore.

Gaskin, R. (1992) "Turnus, Mezentius and the Complexity of Virgil's *Aeneid*," pp. 295-315 in C. Deroux (ed.), *Studies in Latin Literature VI*. Collection Latomus 217. Bruxelles.

George, E.V. (1974) Aeneid *VIII and the* Aitia *of Callimachus*. Mnem. Suppl. 27. Leiden.

Geymonat, M. (ed.) (2008) *P. Vergili Maronis opera. Post Remigium Sabbadini et Aloisium Castiglioni recensuit Marius Geymonat*. Paravia and Rome.

Gildenhard, I. (2004) "Confronting the Beast: From Virgil's Cacus to the Dragons of Cornelis van Haarlem," *Proceedings of the Virgil Society* 25: 27-48.

Goldschmidt, N. (2013) *Shaggy Crowns: Ennius'* Annales *and Virgil's* Aeneid. Oxford.

Goold, G.P. (1990) "Servius and the Helen Episode," pp. 60-126 in Harrison, ed. (1990). Repr. from *Harvard Studies in Classical Philology* 74 (1970): 101-68.

———. (2002) "Hypermeter and Elision in Virgil," pp. 76-89 in J.F. Miller, C. Damon, and K.S. Myers (eds.), *Vertis in usum: Studies in Honor of Edward Courtney.* Beiträge zur Altertumskunde 161. Munich.

Görler, W. (1999) "Rowing Strokes: Tentative Considerations on 'Shifting' Objects in Virgil and Elsewhere," pp. 269-86 in R. Mayer and J.N. Adams (eds.), *Aspects of the Language of Latin Poetry.* London.

Grandazzi, A. (1997) *The Foundation of Rome: Myth and History.* Trans. J.M. Todd. Ithaca.

Gransden, K.W. (1976) *Virgil.* Aeneid *Book VIII.* Cambridge.

———. (1984) *Virgil's* Iliad: *An Essay on Epic Narrative.* Cambridge.

Green, S.J. (2004) *Ovid,* Fasti *1: A Commentary.* Leiden.

Gruen, E. (1992) *Culture and National Identity in Republican Rome.* Ithaca.

Gurval, R.A. (1995) *Actium and Augustus: The Politics and Emotions of Civil War.* Ann Arbor.

Habinek, T. (2005) *The World of Roman Song: From Ritualized Speech to Social Order.* Baltimore.

Hall, J. (2005) *"Arcades his oris*: Greek Projections on the Italian Ethnoscape?" pp. 259-84 in E. Gruen (ed.), *Cultural Borrowings and Ethnic Appropriations in Antiquity.* Stuttgart.

Harder, A. (2012) *Callimachus:* Aetia. 2 vols. Oxford.

Hardie, P.R. (1986) *Virgil's* Aeneid: *Cosmos and Imperium.* Oxford.

———. (1990) "Ovid's Theban History: The First Anti-*Aeneid,*" *Classical Quarterly* 40: 224-35.

———. (1991) "The *Aeneid* and the *Oresteia,*" *Proceedings of the Virgil Society* 20: 29-45.

———. (1993) *The Epic Successors of Virgil: A Study in the Dynamics of a Tradition.* Cambridge.

———. (1994) *Virgil,* Aeneid: *Book IX.* Cambridge.

———. (1997) "Virgil and Tragedy," pp. 312-26 in Martindale, ed. (1997).

———. (1998) *Virgil.* Greece & Rome New Surveys in Classics 28. Oxford.

———. (2006) "Virgil's Ptolemaic Relations," *Journal of Roman Studies* 96: 25-41.

———. (2012) *Rumour and Renown: Representations of 'Fama' in Western Literature.* Cambridge.

Harrison, S.J. (1984) "Evander, Jupiter and Arcadia," *Classical Quarterly* 34: 487-8.

———. (1989) Rev. of Novara (1989). *CR* n.s. 39.2: 390-1.

———. (ed.) (1990) *Oxford Readings in Vergil's* Aeneid. Oxford.

———. (1991) *Vergil,* Aeneid *10: With Introduction, Translation, and Commentary.* Oxford.

———. (1997) "The Survival and Supremacy of Rome: The Unity of the Shield of Aeneas," *Journal of Roman Studies* 87: 70-6.

Heckenlively, T.S. (2013) "*Clipeus Hesiodicus: Aeneid 8* and the *Shield of Heracles,*" *Mnemosyne* 66/4-5: 649-65.

Heffernan, J.A.W. (1993). *Museum of Words: The Poetics of Ekphrasis from Homer to Ashbery.* Chicago.

Heiden, B. (1987) "*Laudes Herculeae:* Suppressed Savagery in the Hymn to Hercules, Verg. *A.* 8.285-305," *American Journal of Philology* 108: 661-71.

Heinze, R. (1993) *Virgil's Epic Technique.* Berkeley. Translation of *Vergils epische Technik* by H. Harvey, D. Harvey, and F. Robertson (Leipzig, 3rd ed., 1928).

Henderson, J.G.W. (1998) "Lucan: The Word at War," pp. 165-211 in Henderson, *Fighting for Rome: Poets and Caesars, History and Civil War.* New York. Revised from Henderson (1987) *Ramus* 16: 122-64.

Henry, J. (1889) *Aeneidea, or Critical, Exegetical, and Aesthetical Remarks on the* Aeneid. Vol. 3. Dublin.

Heubeck, A., S. West, and J.B. Hainsworth. (1988) *A Commentary on Homer's* Odyssey, *Vol. I: Introduction and Books I-VIII.* Oxford.

Heyworth, S. (2005) "Pastoral," pp. 148-58 in S.J. Harrison (ed.), *A Companion to Latin Literature.* Oxford.

Hickson, F.V. (1993) *Roman Prayer Language: Livy and the* Aeneid *of Vergil.* Stuttgart.

Hinds, S. (1998) *Allusion and Intertext: Dynamics of Appropriation in Roman Poetry.* Cambridge.

Hirtzel, F.A. (ed.) (1900) *P. Vergili Maronis Opera.* Oxford.

Holloway, R.R. (1994) *The Archaeology of Early Rome and Latium.* London.

Horsfall, N. (1971) "Numanus Remulus: Ethnography and Propaganda in *Aeneid* 9.598ff.," *Latomus* 30 (1971): 1108-16. Repr. pp. 305-15 in Harrison, ed. (1990).

———. (1981) "From History to Legend: M. Manlius and the Geese," *Classical Journal* 76.1: 298-311.

———. (1984) Rev. of Small (1982), *Classical Review* 34: 226-9.

———. (1990) "Virgil and the Illusory Footnote," *Proceedings of the Liverpool Latin Seminar* 6: 49-63.

———. (1991) "*Externi duces,*" *Rivista di Filologia e Istruzione Classica* 119: 188-92.

———. (1995) *A Companion to the Study of Virgil.* Leiden.

———. (2000) *Virgil,* Aeneid *7: A Commentary.* Mnemosyne Suppl. 198. Leiden.

————. (2003) *Virgil, Aeneid 11: A Commentary.* Leiden.

————. (2006) *Virgil, Aeneid 3: A Commentary.* Leiden.

————. (2013) *Virgil, Aeneid 6: A Commentary.* Berlin.

————. (2016) *The Epic Distilled: Studies in the Composition of the* Aeneid. Oxford.

Hui, A. (2011) "The Textual City: Epic Walks in Virgil, Lucan, and Petrarch," *Classical Receptions Journal* 3(2): 148-65.

Hunter, R.L. (2006) *The Shadow of Callimachus: Studies in the Reception of Hellenistic Poetry at Rome.* Cambridge.

Huskey, S. (2006) "Ovid's (Mis)Guided Tour of Rome: Some Purposeful Omissions in *Tr.* 3.1," *CJ* 102.1: 17-39.

Jackson Knight, W.F. (1944) *Roman Vergil.* London.

Janko, R. (1992) *The Iliad: A Commentary.* Vol. 4: *Books 13-16.* Cambridge.

Johanson, C. (2009) "Visualizing History: Modeling in the Eternal City," *Visual Resources: An International Journal of Documentation* 25(4): 403-18.

Johnson, W.R. (1976) *Darkness Visible: A Study of Vergil's* Aeneid. Berkeley.

————. (1987) *Momentary Monsters: Lucan and His Heroes.* Ithaca.

————. (2001) "Imaginary Romans: Vergil and the Illusion of National Identity," pp. 3-16 in S. Spence (ed.), *Poets and Critics Read Vergil.* New Haven.

————. (2004) "Robert Lowell's American Aeneas," *Materiali e discussioni per l'analisi dei testi classici* 52: *Re-Presenting Virgil.* Special Issue in Honor of Michael C. J. Putnam, 227-39.

————. (2005) "Introduction," pp. xv-lxxi in *Virgil: Aeneid,* trans. by S. Lombardo. Indianapolis.

Johnston, P.A. (1980) *Vergil's Agricultural Golden Age: A Study of the* Georgics. Leiden.

————. (1996) "Under the Volcano: Volcanic Myth and Metaphor in Vergil's *Aeneid,*" *Vergilius* 42: 55-65.

Jones, A.H.M. (1970) *Augustus.* London.

Joshel, S. (1992) "The Body Female and the Body Politic: Livy's Lucretia and Verginia," pp. 112-30 in A. Richlin (ed.), *Pornography and Representation in Greece and Rome.* Oxford. Repr. pp. 16-90 in L.K. McClure (ed.), *Sexuality and Gender in the Classical World.* Blackwell, 2002.

Kalligeropoulos, D., and S. Vasileiadou. (2008) "The Homeric Automata and Their Implementation," pp. 77-84 in S.A. Paipetis (ed.), *Science and Technology in Homeric Epics.* Patras, Greece.

Kania, R. (2016) "'Unbounded Views': Incomplete Ekphrasis and the Visual Imagination in Virgil," *Ramus* 45.1: 74-101.

Kaster, R.A. (ed.) (2011) *Macrobius: Saturnalia.* Vol. 1: *Books 1-2.* Cambridge, MA.

Keith, A.M. (2000) *Engendering Rome: Women in Latin Epic.* Cambridge.

Kennedy, D. (1992) "'Augustan' and 'Anti-Augustan': Reflections on Terms of Reference," pp. 26-58 in A. Powell (ed.), *Roman Poetry and Propaganda in the Age of Augustus*. Bristol.

Kinsey, T.E. (1990) "Virgil, *Aeneid* VIII, 497-504," *RBPh* 68: 84-5.

Kirk, G.S. (1990) *The* Iliad*: A Commentary*, Vol. 2: *Books 5-8*. Cambridge.

Klodt, C. (2001) *Bescheidene Grosse: Die Herrschergestalt, der Kaiserpalast und die Stadt Rom; Literarische Reflexionen monarchischer Selbstdarstellung*. Göttingen.

Knauer, G.N. (1964a) *Die* Aeneis *und Homer: Studien zur poetischen Technik Vergils mit Listen der Homerzitate in der* Aeneis. Hypomnemata 7. Göttingen.

———. (1964b) "Vergil's *Aeneid* and Homer," *Greek, Roman and Byzantine Studies* 5: 61-84. Repr. pp. 390-412 in S.J. Harrison, ed. (1990), *Oxford Readings in Vergil's* Aeneid. Oxford.

Knox, P.E. (1997) "Savagery in the *Aeneid* and Virgil's Ancient Commentators," *Classical Journal* 92.3: 225-33.

Kondratieff, E. (2014) "Future City in the Heroic Past: Rome, Romans, and Roman Landscapes in *Aeneid* 6-8," pp. 165-228 in A. Kemezis (ed.), *Urban Dreams and Realities in Antiquity: Remains and Representations of the Ancient City*. Leiden.

Kopff, E.C. (1981) "Vergil and the Epic Cycle," *Aufstieg und Niedergang der römischen Welt* 2.31.2: 919-47.

Kraggerud, E. (1997) "*Disiectorum voces poetarum*: On Imitation in Vergil's *Aeneid*," *Symbolae Osloenses* 72: 105-17.

Kristol, S.S. (1990) Labor *and* Fortuna *in Virgil's* Aeneid. New York.

Kron, G. 2013. "Fleshing Out the Demography of Etruria," pp. 56-75 in J. M. Turfa (ed.), *The Etruscan World*. Routledge.

Kronenberg, L. (2005) "Mezentius the Epicurean," *Transactions of the American Philological Association* 135: 403-31.

Labate, M. (2006) "Erotic Aetiology: Romulus, Augustus, and the Sabine Women," pp. 193-215 in R. Gibson, A. Sharrock, and S. Green (eds.), *The Art of Love: Bimillennial Essays on Ovid's* Ars Amatoria *and* Remedia Amoris. Oxford.

Lada-Richards, I. (2006) "*Cum femina primum*…: Venus, Vulcan, and the Politics of Male *mollitia* in *Aeneid* 8," *Helios* 33.1: 27-72.

Laird, A. (1993) "Sounding Out Ecphrasis: Art and Text in Catullus 64," *Journal of Roman Studies* 83: 18-30.

———. (1996) "*Vt figura poesis*: Writing Art and the Art of Writing in Augustan Poetry," pp. 75-102 in J. Elsner (ed.), *Art and Text in Roman Culture*. Cambridge.

Lanham, R.A. (1991) *A Handlist of Rhetorical Terms*. Second edition. Berkeley.

Leach, E.W. (1997) "Venus, Thetis and the Social Construction of Maternal Behavior," *Classical Journal* 92.4: 347-72.

Lenssen, J.G.A.M. (1990) *"Hercules exempli gratia*: De Hercules-Cacus-episode in Vergilius *Aeneis* 8.185-305," *Lampas* 23: 50-73.

Lessing, G.E. (1984) *Laocoon: An Essay on the Limits of Painting and Poetry*. Trans. E.A. McCormick. Baltimore.

Liversidge, M.J.H. (1997) "Virgil in Art," pp. 91-104 (with plates after p. 110) in Martindale, ed. (1997).

Lloyd, C. (1999) "The Evander-Anchises Connection: Fathers, Sons, and Homoerotic Desire in Virgil's *Aeneid*," *Vergilius* 45: 3-21.

Loar, M.P. (2017) "Hercules, Mummius, and the Roman Triumph in *Aeneid* 8," *Classical Philology* 112.1: 45-62.

Lowrie, M. (2009) *Writing, Performance, and Authority in Augustan Rome*. Oxford.

———. (2010) "Vergil and Founding Violence," pp. 391-403 in Farrell and Putnam, eds. (2010).

Lyne, R.O.A.M. (1978) *Ciris: A Poem Attributed to Vergil*. Cambridge.

———. (1987) *Further Voices in Vergil's* Aeneid. Oxford.

———. (1989) *Words and the Poet: Characteristic Techniques of Style in Vergil's* Aeneid. Oxford.

Mahoney, A. (2001) *Allen and Greenough's New Latin Grammar*. Newburyport, MA. Reprint with additional material of 1903 edition.

Maltby, R. (1991) *A Lexicon of Ancient Latin Etymologies*. Leeds.

———. (2002) *Tibullus: Elegies. Text, Introduction and Commentary*. Cambridge.

Manning, S.W. (1988) "Augustus and the Araxes (Virgil, *Aeneid* 8.728 ...*et pontem indignatus Araxes*)," *Liverpool Classical Monthly* 13: 27-9.

Marincola, J. (2010) "Eros and Empire: Virgil and the Historians on Civil War," pp. 183-204 in C. Kraus, J. Marincola, and C. Pelling (eds.), *Ancient Historiography and Its Contexts: Studies in Honour of A. J. Woodman*. Oxford.

Martindale, C. (1993) "Descent into Hell: Reading Ambiguity, or Virgil and the Critics," *Proceedings of the Virgil Society* 21: 111-50.

———. (1993) *Redeeming the Text: Latin Poetry and the Hermeneutics of Reception*. Cambridge.

———. (ed.) (1997) *The Cambridge Companion to Virgil*. Cambridge.

Mastronarde, D.J. (2002) *Euripides: Medea*. Cambridge.

Mayer, R. (2012) *Horace: Odes Book I*. Cambridge.

McCarter, S. (2012) "The Forging of a God: Venus, the Shield of Aeneas, and Callimachus's Hymn to Artemis," *Transactions of the American Philological Association* 142.2: 355-81.

McKay, A.G. (1970) *Vergil's Italy*. Greenwich, CT.

———. (1998) "*Non enarrabile textum?* The Shield of Aeneas and the Triple Triumph of 29 BC: *Aeneid* 8.630-728," pp. 199-221 in Stahl, ed. (1998).

McPhee, B. (n.d.) "Erulus and the Moliones: An Iliadic Intertext in *Aeneid* 8.560-567," forthcoming in *Harvard Studies in Classical Philology.*

Miles, G. (1995) *Livy: Reconstructing Early Rome.* Ithaca.

Miller, J.F. (2009) *Apollo, Augustus, and the Poets.* Cambridge.

———. (2014) "Virgil's Salian Hymn to Hercules," *Classical Journal* 109.4: 439-63.

Milnor, K. (2005) *Gender, Domesticity, and the Age of Augustus: Inventing Private Life.* Oxford.

Morgan, L. (2005) "A Yoke Connecting Baskets: *Odes* 3.14, Hercules, and Italian Unity," *Classical Quarterly* 55: 190-203.

———. (1998) "Assimilation and Civil War: Hercules and Cacus (*Aen.* 8.185-267)," pp. 175-97 in Stahl, ed. (1998).

Mueller, H.-F. (2002) "The Extinction of the Potitii and the Sacred History of Augustan Rome," pp. 313-29 in D.S. Levene and D.P. Nelis (eds.), *Clio and the Poets: Augustan Poetry and the Traditions of Ancient Historiography.* Leiden.

Mynors, R.A.B. (ed.) (1969) *P. Vergili Maronis Opera.* Oxford.

———. (1990) *Virgil. Georgics.* Oxford.

Nakata, S. (2012) "*Egredere o quicumque es*: Genealogical Opportunism and Trojan Identity in the *Aeneid,*" *Phoenix* 66.3/4: 335-63.

Nappa, C. (2005) *Reading after Actium: Vergil's Georgics, Octavian, and Rome.* Ann Arbor.

Nelis, D. (2001) *Vergil's* Aeneid *and the* Argonautica *of Apollonius Rhodius.* Leeds.

Newman, J.K. (2002) "Hercules in the *Aeneid*: The *dementia* of Power," pp. 398-411 in *Hommages à Carl Deroux,* vol. 1: *Poésie.* Collection Latomus 266. Bruxelles.

Nicoll, W.S.M. (1988) "The Sacrifice of Palinurus." *CQ* 38: 459-72.

Nisbet, R.G.M., and M. Hubbard. (1970) *A Commentary on Horace* Odes I. Oxford.

———. (1978) *A Commentary on Horace* Odes II. Oxford.

Nisbet, R.G.M., and N. Rudd. (2004) *A Commentary on Horace,* Odes Book III. Oxford.

Nisetich, F. (2001) *The Poems of Callimachus.* Oxford.

Novara, A. (1989) *Poésie virgilienne de la mémoire: questions sur l'histoire dans l'*Enéide 8. Vates 1. Clermont-Ferrand.

Nünlist, R. (2009) *The Ancient Critic at Work: Terms and Concepts of Literary Criticism in Greek Scholia.* Cambridge.

O'Hara, J. (1990) *Death and the Optimistic Prophecy in Vergil's* Aeneid. Princeton.

———. (1993) "Dido as 'Interpreting Character' in *Aeneid* 4.56-66," *Arethusa* 26: 99-114.

———. (1996) "Vergil's Best Reader? Ovidian Commentary on Vergilian Etymological Wordplay," *Classical Journal* 91: 255-76. Repr. pp. 100-22 in P. Knox, ed. (2007), *Oxford Readings in Ovid*. Oxford.

———. (1997) "Virgil's Style," pp. 241-58 in Martindale, ed. (1997).

———. (2001) "Callimachean Influence on Vergilian Etymological Wordplay," *Classical Journal* 96: 369-400.

———. (2007) *Inconsistency in Roman Epic: Studies in Catullus, Lucretius, Vergil, Ovid and Lucan*. Cambridge.

———. (2010) "The Unfinished *Aeneid*?" pp. 96-106 in Farrell and Putnam, eds. (2010).

———. (2011) *Vergil:* Aeneid *Book 4*. Newburyport, MA.

———. (2017) *True Names: Vergil and the Alexandrian Tradition of Etymological Wordplay*. Expanded from 1996 edition. Ann Arbor.

———. (2018) "Evander's Love of Gore and Bloodshed in *Aeneid* 8," forthcoming in M.C. English and L.M. Fratantuono (eds.), *Pushing the Boundaries of* Historia: *Essays on Greek and Roman History and Culture in Honor of Blaise Nagy*. Routledge.

———. (n.d.) "*Triumphati magis quam victi?* Possible Responses to Lying and Exaggeration in *Aeneid* 8, with Special Focus on Aeneas' Shield." Unpublished paper.

Ogilvie, R.M. (1970) *A Commentary on Livy Books 1-5*. Oxford.

Oliensis, E. (2009) *Freud's Rome: Psychoanalysis and Latin Poetry*. Cambridge.

Osgood, J. (2006) *Caesar's Legacy: Civil War and the Emergence of the Roman Empire*. Cambridge.

Östenberg, I. (1999) "Demonstrating the Conquest of the World: The Procession of Peoples and Rivers on the Shield of Aeneas and the Triple Triumph of Octavian in 29 B.C. (*Aen.* 8.722-728)," *Opuscula Romana* 24: 155-62.

———. (2009) *Staging the World: Spoils, Captives, and Representations in the Roman Triumphal Procession*. Oxford.

Otis, B. (1964) *Virgil: A Study in Civilized Poetry*. Oxford.

Page, T.E. (ed.) 1900. *The* Aeneid *of Vergil: Books VII-XII*. London.

Pandey, N.B. (2013) "Caesar's Comet, the Julian Star, and the Invention of Augustus," *Transactions of the American Philological Association* 143.2: 405-49.

Panoussi, V. (2002) "Vergil's Ajax: Allusion, Tragedy, and Heroic Identity in the *Aeneid*," *Classical Antiquity* 21: 95-134.

———. (2009) *Greek Tragedy in Vergil's* Aeneid: *Ritual, Empire, and Intertext*. Cambridge.

Papaioannou, S. (2003) "Founder, Civilizer and Leader: Vergil's Evander and His Role in the Origins of Rome," *Mnemosyne* 56: 680-702.

Papanghelis, T.D. (1993) "A Note on *Aeneid* 8.514-517," *Classical Quarterly* 43: 339-41.

Parkes, R. (2007) "Where Was Hercules? A Note on Vergil *Aeneid* 8.201-212," *Vergilius* 53: 102-5.

———. (2009) "Hercules and the Centaurs: Reading Statius with Vergil and Ovid," *Classical Philology* 104.4: 476-94.

Parry, A. (1966) "The Two Voices of Vergil's *Aeneid*," pp. 107-23 in Commager, ed. (1966). Repr. from *Arion* 2 (1963): 266-80.

Pavlock, B. (1985) "Epic and Tragedy in Vergil's Nisus and Euryalus Episode," *Transactions of the American Philological Association* 115: 207-24.

Pease, A.S. (1979) *M. Tulli Ciceronis De Natura Deorum*. 2 vols. New York. Reprint of Cambridge, MA. 1958 edition.

Pelling, C. (1996) "The Triumviral Period," pp. 1-69 in A. Bowman, E. Champlin, and A. Lintott (eds.), *The Augustan Empire: 43 B.C.–A.D. 69*. The Cambridge Ancient History 10. 2nd ed. Cambridge.

Perkell, C. (1989) *The Poet's Truth: A Study of the Poet in Virgil's* Georgics. Berkeley.

———. (1994) "Ambiguity and Irony: The Last Resort?" *Helios* 21: 63-74.

———. (ed.) (1999) *Reading Vergil's* Aeneid: *An Interpretive Guide*. Norman, OK.

———. (1999) "*Aeneid* 1: An Epic Programme," pp. 29-49 in Perkell, ed. (1999).

———. (2002) "The Golden Age and Its Contradictions in the Poetry of Vergil," *Vergilius* 48: 3-39.

———. (2010) *Vergil:* Aeneid *Book 3*. Newburyport, MA.

Petrini, M. (1997) *The Child and the Hero: Coming of Age in Catullus and Vergil*. Ann Arbor.

Pöschl, V. (1950) *Die Dichtkunst Vergils: Bild und Symbol in der* Aeneis. Innsbruck.

———. (1962) *The Art of Vergil: Image and Symbol in the* Aeneid. Trans. G. Seligson. Ann Arbor.

Powell, A. (ed.) (1992) *Roman Poetry and Propaganda in the Age of Augustus*. Bristol.

Putnam, M.C.J. (1965) *The Poetry of the* Aeneid: *Four Studies in Imaginative Unity and Design*. Cambridge, MA. Repr. Ithaca, 1990.

———. (1979) *Virgil's Poem of the Earth: Studies in the* Georgics. Princeton.

———. (1993) "The Languages of Horace, *Odes* 1.24," *Classical Journal* 88.2: 123-35.

———. (1995) *Virgil's* Aeneid: *Interpretation and Influence*. Chapel Hill.

———. (1998) *Virgil's Epic Designs: Ekphrasis in the* Aeneid. New Haven.

Quint, D. (1993) *Epic and Empire: Politics and Generic Form from Virgil to Milton*. Princeton.

———. (2015) "Culture and Nature in Book 8 of the *Aeneid*," *Materiali e discussioni per l'analisi dei testi classici* 75.2: 9-48.

Race, W.R. (2008) *Apollonius Rhodius:* Argonautica. Cambridge, MA.

Ramsey, J., and A.L. Licht (1997) *The Comet of 44 B.C. and Caesar's Funeral Games.* Atlanta.

Ready, J.L. (2010) "Why Odysseus Strings His Bow," *Greek, Roman and Byzantine Studies* 50: 133-57.

Rebeggiani, S. (2013) "Reading the Republican Forum: Virgil's Aeneid, the Dioscuri and the Battle of Lake Regillus," *Classical Philology* 108: 53-69.

Reed, J. (2007) *Virgil's Gaze: Nation and Poetry in the* Aeneid. Ann Arbor.

Rees, R. (1996) "Revisiting Evander at *Aeneid* 8.363," *Classical Quarterly* 46.2: 583-6.

Reinhold, M. (1988) *From Republic to Principate: An Historical Commentary on Cassius Dio.* Atlanta.

Richardson, L., Jr. (1992) *A New Topographical Dictionary of Ancient Rome.* Baltimore.

Rogerson, A. (2017) *Virgil's Ascanius: Imagining the Future in the* Aeneid. Cambridge.

Rosenmeyer, P. (1999) "Tracing *medulla* as a Locus Eroticus in Greek and Latin Poetry," *Arethusa* 32: 19-47.

Ross, D.O., Jr. (1969) *Style and Tradition in Catullus.* Cambridge.

———. (1975). *Backgrounds to Augustan Poetry: Gallus, Elegy and Rome.* Cambridge.

———. (1987) *Virgil's Elements: Physics and Poetry in the* Georgics. Princeton.

———. (2007) *Virgil's* Aeneid: *A Reader's Guide.* Malden, MA.

Rossi, A. (2010) "*Ab urbe condita*: Roman History on the Shield of Aeneas," pp. 145-56 in B.W. Breed, C. Damon, and A. Rossi (eds.), *Citizens of Discord: Rome and Its Civil Wars.* Oxford.

Rudd, N. (1989) *Horace:* Epistles *Book II and* Epistle to the Pisones (Ars Poetica). Cambridge.

Sansone, D. (1991) "Cacus and the Cyclops: An Addendum," *Mnemosyne* 44: 171.

Sayers, D. (ed.) (1928) "The Story of Hercules and Cacus," pp. 56-7 in *Great Short Stories on Detection, Mystery, and Horror.* Vol. 1. London. Also pp. 45-6 in Sayers (1929), *The Omnibus of Crime.* Garden City, NY.

Scodel, R.S., and R.F. Thomas. (1984) "Virgil and the Euphrates," *American Journal of Philology* 105.3: 339.

Scullard, H.H. (1981) *Festivals and Ceremonies of the Roman Republic.* Ithaca.

———. (1982) *From the Gracchi to Nero: A History of Rome from 133 B.C. to A.D. 68.* 5th ed. London.

Secci, D.A. (2013) "Hercules, Cacus and Evander's Myth-Making in *Aeneid* 8," *Harvard Studies in Classical Philology* 107: 197-227.

———. (2014) "On Vergil's Lightning, Comets, and Libyan She Bears," *Classical Quarterly* 64.2: 707-24.

Sedley, D.N. (1998) *Lucretius and the Transformation of Greek Wisdom.* Cambridge.

Shotter, D. (2005) *Augustus Caesar.* 2nd ed. London.

Skutsch, O. (1985) *The Annals of Quintus Ennius*. Oxford.

Small, J.P. (1982) *Cacus and Marsyas in Etrusco-Roman Legend*. Princeton.

Smith, R.A. (2011) *Virgil*. Malden, MA.

Smolenaars, J.J. (1994) *Statius, Thebaid VII: A Commentary*. Leiden.

———. (2004) "A Disturbing Scene from the Marriage of Venus and Vulcan: *Aeneid* 8.370-415," *Vergilius* 50: 96-107.

Smyth, H.W. (1920) *A Greek Grammar for Colleges*. Cambridge, MA.

Soubiran, J. (1966) *L'Élision dans la poésie latine*. Paris.

Southern, P. (1998) *Augustus*. New York.

Sparrow, J. (1931) *Half-Lines and Repetitions in Virgil*. Oxford.

Stafford, E. (2012) *Herakles*. London.

Stahl, H.-P. (ed.) (1998) *Vergil's Aeneid: Augustan Epic and Political Context*. London.

Sutton, D. (1977) "The Greek Origins of the Cacus Myth," *Classical Quarterly* 27.2: 391-3.

Syme, R. (1939) *The Roman Revolution*. Oxford.

Syson, A. (2013) *Fama and Fiction in Vergil's Aeneid*. Columbus, OH.

Taylor, M.E. (1955) "Primitivism in Virgil," *American Journal of Philology* 79.1: 261-78.

Tetlow, J. (1893) *The Eighth Book of Virgil's Aeneid*. Boston.

Thibodeau, P. (2011) *Playing the Farmer: Representations of Rural Life in Vergil's Georgics*. Berkeley.

Thomas, R.F. (1983) "Callimachus, the Victoria Berencies, and Roman Poetry," *Classical Quarterly* 33: 92-113 = (1999) 68-100.

———. (1982) *Lands and Peoples in Roman Poetry: The Ethnographical Tradition*. Cambridge.

———. (1986) "Virgil's *Georgics* and the Art of Reference," *Harvard Studies in Classical Philology* 90: 171-98.

———. (1988) *Virgil: Georgics*. 2 vols. Cambridge.

———. (1999) *Reading Virgil and His Texts: Studies in Intertextuality*. Ann Arbor.

———. (2001) *Virgil and the Augustan Reception*. Cambridge.

———. (2004-5) "Torn between Jupiter and Saturn: Ideology, Rhetoric and Culture Wars in the *Aeneid*," *Classical Journal* 100.2: 121-47.

Thomas, R.F., and J. Ziolkowski. (eds.) (2014) *The Virgil Encyclopedia*. Malden, MA. Abbreviated in the notes as *VE*.

Timpanaro, S. (1967) "Note a interpreti virgiliani antichi," *Rivista di Filologia e Istruzione Classica* 95: 428-45.

Toll, K. (1997) "Making Roman-ness and the *Aeneid*," *Classical Antiquity* 16.1: 34-56.

Tracy, H.L. (1963) "Seven Homecomings," *Vergilius* 9: 28-31.

Tronson, A. (1998) "Vergil, the Augustans, and the Invention of Cleopatra's Suicide: One Asp or Two?" *Vergilius* 44: 31-50.

Tueller, M.A. (2000) "Well-Read Heroes: Quoting the *Aetia* in *Aeneid* 8," *Harvard Studies in Classical Philology* 100: 361-80.

Van Sickle, J. (1992) *A Reading of Virgil's Messianic* Eclogue. New York.

Vernant, J.-P., and P. Vidal-Naquet. (1988) *Myth and Tragedy in Ancient Greece.* Trans. J. Lloyd. New York.

Versnel, H.S. (1970) *Triumphus: An Inquiry into the Origin, Development and Meaning of the Roman Triumph.* Leiden.

Volk, K. (ed.) (2008a) *Vergil's* Eclogues. Oxford.

———. (ed.) (2008b) *Vergil's* Georgics. Oxford.

Wallace-Hadrill, A. (1982) "The Golden Age and Sin in Augustan Ideology," *Past & Present* 95: 19-36.

———. (1993) *Augustan Rome.* London.

———. (2008) *Rome's Cultural Revolution.* Cambridge.

Warmington, E. H. (1935-40) *Remains of Old Latin.* Rev. ed. 4 vols. Cambridge, MA.

Watson, L.C. (2003) *A Commentary on Horace's* Epodes. Oxford.

Weber, C. (1969) "The Diction of Death in Latin Epic," *Agon* 3: 45-68.

———. (2014) "Bureaucratese in Vergil, *Aeneid* 8.721," *Vergilius* 60: 117-25.

West, D.A. (1990a) "Multiple-Correspondence Similes in the *Aeneid*," pp. 429-44 in Harrison, ed. (1990). Repr. from *Journal of Roman Studies* 59 (1969): 40-9.

———. (1990b) "*Cernere erat*: The Shield of Aeneas," pp. 295-304 in Harrison, ed. (1990).

White, P. (1993) *Promised Verse: Poets in the Society of Augustan Rome.* Cambridge, MA.

———. (2005) "Poets in the New Milieu: Realigning," pp. 321-39 in K. Galinsky (ed.), *The Cambridge Companion to the Age of Augustus.* Cambridge.

Wiesen, D.S. (1973) "The Pessimism of the Eighth *Aeneid*," *Latomus* 32: 737-65.

Wigodsky, M. (1972) *Vergil and Early Latin Poetry.* Wiesbaden.

Wilkinson, L.P. (1963) *Golden Latin Artistry.* Cambridge.

———. (1969) *The* Georgics *of Virgil: A Critical Survey.* Cambridge.

Williams, R.D. (1972-3) *Virgil:* Aeneid. 2 vols. London.

Williams, C. (2010) *Roman Homosexuality.* 2nd ed. Orig. pub. 1999. Oxford.

Williams, G.W. (1968) *Tradition and Originality in Roman Poetry.* Oxford.

———. (1983) *Technique and Ideas in the* Aeneid. New Haven.

Wills, J. (1987) "Scyphus, a Homeric *hapax* in Virgil," *American Journal of Philology* 108: 455-7.

———. (1996) *Repetition in Latin Poetry: Figures of Allusion.* Oxford.

Wiltshire, D.C.A. (2012) *"Hopeful Joy": A Study of* Laetus *in Vergil's* Aeneid. Dissertation, University of North Carolina–Chapel Hill.

Wimperis, T. (2017) *Cultural Memory and Constructed Ethnicity in Vergil's* Aeneid. Dissertation, University of North Carolina–Chapel Hill.

Winter, J.G. (1910) *The Myth of Hercules at Rome.* New York.

Wirszubski, C. (1950) Libertas *as a Political Idea at Rome during the Late Republic and Early Principate.* Cambridge.

Wiseman, T.P. (2009) "Cybele, Virgil, and Augustus," pp. 381-98 in J. Edmondson (ed.), *Augustus.* Edinburgh. Reprint of pp. 117-128 in T. Woodman and D. West, eds. (1984), *Poetry and Politics in the Age of Augustus.* Cambridge.

Wlosok, A. (1999) "The Dido Tragedy in Virgil: A Contribution to the Question of the Tragic in the *Aeneid*," pp. 158-81 in P. Hardie (ed.), *Virgil: Critical Assessments of Classical Authors*, vol. 4. Originally published as "Vergils Didotragödie: ein Beitrag zum Problem des Tragischen in der *Aeneis*," pp. 228-50 in H. Görgemanns and E. A. Schmidt, eds. (1976), *Studien zum antiken Epos.* Meisenheim.

Woodman, A.J. (1989) "Virgil the Historian: *Aeneid* 8.626-62 and Livy," pp. 132-45 in J. Diggle, J.B. Hall, and H.D. Jocelyn (eds.), *Studies in Latin Literature and Its Tradition: In Honour of C.O. Brink.* Cambridge.

Worthington, I. (1986) "Should *Aeneid* 8.727 and 728 Be Transposed?" *Eranos* 84: 167-9.

Wyke, M. (2007) "Meretrix Regina: Augustan Cleopatras," pp. 197-243 in Wyke, *The Roman Mistress: Ancient and Modern Representations.* Oxford. Repr. pp. 334-80 in J. Edmondson, ed. (2009), *Augustus.* Edinburgh.

Yardley, J.C. (1981) "Evander's *altum limen*: Virgil *Aen.* 8.461-2," *Eranos* 79: 147-8.

Zanker, P. (1988) *The Power of Images in the Age of Augustus.* Trans. A. Shapiro. Ann Arbor.

Zetzel, J.E.G. (1994) "Looking Backward: Past and Present in the Late Roman Republic," *Pegasus* (Journal of the Exeter University Classics Society) 37: 20-32.

———. (1996) "Natural Law and Poetic Justice: A Carneadean Debate in Cicero and Virgil," *Classical Philology* 91.4: 297-319.

———. (1997) "Rome and Its Traditions," pp. 188-203 in Martindale, ed. (1997).

List of Abbreviations

abl.	= ablative	interrog.	= interrogative
acc.	= accusative	m.	= masculine
adj.	= adjective	meton.	= metonymy
adv.	= adverb	n.	= neuter
cf.	= *confer*, i.e., compare	nom.	= nominative
comp.	= comparative	num.	= numeral
conj.	= conjunction	opp.	= opposed
correl.	= correlative	part.	= participle
dat.	= dative	pass.	= passive
defect.	= defective	perf.	= perfect
dem.	= demonstrative	pers.	= personal
dep.	= deponent	pl.	= plural
dissyl.	= disyllabic	plup.	= pluperfect
dist.	= distributive	poss.	= possessive
enclit.	= enclitic	prep.	= preposition
f.	= feminine	pron.	= pronoun
fig.	= figurative	reflex.	= reflexive
freq.	= frequentative	rel.	= relative
fut.	= future	sc.	= scilicet, "of course," "namely"
gen.	= genitive		
i.e.	= *id est*, that is	sing.	= singular
indecl.	= indeclinable	subst.	= substantive
indef.	= indefinite	superl.	= superlative
indic.	= indicative	tr.	= transitive
inf.	= infinitive	trisyl.	= trisyllabic
intens.	= intensive	v.	= verb
interj.	= interjection	voc.	= vocative
intr.	= intransitive		

Vocabulary for *Aeneid* 8

Adapted from Tetlow (1893) with the aid of Ganiban (2009), Perkell (2010), O'Hara (2011), and the *OLD*.

A

ā, ab, prep. with abl., *from, by.*

abiēs, -etis (abl. **abiete**, trisyl., 599), **f.**, *fir, fir-wood, ship, vessel.*

abigō, -ere, -ēgī, -actum, *drive away;* perf. part. **abactus** (of the night), *driven away, flying.*

abitus, -ūs, m., *going away, departure, removal.*

abiūrō, -āre, -āvī, -ātum, *deny or disavow on oath.*

abrumpō, -ere, -rūpī, -ruptum, *break off.*

absistō, -ere, -stitī, —, *withdraw, depart, cease, draw back, shrink, hesitate.*

abstrahō, -ere, -traxī, -tractum, *drag off, draw away.*

absum, abesse, āfuī, āfutūrum (fut. inf. **āfore**), *be away, be absent.*

āc, conj., short form of **atque**, used only before consonants, *and;* (after words of comparison) *as, than.*

accēdō, -ere, -cessī, -cessūrum, *go to, approach, draw near.*

accendō, -ere, -cendī, -censum, *set fire to, kindle, inflame.*

accessus, -ūs, m., *approach; means or avenue of approach, inlet, entrance.*

accipiō, -ere, -cēpī, -ceptum, *receive, accept, welcome.*

ācer, ācris, ācre, adj., *sharp; eager, spirited.*

acernus, -a, -um, adj., *of maple wood, maple.*

acervus, -ī, m., *heap, pile.*

Achātēs, -ae, m., *companion of Aeneas.*

aciēs, -ēī, f., *edge; line of battle, line, army.*

Actius, -a, -um, adj., *of Actium, Actian.*

acuō, -ere, -uī, -ūtum, *sharpen, whet.*

acūtus, -a, -um, adj., *sharpened, pointed.*

ad, prep. with acc., *to, toward, at, for.*

addō, -ere, -didī, -ditum, *add, join to, give, lend.*

adeō, adv., *to that extent, thus far.*

adeō, -īre, -iī or -īvī, -itum, *go or come to, draw nigh, approach, visit.*

adferō, -ferre, attulī, adlātum, *bring to, bring;* (with reflex. pron.) *make one's way, go, come.*

adfīgō, -ere, -fīxī, -fixum, *fix, fasten.*

(adfor), -fārī, -ātum, defect., *speak to, address, accost.*

adhibeō, -ēre, -uī, -itum, *hold towards; furnish, add, cause to join.*

adiciō, -ere, -iēcī, -iectum, *throw to; add.*

adimō, -ere, -ēmī, -emptum, *take away.*

adiungō, -ere, -iunxī, -iunctum, *join to, attach to, unite with.*

adlābor, -ī, -lapsus, *glide towards.*

adloquor, -ī, -cūtus, *speak to, address.*

adluō, -ere, -luī, —, *wash against, wash.*

adsiduē, adv., *continually, incessantly.*

adsuescō, -ere, -ēvī, -ētum, *make accustomed.*

adsum, adesse, adfuī, —, *be at hand, be present.*

advehō, -ere, -vexī, -vectum, *carry to;* (in pass.) *come to or among, arrive.*

adventus, -ūs, m., *arrival.*

adversus, -a, -um, adj., *facing, in front; adverse, opposing, opposite.*

advertō, -ere, -tī, -sum, *turn towards.*

advocō, -āre, -āvī, -ātum, *call, summon; call to one's aid.*

aedis or aedēs, -is, f., *temple;* (pl.) *house, mansion.*

aegis, -idis (acc. aegida), f., *aegis or shield of Jupiter; aegis or breast plate of Pallas.*

Aegyptius, -a, -um, adj., *of Egypt, Egyptian.*

Aegyptus, -ī, f., *Egypt.*

Aeneadēs, -ae, m., *son or descendant of Aeneas.*

Aenēās, -ae (acc. Aenēān), m., *Aeneas.*

aēnus, -a, -um, adj., *of copper, copper* (adj.), *of bronze, bronze* (adj.).

Aeolius, -a, -um, adj., *of or belonging to Aeolus, god of the winds, Aeolian.*

aequō, -āre, -āvī, -ātum, *make equal, make to match, mate.*

aequor, -oris, n., *level surface, surface* (of the sea or a river), *expanse.*

aerātus, -a, -um, adj., *of bronze, wrought in bronze, with bronze beak.*

āerius, -a, -um, adj., *belonging to the air, aerial; lofty, high.*

aes, aeris, n., *copper, bronze.*

aestuō, -āre, -āvī, -ātum, *burn, rage;* (of waves) *surge, heave, swell.*

aestus, -ūs, m., *(blast of) heat, glow, surge, swell, tide, waves.*

aetās, -ātis, f., *age, lifetime, generation, age, lapse of time, time.*

aeternus, -a, -um, adj., *eternal, everlasting, permanent.*

aethēr, -eris, m., *the upper air, sky, heaven.*

aetherius, -a, -um, adj., *of the upper air, of heaven, celestial, heavenly.*

Aetnaeus, -a, -um, adj., *of or belonging to Aetna, Aetnaean.*

aevum, -ī, n., *lifetime, generation, period of time, age, time.*

Āfer, Āfrī, m., *an African.*

āfore, fut. inf. of absum.

ager, -grī, m., *land, field; territory.*

agmen, -inis, n., *that which is led, band, troop, army, naval force.*

agnoscō, -ere, -gnōvī, -gnitum, *recognize.*

agō, -ere, ēgī, actum, *put in motion, drive;* sē agere, *bestir oneself, move, come.*

agrestis, -e, adj., *of the fields, rustic.*

Agrippa, -ae, m., *Marcus Vipsanius Agrippa, son-in-law of Augustus and his best general.*

Agyllīnus, -a, -um, adj., *of Agylla.*

āiō, defect., *say.*

āla, -ae, f., *wing.*

Alba, -ae, f., *the town of Alba Longa, the mother city of Rome.*

Albānus, -a, -um, adj., *of Alba, Alban.*

Albula, -ae, f., *Albula, ancient name of Tiber.*

albus, -a, -um, adj., *white.*

Alcīdēs, -ae, m., *descendant of Alceus, Hercules.*

āles, -itis (gen. pl. **ālituum**), adj., *winged*; (used subst.) *winged creature, bird.*

aliquandō, adv., *at some time, at one time.*

aliquī, -qua, -quod, indef. adj., *some.*

alius, -a, -ud, adj., *other, another*; **aliī... aliī**, *some...others.*

almus, -a, -um, adj., *nourishing, genial, kindly.*

alō, -ere, aluī, altum or **alitum**, *feed, nourish, sustain, support.*

Alpīnus, -a, -um, adj., *of the Alps, Alpine.*

altāria, -ium, n. pl., *high altar, altar.*

alternus, -a, -um, adj., *one after another, in turn, by turns.*

altus, -a, -um, adj., *high, tall, lofty, deep*; (n. sing. or pl. used subst.) *the deep, the sea.*

ambiguus, -a, -um, adj., *uncertain, doubtful, wavering.*

ambō, ambae, ambō, num. adj., *both.*

amictus, -ūs, m., *outer garment, wrap, mantle, drapery.*

amīcus, -a, -um, adj., *loving, friendly, kindly*; (m. used subst.) *friend.*

āmittō, -ere, -mīsī, -missum, *lose, send or let go away, let go.*

amnis, -is, m., *river, stream; current.*

amoenus, -a, -um, adj., *pleasant, agreeable, charming.*

amor, -ōris, m., *love, affection; eager desire, ardent longing, greed.*

Amphitryōniadēs, -ae, m., *son of Amphitryon, Hercules.*

amplector, -ī, -plexus, *encircle, embrace, enfold, clasp.*

amplexus, -ūs, m., *enfolding, embrace.*

an, conj. introducing the second part of a disjunctive question, *or.*

Anchīsēs, -ae, m., *a Trojan, father of Aeneas.*

Anchīsiadēs, -ae, m., *son of Anchises, i.e., Aeneas.*

ancīle, -is, n., *small shield* (oval, but curved inward at the sides), *sacred shield.*

angō, -ere, — , —, *squeeze, draw tight, compress.*

anguis, -is, m. or **f.**, *serpent.*

angustus, -a, -um, adj., *narrow, contracted, confined.*

anhēlō, -āre, -āvī, -ātum, *pant, gasp for breath.*

anima, -ae, f., *breath, air, wind, blast; life.*

animal, -ālis, n., *living creature, animal.*

animus, -ī, m., *soul; mind, heart, feeling, passion, spirit, courage.*

annus, -ī, m., *year.*

annuus, -a, -um, adj., *lasting a year, annual.*

anser, -eris, m., *goose.*

ante, prep. with acc., (of space) *before, in front of*; (in comparisons) *before, above.*

Antōnius, -ī, m., *Mark Antony, the triumvir, defeated at Actium.*

antrum, -ī, n., *cave, cavern, den, recess.*

Anūbis, -is or **-idis, m.**, *Anubis, Egyptian deity represented with the head of a dog.*

aperiō, -īre, -eruī, -ertum, *open, uncover, lay bare, expose to view.*

apertus, -a, -um, adj., *uncovered, open, clear.*

apex, -icis, m., *tip, point, peak; peaked cap* (worn by flamens and also by the Salii).

Apollō, -inis, m., *god of prophecy, archery, healing, music and poetry.*

appāreō, -ēre, -uī, -itūrum, *come into view, show onself, appear, be seen.*

aptō, -āre, -āvī, -ātum, *fit, attach, fasten, hang up, supply, equip, fit.*

aqua, -ae, f., *water.*

aquōsus, -a, -um, adj., *abounding in water, watery.*

āra, -ae, f., *altar.*

Arabs, -abis, m., *an Arab.*

Araxēs, -is, m., *river of Armenia.*

arbor , -oris, f., *tree.*

Arcadia, -ae, f., *central region of the Peloponnese in Greece.*

Arcadius, -a, -um, adj., *of Arcadia, Arcadian.*

Arcas, -adis (acc. pl. **Arcadǎs**), adj., *Arcadian.*

arceō, -ēre, -uī, —, *shut up, confine, enclose; protect, shield.*

arcus, -ūs, m., *a bow.*

ardeō, -ēre, -sī, -sum, *burn, glow, blaze, kindle.*

arduum, -ī, n., *steep place, steep side, height.*

arduus, -a, -um, adj., *steep, high, towering.*

argenteus, -a, -um, adj., *made of silver.*

argentum, -ī, n., *silver.*

Argīlētum, -ī, n., *district in Rome.*

Argolicus, -a, -um, adj., *of Argolis, Argolic, Greek.*

Argus, -ī, m., *a guest of Evander.*

arma, -ōrum, n., *arms, weapons, armor, war.*

armātus, -a, -um, adj., *armed, in arms.*

armentum, -ī, n., (usually pl.) *cattle for ploughing, cattle, oxen, herd.*

armō, -āre, -āvī, -ātum, *give arms to, furnish with arms, arm.*

ars, artis, f., *skill, art, workmanship, cunning.*

artūs, -uum, m. pl., *joints, limbs, frame.*

arvum, -ī, n., *ploughed land, cultivated land.*

arx, arcis, f., *fortress, stronghold, tower; citadel.*

Ascanius, -ī, m., *son of Aeneas and Creusa* (also called Iulus).

asper, -era, -erum, adj., *rough, rude, harsh, savage, severe.*

aspiciō, -ere, -exī, -ectum, *look at, see.*

aspīrō, -āre, -āvī, -ātum, *breathe upon or into.*

astrum, -ī, n., *heavenly body, star.*

asȳlum, -ī, n., *place of refuge, asylum.*

at, conj., *but.*

āter, -tra, -trum, adj., *black, dark, gloomy, murky.*

Atlantis, -idis, f., *daughter of Atlas, i.e., Electra.*

Atlās, -antis, m., *son of Iapetus and Clymene, father of the Pleiades, and upholder of the pillars that support the heavens.*

atque or (before consonants only) **āc**, conj., *and, and also;* (after words of comparison) *as, than.*

Atrīdēs, -ae, m., *son of Atreus;* (in pl.) *Agamemnon and Menelaus.*

attollō, -ere, — , —, *raise, lift.*

auctor, -ōris, m., *promoter, author, adviser, founder.*

audax, -ācis, adj., *daring, bold.*

audeō, -ēre, ausus, *dare, have the courage, be bold.*

audiō, -īre, -iī or **-īvī, -ītum**, *hear, listen to, hear about.*

auferō, -ferre, abstulī, ablātum,
bear or take away, carry off,
remove.
augustus, -a, -um, adj., *magnified,*
exalted, venerable; (m. used subst.)
Augustus.
aura, -ae, f., (moving) *air, wind.*
aurātus, -a, -um, adj., *gilded.*
aureus, -a, -um, adj., *of gold, golden.*
auris, -is, f., *ear.*
aurōra, -ae, f., *morning, dawn*;
(personified) *Aurora, goddess of*
the morning; (meton.) *the East.*
aurum, -ī, n., *gold.*
Ausonius, -a, -um, adj., *Ausonian,*
Italian.
Auster, -trī, m., *the south wind.*
aut, conj., *or*; **aut . . . aut,** *either . . . or.*
autem, conj., (postpositive and
expressing contrast) *but, however.*
auxilium, -ī, n., *help, assistance,*
reinforcement; (pl.) *auxiliary forces.*
āvellō, -ere, -vellī or **vulsī, -vulsum,**
tear away, tear out.
Aventīnus, -ī, m., *the Aventine, one of*
the seven hills of Rome.
āvertō, -ere, -tī, -sum, *turn away; carry*
off, remove.
axis, -is, m., *axle-tree; celestial axis;*
pole; heaven.

B

Bacchus, -ī, m., *god of wine*; (meton.)
wine.
Bactra, -ōrum, n., *chief city of Bactria.*
barathrum, -ī, n., *pit, abyss, gulf.*
barbaricus, -a, -um, adj., *foreign,*
uncivilized.
bellō, -āre, -āvī, -ātum, *wage or carry*
on war.
Bellōna, -ae, f., *goddess of war.*
bellum, -ī, n., *war.*

bicolor, -ōris, adj., *two-colored.*
bicornis, -e, adj., *two-horned.*
bidens, -entis, adj., *having two teeth*;
(f. used subst.) *animal for sacrifice,*
sheep.
bimembris, -e, adj., *having varied*
limbs, two-formed, hybrid.
bīnī, -ae, -a, distr. num. adj., *two by*
two, two apiece; (for **duo**) *two.*
birēmis, -e, adj., *two-oared*; (f. used
subst.) *ship with two banks of oars,*
bireme.
bis, num. adv., *twice.*
bōs, bŏvis, m. or **f.,** *bull, ox, cow.*
bracchium, -ī, n., *arm.*
Brontēs, -ae, m., *a Cyclops, one of*
Vulcan's workmen.

C

Cācus, -ī, m., *giant monster slain*
by Hercules, a son of Vulcan.
cadāver, -eris, n., *dead body, corpse,*
carcass.
cadō, -ere, cecidī, cāsūrum, *fall; set,*
sink, fade, disappear.
caecus, -a, -um, adj., *blind; dark, thick,*
blinding, pitchy.
caedēs, -is, f., *a cutting down; slaughter,*
bloodshed, carnage, murder.
caedō, -ere, cecīdī, caesum, *cut down;*
kill, slay, slaughter.
caelō, -āre, -āvī, -ātum, *engrave, carve*
in relief, emboss.
caelum, -ī, n., *sky, heaven.*
Caere (usually indecl., but gen.
Caeritis, 597), **n.,** *town in Etruria*
= *Agylla.*
caeruleus, -a, -um, adj., *like the sky,*
blue, dark blue, dark green, sea-
green.
caerulus, -a, -um, adj., *same meanings*
as foregoing word; dark, gloomy;

(n. pl. used subst.) *dark blue waters, sea.*

Caesar, -aris, m., *Caesar, princeps of Rome.*

caesariēs, -ēī, f., *hair, flowing locks.*

cālīgō, -inis, f., *thick air, mist; darkness, gloom.*

calor, -ōris, m., *warmth, heat.*

camīnus, -ī, m., *furnace, forge.*

campus, -ī, m., *plain.*

candens, -entis, adj., *glistening, dazzling, shining, white, bright.*

candidus, -a, -um, adj., *glistening white, white, bright.*

canis, -is, m. or **f.**, *dog.*

canistrum, -ī, (usually pl.) **n.**, *basket of plaited reeds, basket.*

canō, -ere, cecinī, —, *sing; foretell, predict, prophesy in song.*

cantus, -ūs, m., *song, music.*

cānus, -a, -um, adj., *white, whitening, gray.*

capessō, -ere, -īvī or **-iī, - itūrum**, *take eagerly, seize, lay hold of.*

capiō, -ere, cēpī, captum, *take, seize, lay hold of, contain, suffice for.*

Capitōlium, -ī, n., *Capitol, temple of Jupiter on Capitoline hill.*

caput, -itis, n., *head, person, spring, fountain-head.*

carbasus, -ī, f.; pl. **carbasa, -ōrum, n.**, *fine flax or linen.*

Cārēs, -um (acc. **Cāras**), **m.**, *the Carians, from Asia Minor.*

carīna, -ae, f., *keel; boat, ship, vessel.*

Carīnae, -ārum, f., *the Keels, a quarter in Rome between the Caelian and Esquiline hills.*

carmen, -inis, n., *song.*

Carmentālis, -e, adj., *of or belonging to Carmentis, Carmental.*

Carmentis, -is, f., *a prophetic nymph, mother of Evander.*

cārus, -a, -um, adj., *dear, beloved, darling.*

castra, -ōrum, n. pl., *camp, encamped army.*

castus, -a, -um, adj., *pure, spotless, chaste, stainless.*

cāsus, -ūs, m., *fall, chance, mischance, misfortune, disaster.*

catēna, -ae, f., *chain.*

caterva, -ae, f., *throng, band, troop, body of troops.*

Catilīna, -ae, m., *Catiline, whose conspiracy Cicero as consul crushed, BCE 63.*

Catō, -ōnis, m., *great-grandson of Cato the Censor; committed suicide at Utica after being defeated by Caesarians at Thapsus, BCE 46.*

cauda, -ae, f., *tail.*

causa, -ae, f., *cause, reason, motive, argument.*

cavea, -ae, f., *cavity, enclosure;* (at the theatre or circus) *seating area;* (meton.) *amphitheatre, circus.*

caverna, -ae, f., *cavity, cavern, depth, recess.*

cavus, -a, -um, adj., *concave, hollowed out, hollow; valley-forming.*

cēdō, -ere, cessī, cessum, *go away, depart.*

celebrō, -āre, -āvī, -ātum, *throng, frequent, celebrate.*

celer, -eris, -ere, adj., *swift.*

celerō, -āre, -āvī, -ātum, *hasten, quicken, speed.*

celsus, -a, -um, adj., *towering, high, tall, lofty.*

centum, indecl. num. adj., *hundred.*

Cerēs, -eris, f., *goddess of agriculture;* (meton.) *grain, bread.*

cernō, -ere, crēvī, certum, *sift, separate; distinguish, see.*

certāmen, -inis, n., *contest, struggle, dispute.*

certātim, adv., *in competition or rivalry, zealously.*

certus, -a, -um, adj., *assured, settled, fixed, established.*

cervix, -īcis, f., *neck.*

ceterus, -a, -um, adj., *the remaining, the other, the rest of.*

Chalybes, -um, m., *a people of Pontus.*

chalybs, -ybis, m., *steel.*

chlamys, -ydis, f., *cape, mantle, cloak.*

chorus, -ī, m., *dance in a circle, dance; band, troop, company.*

cieō, -ēre, cīvī, citum, *rouse, stir, drive, call up.*

cingō, -ere, -nxī, -nctum, *surround, encompass, gird; crown, wreathe.*

cinis, -eris, m., *ashes, embers.*

Circensis, -e, adj., *of the Circus;* (m. pl. used subst., sc. **ludī**) *games of the Circus Maximus.*

circum, adv. and prep. with acc., *round about, around, about.*

circumdō, -dare, -dedī, -datum, *put round or on.*

circumsonō, -āre, -āvī, -ātum, *thunder about, make resound, make echo.*

circumstō, -stāre, -stetī, or -stitī, —, *stand around, surround, threaten.*

cīvis, -is, m. or f., *citizen, inhabitant; subject.*

clāmor, -ōris, m., *shouting, shout, outcry.*

clangor, -ōris, m., *sound, noise, clang, bray.*

clārus, -a, -um, adj., *clear, bright, illustrious, renowned.*

classis, -is, (abl. **classe** usually, as in 8.79; but **classī** in 8.11) f., *class, division of the people; flee.*

claudō, -ere, -sī, -sum, *shut, close; shut in, confine, bound, hem in.*

clipeus, -ī, m., *round shield, shield.*

coeō, -īre, -īvī or iī, -itum, *go together, assemble, muster.*

coepiō, -ere, coepī, coeptum, *begin.*

coeptum, -ī, n., *a thing begun; beginning, proceeding, undertaking.*

cognātus, -a, -um, adj., *related by blood, kindred.*

cognōmen, -inis, n., *additional name, surname; name.*

cōgō, -ere, coēgī, coactum, *drive together, bring together, collect, muster.*

collis, -is, m., *hill.*

collum, -ī, n., *neck.*

colus, (-ī or -ūs), f., *distaff, staff for holding thread to be spun.*

coma, -ae, f., *hair, locks.*

comes, -itis, m. or f., *companion,* comes īre, *to accompany.*

comitor, -ārī, -ātus sum, *attend as companion, accompany.*

commisceō, -ēre, -miscuī, -mixtum, *mix, mingle, blend.*

commūnis, -e, adj., *common.*

cōmō, -ere, compsī, comptum, *arrange, dress, comb; adorn, deck, wreathe.*

compellō, -āre, -āvī, -ātum, *accost, address.*

complector, -ī, -plexus, *embrace, enfold, entwine, clasp.*

complexus, -ūs, m., *embrace.*

compōnō, -ere, -posuī, -positum, *put, bring, or place together, collect.*

comprimō, -ere, -pressī, -pressum, *press together; check, restrain, subdue.*

concēdō, -ere, -cessī, -cessum, *go away, depart, give way, subside.*

concipiō, -ere, -cēpī, -ceptum, *take hold of, take up or in, receive, conceive.*

concolor, -ōris, adj., *of the same color.*

concurrō, -ere, -currī or **-cucurrī, -cursum,** *run together, meet, join battle.*

concutiō, -ere, -cussī, -cussum, *strike together; shake violently.*

condensus, -a, -um, adj., *crowded, swarming, in close order.*

conditor, -ōris, m., *builder, founder.*

condō, -ere, -didī, -ditum, *build, found; bury, plunge.*

cōnectō, -ere, — , -nexum, *bind together, fasten, connect, entwine.*

confugiō, -ere, -fūgī, —, *flee for refuge, flee.*

congredior, -ī, -gressus, *meet.*

coniunctus, -a, -um, adj., *connected, allied, related.*

coniungō, -ere, -iunxī, -iunctum, *connect, unite, join, link, attach.*

coniunx, -iugis, m. or **f.,** *spouse, husband, wife.*

coniūrō, -āre, -āvī, -ātum, *swear together, take an oath together.*

conlābor, -ī, -lapsus, *fall together, fall in ruins, fall helpless, fall fainting.*

conscendō, -ere, -scendī, -scensum, *mount, climb.*

conscius, -a, -um, adj., *knowing in common, knowing, conscious, aware.*

consessus, -ūs, m., *assembly, crowd.*

consistō, -ere, -stitī, -stitum, *come to a halt, take a position, plant oneself.*

consonō, -āre, -uī, —, *sound together, resound, re-echo.*

conspectus, -a, -um, adj., *conspicuous, striking, distinguished.*

conspiciō, -ere, -spexī, -spectum, *catch sight of, see.*

consurgō, -ere, -surrexī, -surrectum, *rise in a body, start up, rise.*

contemnō, -ere, -tempsī, -temptum, *set slight value upon, scorn, despise.*

contemptor, -ōris, m., *despiser, scorner.*

contrā, adv. and prep. with acc., *over against, facing, opposite.*

convellō, -ere, -vellī, vulsum, *tear up, tear to pieces, plough up.*

cor, cordis, n., *heart.*

cōram, adv., *face to face, in the presence of.*

corniger, -gera, -gerum, adj., *having horns, horned.*

cornū, -ūs, n., *horn; trumpet.*

corōna, -ae, f., *wreath, chaplet, crown.*

corpus, -oris, n., *body, form, frame.*

corripiō, -ere, -uī, -eptum, *catch up, seize, lay hold of.*

coruscō, -āre, -āvī, -ātum, *move to and fro, shake, brandish.*

coruscus, -a, -um, adj., *waving, tremulous, quivering, flashing.*

crastinus, -a, -um, adj., *of tomorrow, tomorrow's.*

creātrix, -īcis, f., *she who gives birth to or produces, mother.*

crēdō, -ere, -didī, -ditum, *give credence, believe, trust, think.*

crescō, -ere, crēvī, crētum, *come into being, rise, be born, grow.*

Crēsius, -a, -um, adj., *of Crete, Cretan.*

crīnis, -is, m., *hair, locks.*

crista, -ae, f., *comb, crest.*
crūdēlis, -e, adj., *cruel, unpitying, ruthless, harsh.*
cruentus, -a, -um, adj., *blood-stained, bloody.*
cruor, -ōris, m., *blood* (flowing from a wound).
cubīle, -is, n., *bed.*
culmen, -inis, n., *top, summit; roof, eaves.*
culmus, -ī, m., *stalk, stem, straw, thatch.*
culta, -ōrum, n., *tilled lands, cultivated lands.*
cultor, -ōris, m., *tiller, farmer.*
cultus, -ūs, m., *tillage, cultivation, civilization.*
cum, conj., *when, since:* **cum prīmum,** *as soon as, at the moment when.*
cum, prep. with abl., *with,* (as ending with abl. of person or rel. pron.) **-cum.**
cumulō, -āre, -āvī, -ātum, *heap, pile, load.*
cunctor, -ārī, -ātus, *delay, linger, hesitate.*
cunctus, -a, -um, adj., *all in a body, each and all, all.*
cupidus, -a, -um, adj., *desirous, eager.*
cupiō, -ere, -īvī, -ītum, *desire, long for, hope for.*
cūra, -ae, f., *attention, care, anxiety, concern, solicitude.*
Curēs, -ium, m. or **f.,** *chief Sabine city;* (meton.) *inhabitant of Cures.*
cūrō, -āre, -āvī, -ātum, *care for, look to, take care of.*
curriculum, -ī, n., *small chariot, course.*
currō, -ere, cucurrī, cursum, *run.*
currus, -ūs, m., *car, chariot.*
cursus, -ūs, m., *running, course, speed.*

custōdiō, -īre, *guard, watch.*
custōs, -ōdis, m. or **f.,** *guard, keeper, guardian, custodian.*
Cyclades, -um (acc. **Cycladăs,** 692), **f.,** *islands near Delos in Aegean sea.*
Cyclops, -ōpis (nom. pl. **Cyclōpĕs**), **m.,** *Cyclops, one-eye giant.*
Cyllēnē, -ēs or **-ae, f.,** *mountain in Arcadia sacred to Mercury.*

D

Dahae, -ārum, m., *Scythian people east of the Caspian sea.*
Danaī, -ōrum (**Danaūm,** 129), **m.,** *descendants or followers of Danaus, the Greeks.*
(daps), dapis, f., *sacrificial feast; food.*
Dardania, -ae, f., *city of Dardanus, Troy.*
Dardanius, -a, -um, adj., *Dardanian, Trojan.*
Dardanus, -ī, m., *son of Jupiter and Electra, ancestor of royal house of Troy.*
Daunius, -a, -um, adj., *Daunian, Apulian, Rutulian.*
dē, prep. with abl., *down from, out of, from, derived from.*
dea, -ae, f., *goddess.*
dēbeō, -ēre, -uī, -itum, *owe, destine, doom.*
decem, indecl. num. adj., *ten.*
dēcolor, -ōris, adj., *discolored, tarnished, dull of hue, degenerate.*
decus, -oris, n., *grace, beauty; ornament, glory, honor.*
dēfendō, -ere, -fendī, -fensum, *ward off, avert, protect, defend, shelter, guard.*
dēfīgō, -ere, -fixī, -fixum, *fasten, fix, fix down.*
dēfluō, -ere, -fluxī, -fluxum, *flow down; float down or along.*

dehinc, adv., *from this time forward; hereupon, then.*

dehiscō, -ere, — , —, *yawn open, open.*

dēiciō, -ere, -iēcī, -iectum, *throw, hurl, or cast down; lower, let fall.*

deinde, adv., *next, then, afterwards, thereafter.*

dēlectus, -a, -um, adj., *chosen, picked, choice.*

dēligō, -ere, -lēgī, -lectum, *choose, select.*

delphīn, -īnis, m., *dolphin.*

dēlūbrum, -ī, n., *temple, shrine.*

dēmissus, -a, -um, adj., *drooping, hanging down.*

dēmō, -ere, dempsī, demptum, *take away, remove, dispel.*

dēnī, -ae, -a, distr. num. adj., *ten each;* (= **decem**) *ten.*

dens, dentis, m., *tooth.*

dēprehendō or **dēprendō, -ere, -dī, -ensum,** *take away, seize upon, catch.*

dēscendō, -ere, -dī, -ensum, *descend.*

dēsecō, -āre, -cuī, -ctum, *cut off, sever.*

dēsertus, -a, -um, adj., *deserted, desolate, abandoned.*

dēsuper, adv., *from above.*

dētegō, -ere, -texī, -tectum, *uncover, unroof, lay bare.*

dēterior, -ius, comp. adj., *lower, worse, meaner, inferior.*

deus, -ī (nom. pl. **dī**; gen. pl. **deūm** or **deōrum**; dat. and abl. pl. **dīs**), m., *god, deity.*

dēvehō, -ere, -vexī, -vectum, *carry down or away;* (in pass.) *go down, descend, sink.*

dīvinciō, -īre, -nxī, -nctum, *bind down, bind fast, subdue.*

dexter, -tera, -terum, or **-tra, -trum,** adj., *right, on the right; favorable, propitious.*

dextra, -ae, f., *right hand.*

dīcō, -ere, dixī, dictum, *say, speak, declare, tell, announce; name, call.*

dictum, -ī, n., *what is said, word, promise, agreement.*

dīdō, dīdere, -didī, -ditum, *spread abroad, diffuse.*

diēs, diēī or **diī, m.,** sometimes **f.** in sing., *day.*

differō, -ferre, distulī, dīlātum, *disperse, scatter, tear asunder; defer, postpone.*

dīgnus, -a, -um, adj., *worthy.*

dīgressus, -ūs, m., *parting, separation.*

dīligō, -ere, -lexī, -lectum, *single out, esteem, love.*

dīmittō, -ere, -mīsī, -missum, *send in different directions; send away, let go away.*

Diomēdēs, -is, m., *king of Argos who fought at Troy; settled in Apulia in Italy.*

dīrus, -a, -um, adj., *of evil omen, dreadful, terrible, awe-inspiring, awful;* **Dīrae, -ārum, f.,** *the Dreadful Ones.*

Dīs, -ītis, m., *god of the infernal regions, Dis, Pluto.*

dīs, dat. and abl. pl. of **deus.**

discēdō, -ere, -cessī, -cessum, *go apart, disperse; go away, depart, take one's leave.*

discessus, -ūs, m., *going apart or away, departure.*

discinctus, -a, -um, adj., *without belt, ungirt.*

discordia, -ae, f., *discord, dissension;* **Discordia,** *goddess of discord.*

disiciō, -ere, -iēcī, -iectum, *throw asunder, fling here and there, scatter, disperse.*

dispergō, -ere, -sī, -sum, *scatter, disperse.*

dissultō, -āre, -āvī, -ātum, *leap apart.*

dīva, -ae, f., *goddess.*

dīvellō, -ere, -vellī, -volsum or -vulsum, *tear apart, tear from or away.*

dīversus, -a, -um, adj., *opposite.*

dīvidō, -ere, -vīsī, -vīsum, *force apart, divide, turn in different directions.*

dīvīnus, -a, -um, adj., *of or belonging to a god, divine.*

dīvus, -ī, m., *divine being, god.*

dō, dăre, dĕdī, dătum, *give, hand over, deliver, render:* vēla dare (sc. ventīs), *to spread sails, to make sail;* poenās dare, *pay penalty, suffer punishment.*

doceō, -ēre, -uī, -ctum, *show, teach, recount, explain, tell.*

dolor, -ōris, m., *pain, indignation, resentment, wrath, anger.*

dolus, -ī, m., *craft, artifice, stratagem, wile, trickery, deceit.*

domus, -ūs or -ī, f., *house, abode, home.*

dōnec, conj., *as long as, while; until, till.*

dōnum, -ī, n., *gift, offering.*

dorsum, -ī, n., *back, ridge, roof.*

dubitō, -āre, -āvī, -ātum, *doubt;* (with inf.) *hesitate.*

dūcō, -ere, duxī, ductum, *lead, conduct, lead forward or out, wage, carry on, be engaged in.*

ductor, -ōris, m., *leader, commander, general, chief.*

dulcis, -e, adj., *sweet, charming, dear, loved.*

dum, conj., *during the time in which, while.*

dūmus, -ī, m., *thorn-bush:* (in Verg. always pl.) *thicket, brushwood, undergrowth.*

duo, -ae, -o, num. adj., *two.*

duplicō, -āre, -āvī, -ātum, *double, redouble.*

dūrō, -āre, -āvī, -ātum, *make hard, harden; bear, sustain, endure.*

dūrus, -a, -um, adj., *hard, tough, unyielding, stern, severe.*

dux, ducis, m. or f., *leader, guide, commander, chief.*

E

ē (before consonants only) or ex, *out of, from.*

ecce, interj., *lo, behold.*

edō, edere or esse, ēdī, ēsum, *eat.*

edō, -ere, -didī, -ditum, *put forth; give birth to, beget.*

ēdoceō, -ēre, -uī, -ctum, *show or set forth, teach thoroughly, inform, apprise.*

ēdūcō, -ere, -duxī, -ductum, *lead forth or out; bring up, rear.*

efferō, -ferre, extulī, ēlātum, *bring forth or out; raise, hoist, set high, display.*

efferus, -a, -um, adj., *very wild, savage.*

effētus, -a, -um, adj., *exhausted with giving birth to young, worn out, exhausted.*

(effor), effārī, effātus, defect., *speak out, speak.*

effulgeō, -ēre or -ere, -fulsī, —, *shine forth, flash out, gleam, be ablaze.*

effultus, -a, -um, adj., *propped up, supported.*

effundō, -ere, -fūdī, -fūsum, *pour out or forth, utter.*

ēgelidus, -a, -um, *very cold* (elsewhere means not cold, warm).

egēnus, -a, -um, adj., *needy.*

egeō, -ēre, -uī, — , *need, want, lack.*

egō, gen. **meī;** pl. **nōs,** gen. **nostrum, nostrī,** pers. pron., *I, me, we, us.*

ēgredior, -ī, -gressus, *walk forth, come or go out, depart, disembark, land.*

ēgregius, -a, -um, adj., *select, eminent, extraordinary, distinguished, outstanding.*

ēiciō, -ere, -iēcī, -iectum, *cast out, expel, drive into exile, exile, banish.*

ēlābor, -ī, -lapsus, *slip away, escape, effect one's escape.*

Ēlectra, -ae, f., *daughter of Atlas, mother of Dardanus by Jupiter, sister of Maia.*

ēlectrum, -ī, n., *electrum, a metal made of gold and silver mixed.*

ēlīdō, -ere, -līsī, -līsum, *strike out, dash out, force out, press out, squeeze out; strangle.*

ēmūniō, -īre, -iī, -ītum, *wall off, close up by means of a wall, secure.*

ēn, interj., *lo! behold! see!*

ēnarrābilis, -e, adj., *capable of being (fully) described, describable.*

enim, conj. (postpositive), *for;* (strengthening) *in fact, indeed, yes.*

ēnītor, -ere, -nixus or **-nīsus,** *struggle forth; bring forth, give birth to, bear.*

ensis, -is, m., *sword.*

eō, īre, īvī or **iī, itūrum,** *go, walk, move, flow.*

epulae, -ārum, f., *meats, dishes, feast, banquet.*

eques, -itis, m., *horseman, rider, cavalry soldier, horseman.*

equidem, adv., *indeed, assuredly.*

equitātus, -ūs, m., *cavalry.*

equus, -ī, m., *horse.*

ergō, adv., *therefore, accordingly, so.*

ērigō, -ere, -rexī, -rectum, *raise, erect;* (pass. used reflexively) *rise, mount.*

ēripiō, -ere, -ripuī, -reptum, *snatch from, take away, remove.*

erīlis, -e, adj., *of a master or head of a family, master's.*

Erulus, -ī, m., *king of Praeneste and son of Feronia.*

et, conj., *and, also, even, too;* **et...et,** *both...and;* **-que...et,** *both... and.*

etiam, adv., *now too, still, even yet, besides, even.*

Etrūria, -ae, f., *Etruria, country in central Italy.*

Etruscus, -a, -um, adj., *of Etruria, Etruscan.*

Euphrātēs, -is, m., *the Euphrates, a river rising in Armenia and flowing into the Persian gulf.*

Eurus, -ī, m., *Eurus, the southeast wind.*

Eurystheus, -eī, m., *king of Mycenae who imposed twelve labors on Hercules.*

Evandrus, -ī, m., *Evander, migrated to Italy from Arcadia and founded Pallanteum.*

ēventus, -ūs, m., *outcome, issue, event, result.*

ēvinciō, -īre, -nxī, -nctum, *bind up, bind, wreathe.*

ēvomō, -ere, -uī, -itum, *vomit forth, disgorge, discharge, emit.*

ex or (before consonants only) **ē,** prep. with abl., *out of, from, since, out of, of.*

exardescō, -ere, -arsī, -arsum, *blaze forth, up or out.*

excidium, -ī, n., *destruction.*

excipiō, -ere, -cēpī, -ceptum, *take out of or from; receive, welcome.*

excitō, -āre, -āvī, -ātum, *call out or forth; rouse, excite, stir up, stimulate.*

exedō, -ere, -ēdī, -ēsum, *devour, consume; carve out, hollow.*

exeō, -īre, -iī, -itum, *go forth or out, depart; go or come forth, spring, arise, issue.*

exerceō, -ēre, -uī, -itum, *drive, keep busy, employ, call into requisition, task.*

exhortor, -ārī, -ātus sum, *exhort, encourage.*

exiguus, -a, -um, adj., *scanty, inadequate, paltry; feeble.*

eximō, -ere, -ēmī, -emptum, *take away, remove.*

exin, adv., *after that, next, then.*

expediō, -īre, -īvī or **-iī, -ītum,** *extricate, set free; disentangle, unravel, solve, set right.*

expellō, -ere, -pulī, -pulsum, *drive out or away, expel, banish.*

expleō, -ēre, -ēvī, -ētum, *fill up, fill full, satisfy, satiate.*

exquīrō, -ere, -sīvī, -sītum, *seek out, inquire into, investigate diligently.*

exsors, -rtis, adj., *special, specially selected.*

exspectō, -āre, -āvī, -ātum, *look for, long for, expect, await.*

exstinguō, -ere, -nxī, -nctum, *put out, extinguish, quench.*

exsul, -ulis, m. or **f.,** *exile.*

exsultō, -āre, -āvī, -ātum, *leap up, dance, bound.*

exta, -ōrum, n., *the internal organs, the heart, lungs, and liver.*

extemplō, adv., *forthwith, straightway, at once.*

externus, -a, -um, adj., *external, belonging to another country, foreign.*

exterreō, -ēre, -uī, -itum, *strike with terror, terrify, awe.*

extimescō, -ere, -timuī, —, *fear greatly, fear.*

extrēmus, -a, -um, superl. adj. *most, farthest, remotest, extreme.*

extundō, -ere, -tudī, —, *beat or hammer, forge; execute in relief.*

exuō, -ere, -uī, -ūtum, *take off, strip off.*

F

fabrīlis, -e, adj., *of a workman or artisan.*

faciēs, -ēī, acc. **-em, f.,** *appearance, form, shape.*

facilis, -e, adj., *easy, quick, rapid.*

faciō, -ere, fēcī, factum, *make, construct, form, fashion, do;* (sc. **sacra**) *perform or offer sacrifice.*

factum, -ī, n., *deed, act, exploit.*

fallō, -ere, fefellī, falsum, *deceive, disappoint.*

fāma, -ae, f., *report, rumor, fame, renown.*

famēs, -is, f., *hunger.*

famulus, -ī, m. and **famula, -ae, f.** *servant, attendant.*

fās, n., indecl. *divine law, what is lawful, allowed, permitted, right, proper.*

fastīgium, -ī, n., *point of a gable, point, summit, roof.*

fateor, -ērī, fassus, *confess, admit, acknowledge.*

fātidicus, -a, -um, adj., *prophetic, soothsaying.*

fātifer, -era, -erum, adj., *doom-bringing, death-dealing, deadly.*

fatīgō, -āre, -āvī, -ātum, *make weary, tire out, fatigue, wear out.*

fātum, -ī, n., *that which is spoken, a prophetic utterance; destiny, fate.*

faucēs, -ium, f., *throat.*

Faunus, -ī, m., *Faunus, god of forests and fields, father of Latinus;* (m. pl.) *fauns, sylvan deities.*

faveō, -ēre, fāvī, fautūrum, *be favorably disposed, look kindly upon, favor.*

fel, fellis, n., *gall-bladder, gall.*

fēmina, -ae, f., *woman.*

feriō, -īre, —, —, *strike.*

ferō, ferre, tulī, lātum, *bear, bring, carry, endure, report,* (with **sē**) *move, stride along.*

Fērōnia, -ae, f., *Feronia, an Italian goddess.*

ferrum, -ī, n., *iron, steel; sword.*

fervidus, -a, -um, adj., *glowing, boiling, burning.*

fervō, -ere, —, —, *boil, glow, rage; be aglow, be in a ferment.*

fessus, -a, -um, adj., *tired, wearied, worn out, exhausted.*

fētus, -a, -um, adj., *with young, pregnant, newly delivered, nursing, mother.*

fētus, -ūs, m., *bringing forth; offspring; litter.*

fidēs, fideī, f., *trust, faith, pledge, friendship.*

fidūcia, -ae, f., *trust, confidence, reliance.*

fidus, -a, -um, adj., *trustworthy, trusty, faithful, true.*

fīlia, -ae, f., *daughter;* **fīlius, -ī, m.**, *son.*

fingō, -ere, finxī, fictum, *form, shape, mold, fashion, depict, portray, render.*

fīnis, -is, m. (often **f.** in sing.), *end, boundary, limit, frontier, territory.*

fīnitimus, -a, -um, adj., *bordering on, neighboring, neighbor's.*

fīō, fierī (used as pass. of **faciō**), *become, be made, be done, be wrought.*

firmō, -āre, -āvī, -ātum, *make firm, strengthen; confirm.*

flagellum, -ī, n., *whip, scourge.*

flamma, -ae, f., *flame, blaze, flash of light.*

flectō, -ere, flexī, flexum, *bend; bend to one's will, persuade, prevail upon.*

fleō, -ēre, -ēvī, -ētum, *weep, shed tears;* (used tr.) *weep for, shed tears for.*

flexus, -ūs, m., *bending, bend, winding, winding course.*

flōreō, -ēre, -uī, —, *blossom, flourish, be prosperous.*

flōs, -ōris, m., *flower, blossom, bloom;* (fig.) *flower;* (of the beard) *down.*

fluctuō, -āre, -āvī, -ātum, *move as a wave, be restless, toss.*

fluctus, -ūs, m., *wave, billow.*

flūmen, -inis, n., *a flowing, flood, stream; river, stream.*

fluō, -ere, fluxī, fluxum, *flow; flow, stream, or drip (with).*

fluvius, -ī, m., *river, stream; river god.*

foedus, -eris, n., *bond of faith, treaty, agreement, compact.*

folium, -ī, n., *leaf.*

follis, -is, m., *bellows.*

fons, fontis, m., *spring, fountainhead, fountain.*

(for), fārī, -ātus, defect., *speak.*

forceps, -ipis, f., *tongs.*

forem, imperf. subj. of **sum**, *be.*

foris, -is, f., *door, gate, entrance, portal*, (pl.) *door* (of two leaves).

forma, -ae, f., *form, shape, figure, beauty.*

fornax, -ācis, f., *furnace.*

fors, (**fortis**), abl. **forte, f.**, *chance, accident.*

forte, adv., *by chance.*

fortis, -e, adj., *strong, brave, courageous*; (n. pl. used subst., sc. **facta**) *brave deeds.*

fortūna, -ae, f., *chance, (good) luck, fortune*; *goddess of chance, Fortune.*

forum, -ī, n., *market-place, public square, forum*; (in particular) *the Roman forum.*

foveō, -ēre, fōvī, fōtum, *warm*; *cherish, fondle.*

fragor, -ōris, m., *crashing sound, peal.*

fremō, -ere, -uī, —, *roar, howl, resound, cry out menacingly, complain loudly, clamor angrily.*

frēnum, -ī, n., *bridle, bit.*

frētus, -a, -um, adj., *sustained, relying, trusting.*

frondōsus, -a, -um, adj., *leafy, shaggy, with many leafy branches.*

frons, frondis, f., *leafy bough, foliage*; *leafy garland, chaplet of leaves, leaves.*

fruor, -ī, fructus, *enjoy.*

fuga, -ae, f., *flight.*

fugiō, -ere, fūgī, —, *flee, take flight, take to one's heels, make off, fly, flee from, fly from.*

fulciō, -īre, fulsī, fultum, *prop up, support, secure.*

fulgeō, -ēre, fulsī, —, *flash, shine, gleam.*

fulgor, -ōris, m., *lightning-flash, flash, glare.*

fulmen, -inis, n., *thunderbolt.*

fulvus, -a, -um, adj., *reddish-yellow, tawny.*

fūmifer, -era, -erum, adj., *smoky, smothering, stifling.*

fūmō, -āre, -āvī, -ātum, *smoke, steam.*

fūmus, -ī, m., *smoke.*

fundō, -āre, -āvī, fundātum, *lay the foundation, found, build.*

fundō, -ere, fūdī, fūsum, *pour, bring forth, bear, pour forth.*

fūnis, -is, m., *rope, cord*, (nautical term) *sheet.*

fūnus, -eris, n., *funeral rites, funeral, death.*

furia, -ae, f., *madness, frenzy*; (pl.) *rage, wrath, frenzy*; **Furia**, *goddess of divine vengeance, Fury.*

furō, -ere, —, —, *rage, be furious.*

fuscus, -a, -um, adj., *dark, dusky, sable.*

futūrus, -a, -um, adj., *future, approaching, impending.*

G

gaesum, -ī, n., *heavy javelin.*

galea, -ae, f., *helmet.*

Gallus, -ī, m., *a Gaul.*

gaudeō, -ēre, gāvīsus, *be glad or joyful, rejoice, take pleasure.*

gelidus, -a, -um, adj., *cold, cool.*

Gelōnī, -ōrum, m., *a Scythian nomadic people.*

gelū, abl. **gelū**, *icy coldness, frost, chill.*

geminus, -a, -um, adj., *twin-born, twin*; *two.*

gemitus, -ūs, m., *groaning, groan.*

gemō, -ere, -uī, —, *groan.*

genae, -ārum, f., *cheeks.*

generō, -āre, -āvī, -ātum, *beget, be the father of.*

genitor, -ōris, m., *father.*

genetrix, -īcis, f., *mother.*

gens, gentis, f., *race, stock; tribe, people, nation.*

genus, -eris, n., *race, birth, origin, class, kind, sort, offspring, family, children, descendants.*

Gēryonēs, -ae, m., *a monster having three heads and a threefold trunk.*

glaucus, -a, -um, adj., *bluish-gray, grayish, gray.*

glomerō, -āre, -āvī, -ātum, *wind or roll into a ball, accumulate, collect.*

Gorgō, -onis (acc. **Gorgona**), **f.,** *a Gorgon, esp. Medusa.*

gradior, -ī, gressus, *step, walk, go, move on, proceed.*

Grāī, -ōrum or **-ūm, m.,** *the Greeks.*

Grāiugena, -ae (gen. pl. **Grāiugenūm,** 127), **m.,** *Greek by birth, Greek.*

grāmineus, -a, -um, adj., *of grass, of turf, grassy.*

grātus, -a, -um, adj., *dear, pleasing, agreeable, grateful, appetizing.*

gravis, -e, adj., *heavy; severe, grievous, painful, stern, strenuous.*

gravō, -āre, -āvī, -ātum, *make heavy, load, weight.*

gremium, -ī, n., *lap, bosom.*

gressus, -ūs, m., *stepping, footsteps, steps, course, way.*

grex, gregis, m., *flock, herd, litter.*

guttur, -uris, n., *throat.*

H

habeō, -ēre, -uī, -itum, *have, hold, have in one's keeping, occupy, inhabit.*

habitō, -āre, -āvī, -ātum, *dwell in, inhabit.*

habitus, -ūs, m., *bearing, condition, appearance.*

hāc, adv., *this way, by this road.*

haereō, -ēre, haesī, haesūrum, *cling, stick fast, be rooted to the spot.*

harundō, -inis, f., *reed, cane.*

haruspex, -icis, m., *inspector of entrails of sacrificial victims, soothsayer, diviner.*

hasta, -ae, f., *staff, shaft, spear, lance.*

haud, adv., *not at all, not.*

Herculeus, -a, -um, adj., *Herculean.*

hērōs, -ōis, m., *demi-god, hero.*

Hēsiona, -ae or **Hēsionē, -ēs, f.,** *daughter of Laomedon, sister of Priam, and wife of Telamon, king of Salamis.*

Hesperia, -ae, f., *Hesperia, the western country, i.e., Italy.*

Hesperis, -idis, f., adj., *evening-star, Hesperian, western.*

hesternus, -a, -um, adj., *of yesterday, yesterday's.*

heu, interj. expressing sorrow, *ah! alas!*

hīc, adv., *in this place, here.*

hic, haec, hoc, dem. pron. or adj., *this, this here.*

hinc, adv., *from this place, from this or these, from this source, hence;* **hinc…hinc,** *on this side…on that.*

hōc, adv., *hither, to here.*

homō, -inis, m. and **f.,** *human being, person.*

honōs or **honor, -ōris, m.,** *honor, distinction; mark of honor, homage, worship, sacrifice.*

horrendus, -a, -um, adj., *horrible, fearful.*

horreō, -ēre, -uī, —, *bristle, be rough, stand erect; tremble (at), shudder (at).*

horridus, -a, -um, adj., *bristling,
rough.*
horrifer, -era, -erum, adj., *causing
terror, terrible.*
hospes, -itis, m. (rarely f.), *host, friend;
guest.*
hostis, -is, m. and f., *stranger; public
enemy, enemy, foe.*
hūc, adv., *to this place, hither;* hūc...
illūc, *in this direction...in that,
hither...thither, this way...that
way.*
humilis, -e, adj., *low; lowly, humble.*
humus, -ī, f., *ground, earth.*
Hylaeus, -ī, m., *a centaur.*

I

iaceō, -ēre, -cuī, —, *lie, be outstretched.*
iaciō, -ere, iēcī, iactum, *cast, throw,
fling.*
iactō, -āre, -āvī, -ātum, *throw in
profusion, shower, throw, cast.*
iam, adv., *at this time, now:* iam adeō,
at just this time; iam nunc, *even
now;* iam tum, *even then;* iam
prīmum, *first of all;* cum iam,
when at length.
iamdūdum, adv., *long since, long ere
this, for a long time, long.*
Iāniculum, -ī, n., *Janiculum, one of
the hills of Rome, where Janus built
a citadel.*
iānitor, -ōris, m., *doorkeeper, porter.*
Iānus, -ī, m., *Janus, an old Italian deity
viewed as god of gates, doors, and
beginnings.*
Iāpyx, -ygis, m., *west-northwest wind.*
ictus, -ūs, m., *blow, stroke.*
īdem, eadem, ĭdem, dem. pron., *the
same.*
īgnārus, -a, -um, adj., *ignorant,
unacquainted with.*

īgneus, -a, -um, adj., *of fire, fiery,
blazing.*
īgnipotens, -entis, adj., *having power
over fire.*
īgnis, -is (abl. igne, 255), m., *fire, flame.*
īgnōtus, -a, -um, adj., *unknown,
unfamiliar.*
īlex, -icis, f., *holm-oak, scarlet-oak, oak.*
Īliacus, -a, -um, adj., *of Ilium* (i.e.,
Troy), *Trojan.*
īlicet, adv., *instantly, right away.*
ille, illa, illud, dem. pron. and adj.,
that, those, the former, ex illō
(sc. tempore), *from that time, since
then.*
illīc, adv., *in that place, there.*
illūc, adv., *to that place, thither;* hūc...
illūc, *in this direction...in that, this
way...that way.*
imāgō, -inis, f., *representation, image,
form, idea.*
imber, -bris, m., *rain.*
immānis, -e, adj., *immense, enormous,
vast, giant, huge.*
immittō, -ere, -mīsī, -missum, *send
or let in, admit, introduce; let go,
loose.*
immortālis, -e, adj., *immortal,
undying, deathless, eternal.*
impavidus, -a, -um, adj., *fearless,
intrepid.*
impediō, -īre, *hinder, entangle, fasten
together.*
impellō, -ere, -pulī, -pulsum, *push
forward, drive forward, clash, strike
against.*
imperfectus, -a, -um, adj., *unfinished,
incomplete.*
imperium, -ī, n., *command, order,
control, rule.*
impleō, -ēre, -ēvī, -ētum, *fill
completely, fill.*

impōnō, -ere, -posuī, -positum, *put or place upon, set up, put in place, impose, lay upon.*

imprōvīsō, adv., *unexpectedly, suddenly.*

impulsus, -ūs, m., *striking against, push, shock, force, impulse.*

īmus, -a, -um, adj. superl. of **inferus,** *lowest, deepest.*

in, prep. with abl., *in, on;* with acc., *into, to, for:* **in mōrem,** *after the manner of, like;* **in adversum,** *against;* **in numerum,** *in time, with measured movement;* **in orbem,** *in circles, in curves.*

inaccessus, -a, -um, adj., *inaccessible.*

inardescō, -ere, -arsī, —, *take fire, kindle, glow, redden.*

inausus, -a, -um, adj., *unventured, undared.*

incassum, adv., *to no purpose, in vain, idly.*

incēdō, -ere, -cessī, -cessum, *advance, march, move (in procession).*

incendium, -ī, n., *fire, flame.*

incendō, -ere, -cendī, -censum, *set fire to, kindle, burn.*

incertus, -a, -um, adj., *unsettled, doubtful, uncertain.*

incipiō, -ere, -cēpī, -ceptum, *begin, undertake, begin (to speak).*

inclūdō, -ere, -sī, -sum, *shut in, enclose, confine.*

incolō, -ere, -luī, —, *dwell in, inhabit.*

incolumis, -e, adj., *unharmed, uninjured, safe.*

incommodum, -ī, n., *inconvenience, misfortune, trouble.*

incrēbrescō, -ere, -bruī, *grow, spread, become stronger or more well-known.*

increpō, -āre, -uī, -itum, *rattle, crack, crash, sound, resound.*

incumbō, -ere, -cubuī, -cubitum, *lay onself upon, lean, incline, bend to, ply.*

incūs, -ūdis, f., *anvil.*

inde, adv., *from that place or time, thence, next, after that, then.*

Indī, -ōrum, m. pl., *inhabitants of India, Indians.*

indicium, -ī, n., *pointing out; sign, mark, indication, track.*

indigena, -ae, adj. m. and f., *native.*

indignor, -ārī, -ātus sum, *deem unworthy, be indignant, wrathful or resentful, disdain.*

indocilis, -e, adj., *unteachable, untaught, untamed, rude.*

indomitus, -a, -um, adj., *untamed, unsubdued, indomitable.*

indubitō, -āre, -āvī, -ātum, *throw doubt upon, imply distrust of.*

indūcō, -ere, -duxī, -ductum, *lead in; draw on or over, put on.*

indulgeō, -ēre, -ulsī, -ultum, *be kind, considerate; favor.*

inēluctābilis, -e, adj., *inevitable.*

inexplētus, -a, -um, adj., *unsatisfied.*

infandus, -a, -um, adj., *unspeakable, unheard of, detestable, dreadful.*

infernus, -a, -um, adj., *of the lower regions of the underworld.*

inferō, -ferre, -tulī, inlātum, *bring in, introduce.*

informis, -e, *shapeless, misshapen, unsightly, hideous.*

informō, -āre, -āvī, -ātum, *give shape, shape (in outline), fashion.*

infrā, adv., *on the lower side.*

infrendō -ere, *gnash.* Only in pres. part.

infundō, -ere, -fūdī, -fūsum, *pour in or upon.*

ingens, -gentis, adj., *huge, giant, vast, mighty, enormous.*

ingredior, -ī, -gressus, *step into, enter, go forward, proceed, move, walk.*

ingruō, -ere, -uī, *fall upon, rush in upon, attack violently, burst forth, break out.*

inhaereō, -ēre, -haesī, -haesum, *cling to, cleave to, fasten oneself upon.*

inimīcus, -a, -um, adj., *unfriendly, hostile.*

inīquus, -a, -um, adj., *uneven, unkind, unfriendly, hostile.*

innectō, -ere, -nexuī, -nexum, *fasten to, bind, connect; encircle.*

innō, -āre, -āvī, -ātum, *swim or float in or on, swim.*

inopīnus, -a, -um, adj., *unexpected, unlooked for.*

inops, -opis, adj., *without resources, weak, scant, meagre, wretched.*

inquam, defect., *say.*

inscius, -a, -um, adj., *ignorant.*

insequor, -ī -cūtus, *follow close upon, come next, follow up, pursue.*

insīdō, -ere, -sēdī, -sessum, *take seat, settle in or on.*

insīgne, -is, n., *mark, token, ensign, symbol.*

insīgnis, -e, adj. *marked, remarkable, distinguished, beautiful.*

inspērātus, -a, -um, adj., *unexpected, unlooked for.*

instaurō, -āre, -āvī, -ātum, *establish, institute, renew.*

instō, -āre, -stitī, -statūrum, *be at hand, draw near, threaten, menace.*

instruō, -ere, -uxī, -uctum, *build in,* *insert, set in order, array, draw up, equip.*

insuētus, -a, -um, adj., *unaccustomed, strange.*

insula, -ae, f., *island.*

insultō, -āre, -āvī, -ātum, freq. of **insiliō,** *leap upon, scoff at, insult, dishonor.*

insurgō, -ere, -surrexī, -surrectum, *rise on or over, tower above.*

intendō, -ere, -dī, -tum, *stretch to, stretch,* (with **arcum**) *bend, strain.*

inter, prep. with acc., *between, among;* **inter sē,** *with each other, one after the other, alternately.*

intereā, adv., *in the meantime, meanwhile.*

intertextus, -a, -um, adj., *interwoven, intertwined, embroidered.*

intonō, -āre, -uī, -ātum, *thunder.*

intractātus, -a, -um, adj., *untried, unattempted.*

intrō, -āre, -āvī, -ātum, *go into, enter, penetrate.*

invehō, -ere, -vexī, -vectum, *carry in, introduce, drive in or into, enter.*

invenio, -īre, -vēnī, -ventum, *come upon, find.*

invictus, -a, -um, adj., *unconquered, invincible.*

invideō, -ēre, -vīdī, -vīsum, *look askance at, envy, grudge.*

invīsō, -vīsere, -vīsī, —, *go to see, visit.*

invīsus, -a, -um, adj., *hated, odious.*

invītō, -āre, -āvī, -ātum, *invite, summon.*

involvō, -ere, -volvī, -lūtum, *roll in, roll upon; envelop, involve, wrap.*

ipse, ipsa, ipsum, intens. pron., *self; him-, her-, itself.*

īra, -ae, f., *wrath, anger, ire.*

is, ea, id, dem. pron. and adj., *that; he, she, it.*

ita, adv., *in this manner, thus, so, to such a degree.*

Italus, -a, -um, adj., *Italian.*

Italus, -ī (gen. pl. Italum, 513), m., *an Italian.*

iter, itineris, n., *journey, march, voyage.*

iterum, adv., *again.*

iubeō, -ēre, iussī, iussum, *order, bid, command.*

iugum, -ī, n., *yoke, mountain-ridge, domination symbolized by yoke.*

iungō, -ere, iunxī, iunctum, *yoke, fasten together, unite.*

Iūnō, -ōnis, f., *Juno, daughter of Saturn, sister and wife of Jupiter, queen of heaven.*

Iuppiter, Iovis, m., *Jupiter, son of Saturn, brother and husband of Juno, king of the gods.*

iūs, iūris, n., *right, justice, principle of law, fundamental law, law.*

iustus, -a, -um, adj., *upright, just, righteous.*

iuvenālis, -e, adj., *of a youth, a youth's, youthful.*

iuvencus, -ī, m., *bullock, steer;* iuvenca, -ae, f., *heifer.*

iuvenis, -is, m., *young person, youth, man in the prime of life, warrior.*

iuventās, -ātis, f., *the age of youth, youth.*

iuventūs, -ūtis, f., *youth, young men, men of military age, warriors.*

iuvō, -āre, iūvī, iūtum, *aid, assist, support.*

iuxtā, adv., *close at hand, near to, near, hard by, at the side of.*

L

labefaciō, -ere, -fēcī, -factum, *make totter, shake, loosen, relax.*

lābor, -ī, lapsus, *glide, move easily, slip, fall.*

labor, -ōris, m., *toil, effort, labor, work, task, hardship, trial, suffering.*

labōrō, -āre, -āvī, -ātum, *toil, labor, exert oneself, produce by labor, elaborate.*

labrum, -ī, n., *basin.*

lacertus, -ī, m., *upper arm, arm.*

lacrima, -ae, f., *tear.*

lacrimō, -āre, -āvī, -ātum, *shed tears, weep.*

lacteus, -a, -um, adj., *of milk, milky; milk-white.*

lacus, -ūs, m., *hollow, lake, pool, channel; tank, cooling-trough.*

laetitia, -ae, f., *gladness, joy, rejoicing.*

laetus, -a, -um, adj., *glad, joyful, joyous, rejoicing.*

laeva, -ae, f., *left side, left.*

laevus, -a, -um, adj., *left, on the left.*

lambō, -ere, — , —, *lick, lap.*

lāniger, -era, -erum, adj., *wool-bearing, tufted* (with wool), *woolly.*

lanx, lancis, f., *plate, dish, platter.*

Lāomedontiadēs, -ae, m., *son or descendant of Laomedon.*

Lāomedontius, -a, -um, adj., *of Laomedon, founder of Troy who cheated the gods.*

laqueāria, -ium, n. pl., *sunk panels in a ceiling.*

Lār, Laris, m., (usu. pl.) *a Lar, i.e., household god, guardian divinity of the hearth and home.*

lātē, adv., *widely, extensively, far and wide.*

latebrōsus, -a, -um, adj., *full of hiding-places, cavernous, sheltering.*

lateō, -ēre, -uī, —, *lie concealed, find shelter, find refuge.*

Latīnus, -a, -um, adj., *of Latium, Latin;* (m. pl. used subst.) *the Latins.*

Latium, -ī, n., *area on the west coast of Italy between Etruria and Campania.*

lātrātor, -ōris, m., *barker, dog.*

latus, -eris, n., *side, flank;* (of an island or land mass) *coast.*

lātus, -a, -um, adj., *broad, wide.*

Laurens, -entis, adj., *of Laurentum, Laurentian.*

laus, laudis, f., *praise, merit, service.*

lautus, -a, -um, adj., *elegant, splendid, luxurious.*

laxus, -a, -um, adj., *loose, open, free, slack.*

lectus, -a, -um, adj., *chosen, picked, select, choice.*

lēgātus, -ī, m., *ambassador, envoy.*

legiō, -ōnis, f., *levy of soldiers, the Roman legion; army, force.*

legō, -ere, lēgī, lectum, *gather, collect, pick out, select, choose.*

Leleges, -um (acc. Lelegās, 725), m. pl., *the Leleges, an ancient people of Asia Minor.*

Lemnius, -a, -um, adj., *of Lemnos, Lemnian.*

lēniō, -īre, *soften, soothe, assuage, calm.*

leō, -ōnis, m., *lion.*

Lernaeus, -a, -um, adj., *of Lerna, Lernaean.*

lētum, -ī, n., *death.*

Leucātēs, -ae (acc. -tēn), m., *promontory on the island of Leucadia.*

lēvis, -e, adj., *smooth, polished;* contrast lĕvis, *light.*

levō, -āre, -āvī, -ātum, *lighten, relieve.*

lex, lēgis, f., *law, enactment.*

libens, -entis, adj., *willing, glad, with joy.*

lībertās, -ātis, f., *freedom, liberty.*

lībō, -āre, -āvī, -ātum, *taste, sip; pour a libation, make a drink-offering.*

Libystis, -idis, fem. adj., *of Libya* (Greek name of Africa), *Libyan, African.*

licet, -ēre, -uit and -itum est, *it is lawful, it is permitted.*

licitus, -a, -um, adj., *permitted, unrestrained.*

līmen, -inis, n., *threshold, door, entrance, gate, portal.*

lingua, -ae, f., *tongue, language.*

Liparē, -ēs, f., *Aeolian island off the northern coast of Sicily.*

liquescō, -ere, —, —, *become fluid, melt.*

liquidus, -a, -um, adj., *flowing, liquid, fluid, molten.*

lītoreus, -a, -um, adj., *on the shore, growing on the shore.*

lītus, -oris, n., *sea-shore, shore, river-bank, bank.*

locō, -āre, -āvī, -ātum, *place, dispose.*

locus, -ī, m. (in pl., mostly **loca**, -ōrum, n.), *place, spot, scene; place, site, position.*

longaevus, -a, -um, adj., *aged.*

longē, adv., *at a distance, far off, afar, far.*

longus, -a, -um, adj., *long.*

loquor, -ī, -cūtus, *speak.*

lōrīca, -ae, f., *corselet, breastplate.*

lūceō, -ēre, luxī, —, *shine, gleam.*

lūcifer, -era, -erum, adj., *light-bringing;* (m. used subst.) *Lucifer, morning-star.*

luctāmen, -inis, n., *wrestling, struggle, toil, effort, exertion.*

lūcus, -ī, m., *sacred grove, grove.*

lūdō, -ere, -sī, -sum, *play, sport, frolic.*

lūdus, -ī, m., *game, pastime, diversion.*

lūmen, -inis, n., *ray or beam of light, light, eye, glance.*

lūna, -ae, f., *moon.*

lupa, -ae, f., *she-wolf.*

Lupercal, -ālis, n., *a cave at or not far from the Palatine sacred to Lupercus.*

Lupercī, -ōrum, m. pl., *the Luperci, priests of Lupercus or Pan.*

lustrālis, -e, adj., *of purification, sacrificial.*

lustrō, -āre, -āvī, -ātum, *make bright, light up; survey, scan, observe.*

lux, lūcis, f., *light.*

Lycaeus, -a, -um, adj., *of Mt. Lycaeus* (in Arcadia), *Lycaean.*

Lycius, -a, -um, adj., *of Lycia* (country in Asia Minor), *Lycian.*

Lȳdius, -a, -um, adj., *of Lydia, Lydian.*

M

mactō, -āre, -āvī, -ātum, *sacrifice, slay, kill, magnify, honor, offer up.*

Maeonia, -ae, f., *Maeonia, a district in Lydia; Etruria.*

maereō, -ēre, — , —, *be sorrowful, grieve, mourn.*

magister, -trī, m., *master, director, instructor, teacher.*

magistra, -ae, f., *mistress, instructress, teacher, guide.*

magnus, -a, -um, adj., *large, great, high, spacious, powerful, mighty.*

Māia, -ae, f., *Maia, daughter of Atlas, mother of Mercury by Jupiter.*

māior, comp. of **magnus.**

mālō, malle, māluī, *wish, rather, prefer, choose.*

mandō, -āre, -āvī, -ātum, *put into one's hands, deliver, entrust.*

maneō, -ēre, mansī, mansum, *stay, remain; hold to, abide by.*

Mānēs, -ium, m. pl., *souls of the departed, departed spirits.*

manifestus, -a, -um, adj., *plain, clear, evident, manifest.*

Manlius, -ī, m., Marcus Manlius Capitolinus, *saved the Capitol from the Gauls.*

manus, -ūs, f., *hand; band, host.*

mare, -is, n., *sea.*

Mars, Martis, m., *god of war;* (meton.) *war, battle, forces, troops.*

massa, -ae, f., *lump of dough; mass, lump.*

māter, -tris, f., *mother, matron.*

mātūtīnus, -a, -um, adj., *of morning, morning* (adj.), *early.*

Māvors, -rtis, m., *Mars, the god of war.*

maximus, superl. of **magnus.**

medius, -a, -um, adj., *middle, middle of, interior of.*

medulla, -ae, f., *marrow.*

membrum, -ī, n., *limb.*

meminī, -isse, defect., *call to mind, remember.*

memor, -oris, adj., *heedful, mindful, recalling.*

memorō, -āre, -āvī, -ātum, *call to mind, mention, speak of, recount, say, speak.*

mendax, -ācis, adj., *lying, false.*

mens, mentis, f., *mind, heart, soul.*

mensa, -ae, f., *table, meal.*

Mercurius, -ī, m., *son of Jupiter and Maia, messenger of the gods.*

meritus, -a, -um, adj., *deserving, deserved, due, just, fitting.*

Messāpus, -ī, m., *son of Neptune, ally of Turnus.*

mēta, -ae, f., *pillar in race serving as a turning-post, goal, limit, objective point.*

metallum, -ī, n., *metal.*

Mettus, -ī, m., *Mettus (Fufetius), dictator of Alba in the reign of Tullus Hostilius.*

metus, -ūs, m., *fear, dread, apprehension, alarm.*

meus, -a, -um, poss. adj., *my.*

Mezentius, -ī, m., *king of Etruscan town Agylla (= Caere), expelled by his subjects, ally of Turnus.*

micō, -āre, -uī, —, *dart to and fro, vibrate, gleam, flash.*

mīlitia, -ae, f., *military service.*

mille, indecl. num. adj., *a thousand;* (as subst.) mille, sing., mīlia, pl., n., *thousand.*

minae, -ārum, f., *threats, threatenings, menaces.*

minax, -ācis, adj., *menacing, threatening.*

Minerva, -ae, f., *Minerva, goddess of wisdom and of the arts, esp. spinning and weaving, associated with Greek Pallas Athena;* (meton.) *spinning, weaving.*

ministrō, -āre, -āvī, -ātum, *wait upon, serve, provide, supply, serve.*

minor, -ārī, -ātus sum, *threaten, menace.*

minor, minus, -ōris, adj., *smaller, less;* (used subst. in pl.) *descendants, those of a later day.*

minus, comp. adv., *less:* nec minus, *not less, likewise.*

mīrābilis, -e, adj., *wonderful, marvelous.*

mīror, -ārī, -ātus sum, *wonder at, marvel at, look at with wonder.*

misceō, -ēre, miscuī, mixtum, *mix, mingle, blend.*

miser, -era, -erum, adj., *wretched, miserable, distressed.*

miserescō, -ere, —, —, *take pity, have compassion.*

miseror, -ārī, -ātus sum, *lament, commiserate, pity, feel compassion for.*

mītis, -e, adj., *mellow, ripe; mild, gentle, placid.*

mittō, -ere, mīsī, missum, *let go, send, dispatch.*

moenia, -ium, n., *city walls, walls, walled town or city, city.*

molāris, -is, m., *millstone, or a rock as large as one.*

mōlēs, -is, f., *mass, bulk, labor, difficulty, straining effort, force.*

mollis, -e, adj., *soft, gentle, tender, cushioned, gentle, mild.*

monitum, -ī, n., *warning, admonition, behest, counsel.*

mons, montis, m., *mountain, hill.*

monstrō, -āre, -āvī, -ātum, *show, point out.*

monstrum, -ī, n., *omen, portent, monster;* deum monstra, *gods of monstrous shape.*

monimentum, -ī, n., *means of bringing to mind, memorial, monument, record.*

mora, -ae, f., *hesitation, delay.*

Morīnī, -ōrum, m., *the Morini, tribe of Belgic Gaul.*

mors, -tis, f., *death.*

mortuus, -a, -um, adj., *dead.*

mōs, mōris, m., *way, manner, custom, usage:* sine mōre, *lawlessly.*

moveō, -ēre, mōvī, mōtum, *set in motion, move, remove.*

mox, adv., *soon.*

mūgiō, īre, -īvī, —, *low, bellow;* (of a trumpet) *bray, sound.*

mulceō, -ēre, -sī, -sum, *stroke, fondle, soften, caress.*

Mulciber, -eris or **-erī, m.**, *name of Vulcan as softener of metal.*

multus, -a, -um, adj., *much, great;* (pl.) *many.*

mūnus, -eris, n., *service, function, office, duty, honor.*

mūrus, -ī, m., *wall, rampart.*

N

nam, conj., *for;* **namque**, conj., (stronger than **nam**) *and with reason for, for.*

nascor, -ī, nātus, *be born, spring, proceed, derive origin:* **nascens**, *at birth.*

nātus, -ī, m., *born, offspring, son;* (of brute animals) *young.*

nāvālis, -e, adj., *nautical, naval.*

nāvis, -is, f., *ship.*

-ne, enclit. interrog. part., introducing a question.

nē, adv. with imperative, *not, do not;* conj. with subj., *lest, that not, in order that...not.*

nebula, -ae, f., *mist, vapor, smoke.*

nec or **neque**, conj., *and not, nor;* **nec... nec**, *neither...nor;* **nec nōn**, *and besides, moreover, too;* **nec minus,** *not less, likewise.*

necdum, adv., *and not yet, nor yet.*

necō, -āre, -āvī or **necuī, -ātum,** *kill.*

nefās, indecl., n., *violation of divine law, sacrilege, profanation, sin.*

Nemea, -ae, f., *a town in Argolis near which Hercules killed the Nemean lion.*

nemus, -oris, n., *pasture ground, forest pasture, forest, grove, wood, trees.*

nepōs, -ōtis, m., *grandson, descendant.*

Neptūnius, -a, -um, adj., *of Neptune, god of the sea, Neptune's.*

Neptūnus, -ī, m., *Neptune, god of the sea.*

neque or **nec**, conj., *and not, nor;* **neque...neque**, *neither...nor;* **neque enim,** *for...not.*

nequeō, -īre, -īvī, —, *be unable, cannot.*

nēquīquam, adv., *in vain, without effect, to no purpose.*

Nēreus, -ei (both dissyl.), **m.**, *a sea-god, father of the Nereids including Thetis.*

neu or **nēve**, adv., (the regular continuative after **ne**) *and not, nor.*

nex, necis, f., *death, slaughter.*

nī, conj., *if not, unless.*

nīdus, -ī, m., *nest.*

niger, -gra, -grum, adj., *black, dark.*

nigrans, -antis, adj., *black, dark, gloomy, shadowy.*

nihil or **nīl, indecl., n.**, *nothing.*

Nīlus, -ī, m., *the Nile, great river in Egypt.*

nimbus, -ī, m., *stormcloud, dark cloud, cloud.*

nītor, -ī, nixus and **nīsus**, *press upon; strive, struggle, strain, exert one's strength.*

niveus, -a, -um, adj., *of snow, snowy; snow-white, snowy.*

nōbilis, -e, adj., *well-known, famous, renowned.*

nōdus, -ī, m., *knot.*

Nomas, -adis, m., *wandering herdsman, nomad;* (in pl.) *the Numidians* (of North Africa).

nōmen, -inis, n., *name, fame, renown, authority, account, behalf.*

nōn, adv., *not.*

noscō, -ere, nōvī, nōtum (plup.

nōrant), *come to know, learn;* (perf.) *know.*

noster, -tra, -trum, poss. adj., *our.*

nōtus, -a, -um, adj., *well-known, familiar.*

noverca, -ae, f., *stepmother.*

novō, -āre, -āvī, -ātum, *make new, renew, institute, introduce.*

novus, -a, -um, adj., *new, fresh, recent.*

nox, noctis, f., *night.*

nūbēs, -is, f., *cloud, mist.*

nūbigena, -ae, adj., *cloud-born;* (used subst.) *child of the cloud* (a centaur).

nūdus, -a, -um, adj., *naked, bare.*

nullus, -a, -um, adj., *not any, no.*

nūmen, -inis, n., *command, authority, divine will, divine power, divine presence, divinity.*

numerus, -ī, m., *number; measure, rhythm, time:* in numerum, *in time, with measured movement, in measured cadence.*

numquam or nunquam, adv., *never.*

nunc, adv., *now;* nunc...nunc, *at one time...at another;* iam nunc, *even now.*

nuntius, -a, -um, adj., *making known, bearing tidings, with tidings.*

nuntius, -ī, m., *bearer of tidings, messenger.*

nympha, -ae, f., *nymph.*

O

Ō, interj., *O* (often best left untranslated).

obeō, -īre, īvī, -itum, *go before or to meet; go over, cover, envelop.*

(obex), obicis, m. or f., *bolt, bar.* The abl. is the only case found in the sing.

obiciō, -ere, -iēcī, -iectum, *throw before, offer; expose, risk.*

obserō, -ere, -sēvī, -situm, *sow thickly, sow.*

obsidiō, -ōnis, f., *siege.*

obstipescō, -ere, -puī, —, *be stupefied, be astonished, be struck dumb with amazement.*

obtruncō, -āre, —, obtruncātum, *cut down, cut to pieces, butcher.*

obvius, -a, -um, adj., *in the way, meeting, to meet.*

occultō, -āre, -āvī, -ātum, *secrete, conceal, hide.*

Ōceanus, -ī, m., *the open sea, the ocean, Ocean.*

ōcior, -ius, comp. adj., *swifter, fleeter;* ōcius, comp. adv., *more quickly.*

ocrea, -ae, f., *greave, shinguard.*

oculus, -ī, m., *eye; glance; sight, view.*

Oechalia, -ae, f., *a city of Euboea.*

offerō, offerre, obtulī, oblātum, *bring before, present;* sē *offerre, present onself, appear.*

ōlim, adv., *at that time, then; at times.*

olīva, -ae, f., *olive.*

ollī, archaic form of illī, *those, they.*

Olympus, -ī, m., *Olympus, mountain in Greece, home of the gods, heaven, sky.*

omnigenus, -a, -um, adj., *of all kinds, of all sorts.*

omnipotens, -entis, adj., *all-powerful, omnipotent, almighty.*

omnis, -e, adj., *all, the whole; every.*

onerō, -āre, -āvī, -ātum, *load, freight, fill.*

opācus, -a, -um, adj., *shaded, darkened, dark, shady.*

oppidum, -ī, n., (fortified) *town.*

opportūnus, -a, -um, adj., *fitting, suitable, adapted.*

(ops), opis, f., *help, aid, support, strength, power;* (pl.) *means, resources, supplies, wealth.*

optimus, -a, -um, adj. superl. of bonus, *good, best, worthiest, noblest.*

optō, -āre, -āvī, -ātum, *choose, select; wish, desire, yearn after, long for.*

opulentus, -a, -um, adj., *rich, abounding.*

opus, -eris, n., *work, toil, labor; product of work, a work, thing wrought.*

ōra, -ae, f., *border, margin, boundary; shore, coast, soil, country.*

ōrāculum, -ī, n., *prophetic declaration, oracle.*

ōrātor, -ōris, m., *speaker; envoy, ambassador.*

orbis, -is, m., *ring, circle, circular path, orbit;* **in orbem,** *in circles, in curves;* (of the sky) *arch, vault.*

Orcus, -ī, m., *Orcus, (god of) the underworld.*

ordō, -inis, m., *row, order, series:* **in ordine,** *in regular succession.*

oriens, -entis, m., *the rising sun, dawn, the East, the Orient.*

orior, -īrī, ortus, *rise, become visible, dawn, appear.*

ōrō, -āre, -āvī, -ātum, *speak; pray, entreat, beseech, implore, pray for.*

ōs, ōris, n., *mouth, lips; face, countenance;* **ōra,** *eyes.*

os, ossis, n., *bone;* (pl.) *bones.*

ostentō, -āre, -āvī, -ātum, *show, hold up to view.*

ostendō, -ere, -dī, -tum, *spread out before, show, door, entrance, portal; exhibit, display, expose.*

P

pācifer, -fera, -ferum, adj., *peace-bringing, peaceful.*

palla, -ae, f., *palla, an overgarment worn by women.*

Pallantēum, -ī, n., *Pallanteum, town built by Evander on the Palatine.*

Pallăs, -adis, f., *Pallas, the Greek goddess Athena, identified with Roman Minerva; Greek goddess of wisdom, the arts, and war.*

Pallās, -antis, m., *Pallas:* 1. *king of Arcadia and (great?)grandfather of Evander;* 2. *son of Evander.*

pallens, -entis, adj., *pale, pallid.*

pallidus, -a, -um, adj., *pale, colorless, blanched, pallid, ghastly.*

palma, -ae, f., *palm, hand.*

palūs, -ūdis, f., *swamp, marsh, pool.*

Pān, -os, m., *Pan, god of shepherds, flocks, woods, and fields.*

pandō, -ere, pandī, passum, *spread out, throw open, lay bare, expose to view.*

pangō, -ere, pepigī or **pēgī** (old **panxī**), **pactum,** *make fast, fix, arrange, make.*

panthēra, -ae, f., *panther.*

parcō, -ere, pepercī, parsum, *spare; be sparing of.*

parens, -entis, m. or f., *parent, father or mother.*

pariō, -ere, peperī, partum, *bring forth, bear, give birth to, obtain, acquire.*

pariter, adv., *equally;* **pariter...pariter,** *as well...as, on the one side...on the other.*

parō, -āre, -āvī, -ātum, *make ready, prepare for, prepare, aim at.*

Parrhasius, -a, -um, adj., *Parrhasian, Arcadian.*

pars, partis, f., *part, portion.*

parvus, -a, -um, adj., *little, small.*

passim, adv., *scattered about, all about, in every direction.*

pateō, -ēre, -uī, —, *lie open, be exposed to view.*

pater, -tris, m., *father;* (pl.) *fathers, forefathers, ancestors; senators, senate.*

patera, -ae, f., *shallow dish for liba-tions, sacrificial dish, libation saucer.*

paternus, -a, -um, adj., *of a father, father's.*

patior, -ī, passus, *bear, suffer, endure.*

patria, -ae, f., *fatherland, native country.*

patrius, -a, -um, adj., *of a father, father's; of one's native country, native.*

paucus, -a, -um, adj., (sing.) *small;* (pl.) *few;* (n. pl. used subst.) *few things, few words.*

paulātim, adv., *little by little, gradually.*

pauper, -eris, adj., *poor, of humble means, impoverished.*

pavidus, -a, -um, adj., *trembling, timid, shrinking with fear.*

pax, pācis, f., *compact, treaty of peace; peace.*

pectus, -oris, n., *breast; breast, heart, spirit.*

pecus, -oris, n., *cattle.*

pecus, -udis, f., *brute animal, brute, beast.*

pelagus, -ī, n., *open sea.*

Pelasgī, -ōrum, m., *primitive inhabi-tants of Greece and parts of Italy.*

pellis, -is, f., *skin, hide, pelt.*

pellō, -ere, pepulī, pulsum, *drive, beat, strike, clash, drive out, expel, banish.*

Penātēs, -ium, m. pl., *guardian divinities of the home or state, household gods.*

pendeō, -ēre, pependī, —, *swing, hang, be suspended.*

penitus, adv., *far within, to the inmost depths, thoroughly, completely, utterly.*

pensum, -ī, n., *wool weighed out to be spun, assignment of wool, assign-ment, task.*

per, prep. with acc., *through; through-out, all over, over, on, during.*

percellō, -ere, -culī, -culsum, *strike down, overturn, strike with consternation or awe.*

percurrō, -ere, -cucurrī or -currī, -cursum, *run through, along, or over, traverse quickly.*

perferō, -ferre, -tulī, -lātum, *bear through or to the end, bear, endure.*

perficiō, -ere, -fēcī, -fectum, *bring to an end, finish, complete, accomplish.*

perfundō, -ere, -fūdī, -fūsum, *pour over, wash, moisten, bedew, bathe.*

Pergama, -ōrum, n., *the citadel of Troy, Troy.*

perhibeō, -ēre, -uī, -itum, *say, tell, assert, relate, maintain, call, name.*

perīclum, -ī, n., *danger, peril.*

perpetuus, -a, -um, adj., *unbroken, continuous, entire, whole.*

persolvō, -ere, -solvī, -solūtum, *disentangle, explain, pay, render.*

pervolitō, -āre, -āvī, -ātum, *flit about or over.*

pēs, pedis, m., *foot; heel; footstep, movement, gait.*

petō, -ere, -īvī or -iī, -ītum, *make for, fly to, fly, journey to, seek, request, ask for, court.*

pharetra, -ae, f., *quiver.*

Pheneus, -ī, m., *a town of Arcadia.*

Phoebus, -ī, m., *name of Apollo as god of the sun.*

Pholus, -ī, m., *Pholus, a centaur.*

pictus, -a, -um, adj., *painted, decorated, ornamented.*

pīlentum, -ī, n., *covered carriage.*

Pīnārius, -a, -um, adj., *Pinarian, of the Pinarii, a gens associated with the rites honoring Hercules.*

pinguis, -e, adj., *fat, rich, fertile.*
pius, -a, -um, adj., *devout, pious, reverent, good.*
placidus, -a, -um, adj., *gentle, calm, unruffled, still, peaceful, placid.*
planta, -ae, f., *sole of the foot, sole.*
plausus, -ūs, m., *clapping* (of hands), *flapping* (of wings), *applause.*
plēnus, -a, -um, adj., *full.*
plūrimus, -a, -um, adj. superl. of **multus**, *most, very much, very many.*
plūs, plūris, n., comp. of **multus**, *more.*
pōculum, -ī, n., *drinking-vessel, cup.*
poena, -ae, f., *expiation, punishment, vengeance.*
poliō, -īre, *polish, make bright.*
pōnō, -ere, posuī, positum, *set down, put, place, establish, lay aside, put away.*
pons, pontis, m., *bridge.*
pōpuleus, -a, -um, adj., *of or belonging to the poplar-tree, poplar* (adj.).
pŏpulus, -ī, m., *people, nation, tribe, state.*
pōpulus, -ī, f., *poplar tree, poplar.*
porca, -ae, f., *sow, pig.*
porgite, see **porrigō**.
porrigō, -ere, -rexī, -rectum (2nd pers. pl. imperat. **porgite**), *stretch forth, hold out, offer, present.*
Porsenna, -ae, m., *Lars Porsenna, Etruscan ruler who tried to reinstate the Tarquins.*
porta, -ae, f., *gate.*
portentum, -ī, n., *token, portent, sign, wonder.*
porticus, -ūs, f., *covered walk between rows of columns, colonnade, portico.*
poscō, -ere, poposcī, —, *demand, clamor for, summon.*

possum, posse, potuī, —, *be able, can.*
post, prep. with acc., *after, behind;* adv., *behind, afterwards, later.*
postis, -is, m., *post, door post; doorway, door.*
postquam, conj., *after, when.*
potentia, -ae, f., *might, power.*
Potītius, -ī, m., *one of the Potitii, a gens associated with rites honoring Hercules.*
praecēdō, -ere, -cessī, -cessum, *go before.*
praeceps, -cipitis, adj., *head foremost, headlong.*
praecipitō, -āre, -āvī, -ātum, *throw headlong, jettison, hurry.*
praecipuus, -a, -um, adj., *taken by preference, of special distinction, special.*
praecīsus, -a, -um, adj., *broken off, precipitous, steep and jagged.*
praeclārus, -a, -um, adj., *highly distinguished, of marked excellence, renowned.*
praefulgeō, -ēre, —, —, *gleam in front or at the end.*
Praeneste, -is, f. (and n.), *town of Latium, modern Palestrina.*
praesens, -entis, adj., *at hand, present; instant, immediate.*
praestans, -antis, adj., *preeminent, extraordinary, distinguished, remarkable.*
praetendō, -ere, -dī, -tum, *stretch forth, extend, present.*
praetereā, adv., *besides, too, moreover.*
praeteritus, -a, -um, adj., *gone by, past.*
precor, -ārī, -ātus, *pray, make entreaty; pray to, supplicate.*
premō, -ere, -essī, -essum, *press, press upon, press tight, press hard, crowd.*

(**prex, precis**), **f.**, mostly pl., *prayer, entreaty, supplication.*

Priamus, -ī, m., *Priam, king of Troy, son of Laomedon.*

prīmum, adv., *at first, first, for the first time;* **cum prīmum**, *as soon as.*

prīmus, -a, -um, superl. adj., *first, earliest, the first part of.*

prior, -us, gen. **priōris**, comp. adj., *former, prior, first; belonging to a former age, of old.*

priscus, -a, -um, adj., *of earlier times, ancient.*

prō, prep. with abl., *in front of, before; for, in defense of, in behalf of, in the cause of; in proportion to/ comparison with.*

proavus, -ī, m., *great-grandfather, ancestor.*

procerēs, -um, m. pl., *chiefs, nobles, leaders.*

procul, adv., *at or to a distance, afar off, far, from afar.*

prōcumbō, -ere, -cubuī, -cubitum, *fall forward, lie down, stretch onself out.*

prōdigium, -ī, n., *prophetic sign, portent, prodigy; monster.*

proelium, -ī, n., *battle, combat, conflict, fight.*

profectus, perf. part. of **proficiscor**.

proficiscor, -ī, -fectus, *set forward, set out, depart; originate, spring, be descended.*

profugus, -a, -um, adj., *fugitive, in flight, into exile.*

prōgredior, -ī, -gressus, *step forth, move on, proceed, advance.*

prōlēs, -is, f., *offspring.*

prōmissum, -ī, n., *promise, assurance.*

prōmittō, -ere, -mīsī, -missum, *let go forth, promise, give assurance of.*

prōnus, -a, -um, adj., *bent or leaning forward, inclined, sloping, headlong.*

prope, adv., *near, nearly; visibly, manifestly;* prep. with acc., *near.*

properō, -āre, -āvī, -ātum, 1. intrans., *be quick, hasten;* 2. trans., *quicken, hurry, hasten.*

propinquō, -āre, -āvī, -ātum, *draw near, approach.*

propior, -ius, gen. **-ōris**, comp. adj., *nearer.*

propius, adv., comp. of **prope**.

prōra, -ae, f., *forepart of a ship, ship's head, bow, prow, lot.*

prospectus, -ūs, m., *outlook, prospect, sight.*

prōtegō, -ere, -texī, -tectum, *cover, shelter, protect.*

prōtinus, adv., *right onward, onward, forward.*

prōtrahō, -ere, -traxī, -tractum, *drag forth or out.*

proximus, -a, -um, sup. adj., *nearest.*

pūbēs, -is, f., *full-grown males, young men able to bear arms, youth.*

puer, -erī, m., *boy.*

pugna, -ae, f., *fight, battle, war, struggle.*

pugnō, -āre, -āvī, -ātum, *fight, contend;* (trans.) *fight, wage, carry on.*

pulcher, -chra, -chrum, adj., *beautiful.*

pulvereus, -a, -um, adj., *dusty.*

puppis, -is, f., *stern;* (= **nāvis**) *ship.*

puter, -tris, -tre, adj., *rotten, decaying; crumbling, loose.*

putō, -āre, -āvī, -ātum, *think, cleanse, prune, go over in detail, ponder, brood over.*

Pyracmōn, -onis, m., *a Cyclops, one of Vulcan's workmen.*

Q

quā, rel. adv., *where.*

quadrīgae, -ārum, f. pl., *four-horse team.*

quadripedans, -antis, adj., *going on four feet, galloping, cantering.*

quaerō, -ere, -sīvī, -sītum, *look for, seek, make search; ask, inquire, seek to learn, demand.*

quaesō, archaic form of **quaerō**, found only in first pers. sing, and pl. of pres. indic., *beseech, entreat.*

quālis, -e, adj., *of what sort, like.*

quam, interrog. and rel. adv., *how;* (correl. with **tam**) *as;* (after comp.) *than.*

quamvīs, conj., *although.*

quandō, conj., *since, inasmuch as.*

quantus, -a, -um, adj., *how much, how great, as great as.*

quārē, adv., *wherefore, therefore, and so for this reason.*

quatiō, -ere, —, quassum, *shake.*

quattuor, indecl. num. adj., *four.*

-que, enclitic conj., *and;* **-que...-que**, *both...and.*

quercus, -ūs, f., *oak-tree, oak.*

querella (querēla), -ae, f., *lament, plaint, plaintive cry, wailing.*

quī, quae, quod (dat. pl. **quīs**, 316), interrog. adj. or rel. pron., *who, what, which.*

quia, conj., *because.*

quīcumque, quaecumque, quodcumque, indef. rel. pron. or adj., *whoever, whatever.*

quiēs, -ētis, f., *rest, repose.*

quīn, conj., *why not;* (with **etiam** in climax) *nay even;* (introducing

noun clause after negative expression of preventing) *from, but that, to prevent that.*

quis, quae, quid, interrog. pron., *who, what.*

quid, conj. or adv., *why?*

quis, qua, quid (after **sī, nisī, nē, num**), indef. pron. or adj., *any(one), some(thing).*

quisquam, m., quicquam, n., indef. pron., *anyone, anything;* (adv. acc. neut.) *at all.*

quisque, quaeque, quidque, and (as adj.) **quodque**, indef. pron., *each one, every one*

quisquis, quicquid, indef. rel. pron., *whoever, whatever.*

quīvīs, quaevīs, quodvīs, adj., *any whatever, any, any that you please.*

quō, adv., *to what place, whither.*

quod, conj., *in that, for that, because.* See also **quī, quae, quod**.

quondam, adv., *at one time, once, of old, formerly.*

quoniam, conj., *since, seeing that, because.*

quoque, conj. (placed after an emphatic word), *also, too.*

R

rabiēs, —, f., *frenzy, madness.*

radiō, -āre, -āvī, -ātum, *shine, glisten, be bright.*

radius, -ī, m., *rod, staff, spoke, ray, beam.*

rādix, -īcis, f., *root, base, seat, foundation.*

rāmus, -ī, m., *branch, bough.*

rapidus, -a, -um, adj., *swift.*

rapīna, -ae, f., *robbery, prey, spoil, booty.*

rapiō, -ere, -puī, raptum, *snatch, seize; hurry away or along, hurry.*

raptō, -āre, -āvī, -ātum, *snatch, seize and carry off, drag along.*

rārus, -a, -um, adj., *of coarse texture; scattered, here and there, straggling.*

ratiō, -ōnis, f., *reckoning, account, understanding, reason, judgment, resourcefulness.*

ratis, -is, f., *raft, boat, ship.*

raucus, -a, -um, adj., *hoarse; harsh, grating, discordant.*

recens, -entis, adj., *fresh, new.*

recessus, -ūs, m., *falling back, receding, recess, depth.*

reclūdō, -ere, -clūsī, -clūsum, *unclose, disclose, throw open, expose to view.*

recōgnoscō, -ere, -gnovī, -gnitum, *recall to mind, review, examine, inspect.*

recoquō, -ere, -coxī, -coctum, *boil again; smelt again, forge anew, refine.*

recordor, -ārī, -ātus, *take to heart, call to mind, recall.*

rector, -ōris, m., *ruler.*

rectus, -a, -um, adj., *in a straight line, straight, direct, in undeviating course.*

recubō, -āre, -āvī, -ātum, *lie at full length, be stretched at full length, recline.*

reddō, -ere, -didī, -ditum, *give back, return, restore.*

redeō, -īre, -iī, -itum, *go back, come back, return.*

redūcō, -ere, -duxī, -ductum, *lead back; draw back, pull back.*

reductus, -a, -um, adj., *retired, distant, secluded.*

referō, referre, rettulī, relātum, *bear, bring, or carry back, restore, return, say in answer;* (of sound) *give back, echo;* sē referre, *to return.*

reflectō, -ere, -flexī, -flexum, *bend or turn back or backwards.*

refluō, -ere, —, —, *flow back.*

refulgeō, -ēre, -sī, —, *flash back, reflect light, glisten, gleam.*

rēgia, -ae, f., *royal abode, palace, hall.*

rēgīna, -ae, f., *queen.*

regiō, -ōnis, f., *direction, line, quarter, region.*

rēgnātor, -ōris, m., *ruler, sovereign, monarch.*

rēgnum, -ī, n., *kingdom, domain, sovereignty, realm, power.*

regō, -ere, rexī, rectum, *guide, direct; rule, govern, control.*

rēligiō, -ōnis, f., *religious feeling, reverence, sanctity.*

relinquō, -ere, -līquī, -lictum, *leave behind, leave, abandon, depart from.*

rēliquiae, -ārum, f., *remains, relics.*

rēmigium, -ī, n., *rowing, oars, oarsmen.*

rēmus, -ī, m., *oar.*

repente, adv., *suddenly.*

(repercutiō), -ere, —, -cussum, *strike or beat back;* (of light) *reflect.*

repōnō, -ere, -posuī, -positum, *put back, set on again, replace.*

reposcō, -ere, —, —, *demand back, demand as one's due.*

requiēs, -ētis, f., *rest, repose.*

rēs, reī, f., *thing, matter, affair, means, substance, event, deed.*

reserō, -āre, -āvī, -ātum, *unbolt, unlock, open.*

reservō, -āre, -āvī, -ātum, *keep back, keep in reserve, have in store, reserve.*

resīdō, -ere, -sēdī, —, *sit down, settle down, take up one's station.*

resolvō, -ere, -solvī, -solūtum, *unbind, loose, release, scatter, disperse.*

respiciō, -ere, -spexī, -spectum, *look back (at), look behind (at), pay attention to.*

resultō, -āre, -āvī, -ātum, *rebound, re-echo, resound.*

retineō, -ēre, -inuī, -tentum, *hold or keep back, restrain.*

retorqueō, -ēre, -torsī, -tortum, *turn, throw, or fling back.*

revehō, -ere, -vexī, -vectum, *carry back, bring back.*

revellō, -ere, -vellī, -vulsum, *pull away, tear off, tear away, wrench off, uproot.*

revīsō, -ere, —, —, *revisit, return.*

rex, rēgis, m., *king, monarch.*

Rhēnus, -ī, m., *the Rhine, river separating Gaul from Germany.*

rigens, -entis, adj., *stiff, rigid, unyielding.*

rīma, -ae, f., *cleft, rift, fissure.*

rīpa, -ae, f., *riverbank, bank.*

rīte, adv., *with due observance, in due course or form, duly.*

rīvus, -ī, m., *small stream, stream.*

rōbur, -oris, n., *hard-wood, oak, hard-wood club, club, strength, flower.*

rogō, -āre, -āvī, -ātum, *ask, question, ask for, request, entreat.*

Rōma, -ae, f., *Rome, city of central Italy on the banks of the Tiber.*

Rōmānus, -a, -um, adj., *of Rome, Roman;* (used subst.) **Rōmānī, -ōrum, m.,** *the Romans.*

Rōmuleus, -a, -um, adj., *of Romulus, Romulean.*

Rōmulidae, -ārum, m., *sons, descendants, or followers of Romulus, Romans.*

Rōmulus, -ī, m., *Romulus, son of Mars and Rhea Silvia, founder and first king of Rome.*

rōrō, -āre, -āvī, -ātum, *drop dew, drip* (as with dew), *trickle.*

rostrātus, -a, -um, adj., *furnished with beaks, beaked.*

rostrum, -ī, n., *beak, bill, ship's beak, beak.*

rota, -ae, f., *wheel.*

ruber, -bra, -brum, adj., *red;* (with **lītus**) *the Red Sea* (Indian Ocean).

rubescō, -ere, -buī, —, *grow red, redden.*

rudō, -ere, —, —, *roar, bellow.*

ruīna, -ae, f., *falling down, downfall, fall.*

rūmor, -ōris, m., *sound; shouting, acclamation, cheering, cheers.*

rumpō, -ere, rūpī, ruptum, *break, burst, break off, cut short, interrupt.*

ruō, -ere, ruī, rutum, *fall with a crash, fall in ruins, come down, rush blindly, fling oneself.*

rūpēs, -is, f., *rock, crag, cliff, rocky cavern.*

rutilō, -āre, -āvī, -ātum, *redden, emit a ruddy glow, glow redly.*

rutulus, -a, -um, adj., *red, ruddy.*

Rutulus, -ī, m., *a Rutulian, of the tribe in Latium whose king was Turnus.*

S

Sabaeī, -ōrum, m., *inhabitants of Saba* (chief city of Arabia Felix), *the Sabaeans.*

Sabellus, -a, -um, adj., *of the Sabellians or Sabines, an ancient people of central Italy, Sabine.*

Sabīnus, -a, -um, adj., *of the Sabines, an ancient people of central Italy, Sabine.*

sacer, -era, -crum, adj., *dedicated, consecrated, sacred;* (used subst.) **sacrum, -ī, n.,** *sacred act, rite, object, offering, worship.*

sacerdōs, -ōtis, m. or f., *priest, priestess.*

saeclum, see **saeculum.**

saeculum or saeclum, -ī, n., *race, generation, lifetime, age*

sacrō, -āre, -āvī, -ātum, *consecrate, dedicate.*

saepe, adv., *often, many times*; comp., saepius, *again and again, repeatedly.*

saeta, -ae, f., *stiff or bristly hair, bristle.*

saeviō, īre, -iī, - ītum, *be fierce, be furious, be inflamed, rage, storm.*

saevus, -a, -um, adj., *fierce, savage, cruel.*

sagitta, -ae, f., *arrow.*

sagittifer, -era, -erum, adj., *armed with arrows.*

sagulum, -ī, n., *small military cloak, cloak, mantle.*

Salamīs, -īnis (acc. Salamīna, 158), f., *island off the southeast coast of Greece.*

Saliī, -ōrum, m., *Salii, priests at Rome dedicated to Mars, 663, or Hercules, 285.*

saltus, -ūs, m., *leap, bound, spring.* Only in acc. and abl. sing. and pl.

salūs, -ūtis, f., *soundness, health, safety, deliverance.*

salveō, -ēre, —, —, *be well, be in good health;* (imperat. as greeting) salvē, *hail, be well.*

sanctus, -a, -um, adj., *consecrated, sacred, reverenced, venerated, hallowed.*

sanguineus, -a, -um, adj., *of blood, bloody, dripping with blood, blood-red.*

sanguis, -inis, m., *blood, race, stock.*

saniēs, acc. saniem, abl. saniē, f., *corrupt, diseased blood, bloody matter.*

Sāturnia, -ae, f., *town and citadel built by Saturn on the Capitoline hill.*

Sāturnius, -a, -um, adj., *of Saturn, Saturnian.*

Sāturnus, -ī, m., *Saturn, mythical Golden Age king of Latium; god of agriculture and civilization, identified with Greek Cronos.*

saturō, -āre, -āvī, -ātum, *fill, satiate, satisfy.*

saxeus, -a, -um, adj., *of rock, rocky, of stone, stony.*

saxum, -ī, n., *broken stone, rough stone, rocky fragment, rock, stone; rocky cave, den, or cavern.*

scelus, -eris, n., *wicked act, wickedness, crime.*

sceptrum, -ī, n., *scepter.*

scindō, -ere, scidī, scissum, *split, cleave, rend, tear, divide, separate.*

scopulus, -ī, m., *projecting rock, rock, crag.*

scūtum, -ī, n., *oblong shield, shield.*

scyphus, -ī, m., *large cup supplied with handles, cup.*

sē, see suī.

secō, -āre, -cuī, -ctum, *cut, cut through, pass through, traverse.*

sēcrētus, -a, -um, adj., *separated, apart.*

secundus, -a, -um, adj., *following, next, second, favorable, auspicious.*

secus, adv., *otherwise:* hand secus, *even so,* nōn secus āc or atque, *just as.*

sed, conj., *but, but yet, yet.*

sedeō, -ēre, sēdī, sessum, *sit.*

sēdēs, -is, f., *seat, habitation, dwelling, mansion, temple, site, place, city.*

sedīle, -is, n., *seat.*

sēgnis, -e, adj., *slow, tardy, sluggish, slothful.*

sēmēsus, -a, -um, adj., *half-eaten, half-devoured.*

sēmifer, -fera, -ferum, adj., *half-bestial.*

sēmihomō (trisyl.), **-inis, m.,** *half-man, half-brute.*

semper, adv., *always, forever.*

senātus, -ūs, m., *council of elders, senate.*

senectūs, -ūtis, f., *old age.*

senex, senis, adj., *old, aged;* (used subst.) *old man;* comp. **senior,** *old, aged.*

senior, see **senex.**

sentiō, -īre, sensī, sensum, *perceive by the senses, perceive, feel, see.*

septēnī, -ae, -a, dist. num. adj., *seven each or apiece;* (= **septem**) *seven.*

sequax, -ācis, adj., *following, pursuing, avenging.*

sequor, -ī, secūtus, *follow, attend, journey, or sail to.*

serēnus, -a, -um, adj., *bright, clear, cloudless.*

sermō, -ōnis, m., *speech, conversation.*

serō, -ere, sēvī, satum, *plant, sow;* **satus,** *born, sprung from.*

serpens, -entis (gen. pl. **serpentum,** 436), **f.** or **m.,** *snake, serpent.*

sērus, -a, -um, adj., *late, late-night, too late, inadequate, too far spent.*

servō, servāre, servāvī, servātum, *save, guard, keep, deliver, preserve; observe, keep.*

sēsē, see **suī.**

sevērus, -a, -um, adj., *severe, strict, grave, austere, rugged, hardy.*

sī, conj., *if;* (in wishes) **Ō sī,** *O if, if only, O that, would that.*

sīc, adv., *in this way, thus, to such a degree, so.*

Sīcanius, -a, -um, adj., *Sicanian, Sicilian.*

Sīcānus, -a, -um, adj., *of the Sicani, Sicanian.*

siccus, -a, -um, adj., *dry, drained.*

sīcut, adv., *just as, as.*

sīdus, -eris, n., *group of stars, constellation, heavenly body, star.*

sīgnum, -ī, n., *mark, sign, token, trace; signal;* (military) *standard, banner.*

silex, -icis, usually **m.,** but **f.** in Verg., *flint, granite; granite rock, crag.*

silva, -ae, f., *wood, forest, trees.*

Silvānus, -ī, m., *ancient Italian god associated with woods and uncultivated fields.*

silvestris, -e, adj., *of a wood or forest, thickly wooded; growing wild, untrimmed.*

similis, -e, adj., *like, similar.*

simul, adv., *at the same time, together, simultaneously.*

sīn, conj., *if on the contrary, if however, but if.*

sine, prep. with abl., *without;* **sine mōre,** *lawlessly.*

singulī, -ae, -a, adj., *one by one, individual, separate.*

sinus, -ūs, m., *curved surface, bend, fold, hollow, bay, gulf, lap.*

sistō, -ere, stitī, statum, *make stand, set up, set, place, station.*

sistrum, -ī, n., *sistrum, bronze rattle used by Egyptians in the worship of Isis.*

socius, -a, -um, adj., *associated, allied.*

socius, -ī, m., *associate, companion, comrade, follower, ally.*

sōl, sōlis, m., *sun.*

sōlācium, -ī, n., *comfort, consolation, solace.*

solitus, -a, -um, adj., *accustomed, wonted.*

solium, -ī, n., *official seat, chair of state, seat of honor, throne, chair.*

sollemne, -is, n., *religious or sacred rite, festival, or ceremony, sacrifice, solemnity.*

sollemnis, -e, adj., *yearly, annual.*

solum, -ī, n., *bottom, base, ground, soil.*

sōlus, -a, -um, gen. -īus, *alone, only, sole.*

solvō, -ere, solvī, solūtum, *loose, set free, unfasten, separate.*

somnus, -ī, m., *sleep.*

sonitus, -ūs, m., *sound, noise, clatter.*

sōpiō, -īre, *put to sleep, lull to sleep;* perf. part., sōpītus, (of fires) *slumbering, smoldering.*

sopor, -ōris, m., *sleep, slumber.*

soror, -ōris, f., *sister.*

sortior, -īrī, -ītus, *draw or cast lots; share, divide.*

sospes, -itis, adj., *safe, preserved, uninjured.*

spargō, -ere, sparsī, sparsum, *sprinkle, strew, scatter, cast, moisten.*

spectātus, -a, -um, adj., *tested, tried, proved.*

spectō, -āre, -āvī, -ātum, *look at steadfastly, look at, gaze at, fix the eyes upon.*

specus, -ūs, m. or n., *cave, cavern, den.*

spēlunca, -ae, f., *cave, cavern, den.*

spēs, speī, f., *hope.*

spīrō, -āre, -āvī, -ātum, *breathe, draw breath, pant.*

spolium, -ī, n., *hide, skin;* (pl.) *arms stripped from a conquered enemy, spoils, booty.*

spūmō, -āre, -āvī, -ātum, *foam.*

squāma, -ae, f., *scale.*

stabulum, -ī, n., *standing-place, station, stall, feeding-ground.*

stāgnum, -ī, n., *standing water, pond, lake, pool.*

statuō, -ere, -uī, -ūtum, *set up, place, establish, erect.*

sternō, -ere, strāvī, strātum, *spread out, smooth; strew, strike down, slay, lie stretched on.*

Steropēs, -is, m., *a Cyclops, one of Vulcan's workmen.*

stirps, -pis, f. or m., *trunk, stock, stem, descent, lineage, descendants.*

stō, stāre, stetī, statum, *stand, remain, endure.*

strātum, -ī, n., *covering, couch.*

strepitus, -ūs, m., *confused noise,* (*sound of*) *voices.*

strepō, -ere, -uī, —, *make a (harsh) noise; blare, bray.*

strictūra, -ae, f., *compression;* (of metals), *bar, mass.*

strīdō, -ere, —, —, *make a shrill, harsh or grating sound, hiss.*

stringō, -ere, -inxī, -ictum, *draw tight, touch lightly, graze.*

struō, -ere, struxī, structum, *heap up, build, construct; aim at, have in view.*

stuppeus, -a, -um, adj., *of tow, made of short-fibered material like hemp or flax.*

Stygius, -a, -um, adj., *of the Styx, Stygian.*

sub, adv., prep. with abl. and acc., *below, under, beneath;* sub aurās, *upwards, on high.*

subeō, -īre, -iī or īvī, -itum, *go or come under, enter, approach.*

subigō, -ere, -ēgī, -actum, *drive up, impel, constrain, force, lead.*

subitō, adv., *suddenly, at once.*

subitus, -a, -um, adj., *sudden.*

subiungō, -ere, -iunxī, -iunctum, *fasten under, bring under the yoke, subject to control, subdue.*

sublātus, see tollo.

sublīgō, -āre, -āvī, -ātum, *bind below, fasten, attach.*

subsistō, -ere, -stitī, —, *take a position, come to a pause, stand still, stand.*

subter, prep. with acc. or abl., *under, beneath.*

subvehō, -ere, -vexī, -vectum, *carry or convey up;* (pass.) *sail or journey up.*

succēdō, -ere, -cessī, -cessum, *go or come under; approach, draw near, go to, proceed, join; follow, succeed.*

sūdus, -a, -um, adj., *free from moisture, dry, clear, cloudless;* (n. used subst.) *clear air.*

suī, sibī or **sibi, sē** or **sēsē,** sing. and pl. pron. 3rd pers. reflex., *himself, herself, itself, themselves.*

sum, esse, fuī, *be, exist.*

summoveō, -ēre, -mōvī, -mōtum, *put out of the way, remove, withdraw from sight.*

summus, -a, -um, superl. adj., *uppermost, highest.*

super, adv. and prep., *above, over, from above.*

superbus, -a, -um, adj., *proud, imperious, arrogant, haughty.*

superō, -āre, -āvī, -ātum, *rise above, surmount, overcome, be superior, excel, surpass.*

superstitiō, -ōnis, f., *exaggerated fear of the supernatural, superstition.*

supersum, -esse, -fuī, *be over, be left; remain in life, survive.*

superus, -a, -um, adj., *above, higher;* (m. pl. used subst.) **superī, -ōrum (-um),** *the higher powers, the gods above.*

supplex, -icis, adj., *submissive, suppliant, humble.*

supplicium, -ī, n., *supplication, entreaty, punishment, vengeance.*

suprā, adv., *on the upper side, above.*

suprēmus, -a, -um, adj., *highest, last, final.*

surgō, -ere, surrexī and **subrexī, —,** *rise, arise.*

sūs, suis, m. or **f.,** *swine, hog, sow.*

suscitō, -āre, -āvī, -ātum, *lift up, raise, stir up, rouse, rekindle.*

suspensus, -a, -um, adj., *hung, suspended.*

suspiciō, -ere, -spexī, -spectum, *look up.*

sustineō, -ere, -tinuī, -tentum, *hold up, lift up, bear up, raise, sustain.*

suus, -a, -um, poss. adj., *his (own), her, its, their.*

T

tābum, -ī, n., *corrupt matter, putrid gore.* [abl. sing. only]

tacitus, -a, -um, adj., *silent, hushed, noiseless, still.*

tālis, -e, dem. adj., *of such a kind, such; like this, the following.*

tam, adv., (with correl. **quam,** as, expressed or implied) *so, as.*

tamen, adv., *for all that, nevertheless, yet, still.*

tandem, adv., *at length, at last.*

tantum, adv., *so greatly, so far, so much; only so much, only, but.*

tantus, -a, -um, adj., *of such size, so great; of such importance, so great.*

Tarchōn or **Tarchō, -ontis** or **-ōnis, m.,** *Etruscan leader who aided Aeneas against Turnus.*

tardus, -a, -um, adj., *slow, sluggish, lingering, tardy, inactive, torpid.*

Tarpēius, -a, -um, adj., *Tarpeian.*

Tarquinius, - ī, m., (Lucius) *Tarquinius* (Superbus), *Tarquin* (the Proud), *seventh and last Roman king, banished for tyranny.*

Tartara, -ōrum, n. pl., *Tartarus, part of the underworld where the wicked are punished, underworld.*

Tartareus, -a, -um, adj., *of Tartarus, of the underworld, Tartarean.*

Tatius, -ī, m., *Tatius* (Titus), *king of the Sabines at Cures; warred against Romulus after the seizure of the Sabine women until making peace.*

taurus, -ī, m., *bull; ox, steer,* (in pl.) *cattle.*

tectum, -ī, n., *roofed structure, dwelling, house, covering, roof, ceiling.*

Tegeaeus, -a, -um, adj., *Tegean, Arcadian.*

tegō, -ere, texī, tectum, *cover, shade, shelter.*

tellus, -ūris, f., *earth, land, country.*

tēlum, -ī, n., (*thrown*) *weapon, spear, dart, javelin.*

templum, -ī, n., *place marked off and devoted to sacred uses, sacred enclosure, temple.*

temptamentum, -ī, n., *trial, test, proof.*

temptō, -āre, -āvī, -ātum, *make trial of, try, attempt.*

tempus, -oris, n., *time.*

tempus, -oris, n., *vital place, temple, brow, side of head.*

tenax, -ācis, adj., *tenacious, griping.*

tendō, -ere, tetendī, tentum or **tensum,** *extend, stretch;* (with or without **iter** or **cursum**) *hold one's course, aim, go, proceed.*

tenebrae, -ārum, f., *darkness, blackness, gloom.*

teneō, -ēre, tenuī, —, *hold fast, hold, guard, keep, maintain:* **castra tenēre,** *to be encamped.*

tenuis, -e, adj., *thin, fine, slender, meager, humble.*

tepeō, -ēre, —, —, *be warm, be tepid, steam, reek.*

tepidus, -a, -um, adj., *lukewarm, warm, tepid.*

ter, num. adv., *three times, thrice.*

teres, -etis, adj., *smooth, well-rounded, tapering; flexible, lithe.*

tergeminus, -a, -um, adj., *of three forms, threefold, triple.*

tergum, -ī, n., *back, covering of the back, hide; hinder part, rear.*

ternī, -ae, -a, distr. num. adj., *three each or apiece; three sets of.*

terra, -ae, f., *earth, soil, ground, land, country,* (pl.) *world, earth.*

terreō, -ēre, -uī, -itum, *frighten, terrify, awe, make afraid.*

terribilis, -e, adj., *frightful, terrible, dreadful.*

terrificus, -a, -um, adj., *causing terror, terrible, fearful.*

terror, -ōris, m., *terror, alarm, panic.*

testor, -ārī, -ātus sum, *call to witness, appeal to, invoke.*

Teucrus, -a, -um, adj., *belonging to Teucer, Trojan;* **Teucrī, -ōrum** (**Teucrum,** 154), *the Teucrians, the Trojans.*

textum, -ī, n., *that which is woven, web, texture, fabric, framework.*

thalamus, -ī, m., *inner room, chamber, bedchamber, chamber.*

Thybris, -is and **-idis** (voc. **Thybri;** acc. **Thybrim**), **m.,** *the Tiber, river in Italy.*

Thybris, -is, m., *Thybris, ancient Italian king whose name the Tiber was said to bear.*

Tiberīnus, -ī, m., *the god of the Tiber.*

timeō, -ēre, -uī, —, *fear, be afraid; show fear.*

timor, -ōris, m., *fear, alarm, apprehension.*

tingō, -ere, tinxī, tinctum, *wet, dip, bathe.*

Tīrynthius, -a, -um, adj., *of Tiryns, a town where Hercules was brought up.*

Tithōnius, -a, -um, adj., *of Tithonus.*
tolerō, -āre, -āvī, -ātum, *bear, support, endure, sustain, maintain.*
tollō, -ere, sustulī, sublātum, *lift, raise, sustain, take away.*
tonitrus, -ūs, m., *thunder, thunderclap, thunder-peal.*
tonō, -āre, -uī, —, *make a loud noise, thunder, ring.*
tormentum, -ī, n., *engine for hurling missile weapons; torture.*
torqueō, -ēre, torsī, tortum, *turn, twist, whirl;* **imber tortus** is either hail or hurled rain, 429.
torreō, -ēre, torruī, tostum, *roast.*
torus, -ī, m., *swelling, band or fold of muscle; stuffed mattress, couch, bed, cushion.*
tot, indecl. adj., *so many.*
totidem, indecl. adj., *just as many, the same number of.*
tōtus, -a, -um, gen. **tōtīus**, adj., *whole, complete, all parts of, entire.*
trahō, -ere, traxī, tractum, *draw, drag, drag down, drag along, trail, derive.*
tremendus, -a, -um, adj., *to be dreaded, dread, awful.*
tremō, -ere, -uī, —, *shake, tremble (at).*
tremulus, -a, -um, adj., *shaking, trembling, quivering, flickering.*
trepidō, -āre, -āvī, -ātum, *be agitated, be in confusion, be in a flutter of alarm.*
trepidus, -a, -um, adj., *excited, agitated, alarmed, hurried.*
trēs, tria, num. adj., *three.*
tridens, -entis, adj., *three-pronged, three-fanged, trident.*
triginta, indecl. num. adj., *thirty.*
triplex, -icis, adj., *threefold, triple.*
tristis, -e, adj., *sad, bitter, grim.*

triumphus, -ī, m., *triumphal procession (of a victorious general), triumph, victory.*
Trōia, -ae, f., *Troy.*
Trōiānus, -a, -um, adj., *Trojan.*
Trōiugena, -ae, m., *son of Troy, Trojan.*
Trōius, -a, -um, adj., *Trojan.*
truncus, -ī, m., *trunk of a tree, trunk.*
tū, gen. **tuī**; pl. **vōs**, gen. **vestrum**, **vestrī**, *you;* (used reflex.) *yourself.*
tuba, -ae, f., (straight) *war-trumpet, trumpet.*
tueor, -ērī, tuitus or **tūtus**, *look upon, gaze at.*
Tullus, -ī, m., *Tullus* (Hostilius), *third king of Rome.*
tum, adv., *then, at that time, in those days, on that day, next.*
tumeō, -ēre, —, —, *swell, be swollen.*
tumidus, -a, -um, adj., *swelling, heaving.*
tumor, -ōris, m., *swelling;* (sc. **animī**) *anger, indignation, resentment.*
tumultus, -ūs, m., *uprising, uproar, commotion, tumult.*
tumulus, -ī, m., *rising ground, height, mound, hillock.*
tunc, adv., *at that time, then.*
tunica, -ae, f., *tunic, undergarment.*
turba, -ae, f., *disorder, tumult, throng, crowd, multitude.*
turbō, -āre, -āvī, -ātum, *make an uproar; disturb, trouble, agitate, stir deeply.*
Turnus, -ī, m., *Turnus, king of the Rutuli, a people of Latium.*
turrītus, -a, -um, adj., *furnished with towers, tower-crowned, turreted.*
tūs, tūris, n., *frankincense, incense.*
Tuscus, -a, -um, adj., *Tuscan, Etruscan.*
tūtus, -a, -um, adj., *secure, safe.*
tuus, -a, -um, poss. adj., *your, your own.*
Typhoeus (trisyl.), **-eos, m.**, *Typhoeus,*

a giant defeated by Jupiter with the aid of Hercules.

tyrannus, -ī, m., *ruler, absolute monarch, monarch, tyrant, despot.*

Tyrrhēnī, -ōrum, m., *the Tyrrhenians, early inhabitants of Etruria, Etruscans.*

Tyrrhēnus, -a, -um, adj., *Tyrrhenian, Etruscan, Tuscan.*

U

ūber, -eris, n., *udder, breast.*

ubi (elsewhere **ubī**), rel. adv., *where, when.*

Ūfens, -entis, m., *Ufens, commander of the Aequi, allies of Turnus.*

ullus, -a, -um (gen. **ullīus**), adj., (with negative expressed or implied) *any.*

ultimus, -a, -um, superl. adj., *farthest, remotest, uttermost.*

ultor, -ōris, m., *avenger.*

ultrō, adv., *to the farther side, voluntarily, spontaneously, without waiting to be appealed to.*

umbra, -ae, f., *shade, shadow.*

umbrōsus, -a, -um, adj., *shady, gloomy, dark, casting shadows, bushy.*

umerus, -ī, m., *shoulder.*

umquam, adv., *at any time, ever.*

ūnā, adv., *in the same place or at the same time, in company, together.*

unda, -ae, f., *wave, water, current.*

unde, adv., *whence, from what place.*

undique, adv., *from or on all sides.*

ungō or **unguō, -ere, unxī, unctum**, *besmear, anoint, daub with pitch.*

unguis, -is, m., *(finger- or toe-) nail, claw, talon.*

ungula, -ae, f., *hoof.*

ūnus, -a, -um, gen. **ūnīus** and (poet.) **ūnius**, *one;* **in ūnum**, *to one place, together.*

urbs, -is, f., *city, town.*

ursa, -ae, f., *she-bear, bear.*

usquam, adv., *anywhere, in any instance.*

ūsus, -ūs, m., *use, exercise, enjoyment, need.*

ut, adv. and conj., *as, when, how.*

V

vādō, -ere, —, —, *go, go rapidly, rush, sweep along.*

vadum, -ī, n., *shoal, ford, body of water, (shallow) water.*

valeō, -ēre, -uī, -itum, *be strong, have power, prevail, avail.*

validus, -a, -um, adj., *strong, powerful, vigorous, mighty.*

vallēs or **vallis, -is, f.**, *valley, vale.*

vānus, -a, -um, adj., *hollow, empty, vain, ineffectual.*

varius, -a, -um, adj., *manifold, various, different.*

vastō, -āre, -āvī, -ātum, *make empty, strip, despoil, desolate, dispeople.*

vastus, -a, -um, adj., *empty, waste, vast, enormous, huge, immense, deep.*

vātēs, -is, m., or **f.**, *seer, prophet.*

-ve, enclit. conj., *or;* **-ve...-ve**, *whether... or, either...or.*

vehō, -ere, vexī, vectum, *carry, convey.*

vellō, -ere, —, —, *pluck, tear away, tear down, destroy.*

vēlō, -āre, -āvī, -ātum, *cover, envelop, wrap, veil.*

vēlum, -ī, n., *sail.*

vēnātus, -ūs, m., *hunting.*

veniō, -īre, vēnī, ventum, *come;* **venīre in ūnum**, *meet.*

ventōsus, -a, -um, adj., *full of wind, windy, gasping, puffing.*

ventūrus, -a, -um, adj., *to come, future.*

ventus, -ī, m., *wind.*

Venulus, -ī, m., *native of Tibur serving with Turnus.*

Venus, -eris, f., *goddess of love and sex, mother of Aeneas.*

veprēs, -is, m., *thorn-bush, bush.*

verbum, -ī, n., *word.*

vērō, adv., *in truth, truly, assuredly, you may be sure.*

verrō, -ere, —, —, *sweep, lash.*

versō, -āre, -āvī, -ātum, *turn repeatedly, turn over and over, keep turning.*

vertex, -icis, m., *whirl, eddy top, peak, summit, head, brow.*

vertō, -ere, -tī, -sum, *turn, roll, turn back, reverse.*

vērus, -a, -um, adj., *true, genuine, authentic, original.*

vescor, -ī, —, *feed upon, eat, live upon, feast upon.*

vesper, -erī or -eris, m., *evening-star, evening.*

vester, -tra, -trum, poss. adj., pl., *your.*

vestīgium, -ī, n., *foot-print, track.*

vestiō, -īre, (imperf. vestībat, 160), *clothe.*

vestis, f., *clothes, clothing, raiment, drapery.*

vetō, -āre, -uī, -itum, *not permit, bid not, forbid, prohibit.*

vetus, -eris, adj., *old, aged, ancient.*

vetustus, -a, -um, adj., *ancient.*

via, -ae, f., *way, street, road, path; way, course, journey, march.*

vibrō, -āre, -āvī, -ātum, *put in quivering or tremulous motion; launch, hurl, flash.*

victor, -ōris, m., *conqueror, victor.*

victus, -ūs, m., *means of living, food, sustenance, fare.*

videō, -ēre, vīdī, vīsum, *see, perceive,* (pass.) *be seen, seem, appear.*

viduō, -āre, -āvī, -ātum, *bereave, deprive.*

villōsus, -a, -um, adj., *hairy, shaggy.*

vinclum or vinculum, -ī, n., *means of binding, band, fastening, bond, fetter, sandal.*

vincō, -ere, vīcī, victum, *conquer, vanquish.*

vinculum, see vinclum.

vīnum, -ī, n., *wine.*

vir, virī, m., *man.*

virgātus, -a, -um, adj., *striped.*

viridis, -e, adj., *green, verdant.*

virtūs, -ūtis, f., *manliness, strength, vigor, soul; valor, courage.*

vīs, acc. (vim), and abl. sing. (vī); pl. vīrēs, vīrium, f., *force, violence, power, means, resources.*

viscus, -eris; usually pl. viscera, -um, n., *internal organs, viscera, entrails; flesh.*

vīsō, -ere, -sī, -sum, *go to see, see, visit, view attentively, survey.*

vīsus, -ūs, m., *act of seeing, sight, vision; thing seen, sight, apparition.*

vīta, -ae, f., *life.*

vitta, -ae, f., *(head) band, fillet.*

vīvō, -ere, vixī, —, *live.*

vīvus, -a, -um, adj., *alive, living.*

vix, adv., *with difficulty, scarcely, hardly.*

vocō, -āre, -āvī, -ātum, *call (upon), summon, invoke, invite, woo, name, designate.*

volātilis, -e, adj., *flying, winged.*

Volcānius, -a, -um, adj., *of or belonging to Vulcan, Vulcan's, Vulcan-made.*

Volcānus, -ī, m., *Vulcan, god of fire, husband of Venus.*

volitō, -āre, -āvī, -ātum, *fly to and fro, flit about.*

volō, velle, voluī, *will, wish, choose, be willing, consent.*

volō, -āre, -āvī, -ātum, *fly.*

volucer, -cris, -cre, adj., *flying, winged;*
(fem. used subst., sc. **avis**) *flying
creature, bird.*

voluptās, -ātis, f., *pleasure, delight,
enjoyment.*

volvō, -ere, volvī, volūtum, *make
revolve, roll, toss, send whirling.*

vomō, -ere, -uī, -itum, *vomit, spew
forth, emit, discharge, disgorge.*

vōtum, -ī, n., *solemn promise to a god,
vow.*

vox, vōcis, f., *voice; sound, utterance,
cry; word, language.*

vulgō, -āre, -āvī, -ātum, *spread among
the multitude, publish, broadcast,
make common.*

vulnerō, -āre, -āvī, -ātum, *wound.*

vulnificus, -a, -um, adj., *wound-
inflicting, murderous, deadly.*

vultus, -ūs, m., *face, facial expression.*

Index

Numbers refer to page numbers.